What's Liberal

About the Liberal Arts?

PREVIOUS PUBLICATIONS

The Aesthetics of Cultural Studies
(as editor). Blackwell, 2004.

*The Employment of English: Theory, Jobs, and
the Future of Literary Studies.*
New York University Press, 1998.

Life As We Know It: A Father, a Family, and an Exceptional Child.
Pantheon, 1996. Paper edition published by Vintage, 1998.

*Higher Education Under Fire: Politics, Economics,
and the Crisis of the Humanities*
(as editor, with Cary Nelson). Routledge, 1995.

Public Access: Literary Theory and American Cultural Politics.
Verso, 1994.

*Marginal Forces / Cultural Centers: Tolson, Pynchon,
and the Politics of the Canon.*
Cornell University Press, 1992.

What's Liberal
About the

CLASSROOM POLITICS AND

Liberal Arts?

"BIAS" IN HIGHER EDUCATION

Michael Bérubé

W. W. NORTON & COMPANY

NEW YORK   LONDON

For information about permission to reproduce selections from this book, write to
Permissions, W. W. Norton & Company, Inc., 500 Fifth Avenue, New York, NY 10110

Manufacturing by The Maple-Vail Book Manufacturing Group
Book design by Dana Sloan
Production manager: Anna Oler

Library of Congress Cataloging-in-Publication Data

Bérubé, Michael, 1961–
What's liberal about the liberal arts? : classroom politics and "bias" in higher education
/ Michael Bérubé. — 1st ed.
p. cm.
Includes bibliographical references and index.
ISBN-13: 978-0-393-06037-9 (hardcover)
ISBN-10: 0-393-06037-3 (hardcover)
1. Education, Higher—Political aspects—United States. 2. Education,
Humanistic—United States. 3. Liberalism—United States.
4. Political correctness—United States. I. Title.
LA227.4.B478 2006
378'.0120973—dc22

2006012749

W. W. Norton & Company, Inc., 500 Fifth Avenue, New York, N.Y. 10110
www.wwnorton.com

W. W. Norton & Company Ltd., Castle House, 75/76 Wells Street, London W1T 3QT

1 2 3 4 5 6 7 8 9 0

For my students—all of them

Contents

Acknowledgments

THANKS TO THE WONDERS OF THE INTERNET, I'VE been able to correspond with thousands of people across the political spectrum over the past ten years, and some of them have become critical to my thinking about this book and all the questions it addresses. I want to thank especially Timothy Burke, Sherman Dorn, Todd Gitlin, Maurice Isserman, Graham Larkin, Philip Klinkner, Ralph Luker, and Rick Perlstein for their advice, suggestions, challenges, and hot tips. Christopher Clarke, Roxanne Cooper, John Holbo, Scott Eric Kaufmann, and Amardeep Singh have also been bracing Internet interlocutors, and I am very glad to have met them in real space as well.

The people who have influenced the postmodernism chapter have more or less influenced the way I think about everything else. The chapter is explicit about its debt to Richard Rorty; even where I disagree with him, I disagree with him because I have come to occupy positions defined by his characterizations of the field of thought. But I also want to thank Amanda Anderson, Nancy Fraser, Cary Nelson, Laura Kipnis, and John McGowan; each, in different ways and for different reasons, has led me to rethink how I think about agreement and disagreement.

I would not have so comprehensive a sense of the field of literary studies had I not been elected to the Modern Language Association's Executive Council in 2002. I want to thank especially the MLA staff for all the work they do in running one of the best scholarly organizations in the business, and more especially I want to thank David Laurence, who is very likely the leading authority on employment patterns and practices in the field of English and foreign languages and literatures in North America. And to Rosemary Feal, MLA executive director and multilingual intellectual dynamo, *obrigada*.

As I was writing this book, I was elected to the National Council of the American Association of University Professors. And as I was writing this book, I found many occasions on which to consult the work and the archives of the AAUP as they try to define, maintain, and defend the ideal of academic freedom that is the condition of possibility for everything I do and say as a professor. I can hardly thank the AAUP in an acknowledgment, but I can say this much: from the days of John Dewey and Albert Einstein to the days of Joan Scott and Roger Bowen, the AAUP has done essential intellectual and political work in dark times.

Finally, four very special thanks. To Chris Robinson, assistant professor of political science at Clarkson University, I owe a debt I can hardly express: for reading the manuscript of this book from start to finish—twice!—and gently pointing out my many blind spots in a generous, capacious, and yet unforgiving twelve-page response. Thanks, Chris, I needed that. To Nick, my first-born, for growing up so fast, so wisely, and so well—and for talking to me about Social Security and the welfare state while showing me around St. Louis's University City. To Janet Lyon, my wife and general partner, for insisting that the conclusion was not in fact done, even after the manuscript had endured numerous computer failures, catastrophic data loss traumas, and painstaking rewrites. That was not what I wanted to hear at the time, but it was right on the money. And to Pete Simon, my editor at W. W. Norton, for seeing me through those computer failures, catastrophic data loss traumas, and painstaking rewrites—and for pushing me further on the rewrites even as I mourned the computer failures and data losses.

I have not thanked my son Jamie for his help with this book. But I do thank Jamie every day for being Jamie, and here I thank him also for putting up with an often distracted father who writes books like this.

State College, Pennsylvania, 2006

What's Liberal
About the Liberal Arts?

1. Reasonable Disagreements

THE CLASS STARTED OFF INNOCUOUSLY ENOUGH. We were in the fifth week of an undergraduate honors seminar in postmodernism and American fiction, reading Ishmael Reed's 1972 novel, *Mumbo Jumbo*, and I was starting to explain how the novel is built on a series of deliberate anachronisms. I began with Abdul Hamid's encounter with PaPa LaBas at a rent party (the novel is set in New York during the Harlem Renaissance), where Hamid delivers a tirade that presages the rise of the Nation of Islam and the antiwar protests of the late 1960s:

> This is the country where something is successful in direct proportion to how it's put over; how it's gamed. Look at the Mormons. . . . The most fundamental book of the Mormon Church, the Book of Mormon, is a fraud. If we Blacks came up with something as corny as the Angel of Moroni, something as trite and phony as their story that the book is the record of ancient Americans who came here in 600 B.C. and perished by A.D. 400, they would deride us with pejorative adjectival phrases like "so-called" and "would-be." They would refuse to exempt our priests from the draft, a privilege extended to every White hayseed's fruit stand which calls itself a Church. But regardless of the put-on, the hype, the Mormons got Utah, didn't they?[1]

Most of my students had no idea why Hamid would go off on the Mormons; for them, the passage was just so much mumbo jumbo. I explained briefly that Muhammad Ali's refusal to fight in Vietnam had been incendiary in the late 1960s but eventually led the United States to reconsider its criteria for conscientious-objector status; that the comparison between the Church of Jesus Christ of Latter-Day Saints and the Nation of Islam was a fairly common one when Reed wrote the novel; and that one nationalist group, the Republic of New Africa, had called for the creation of a separate black nation based in five Southern states, as partial reparation for slavery.[2]

At that point, John, a large white student in the back of the room, snorted loudly and derisively. "That's completely ridiculous!" he exclaimed. Startled, the students in the front rows turned to look at John. "It may seem ridiculous to you, yes," I replied, "and for the record, I don't believe there was any possibility that the Republic of New Africa was going to become a reality. I don't endorse it myself. But it was proposed, and some black nationalists pointedly compared their relation with the US government to that of the Mormons."

But John was just getting started. These people are not Africans, he insisted. They are African-*Americans*. The whole "Africa" thing is a charade; racial separatism and identity politics are tearing this country apart; people have to realize that if they live in this country, no matter how they got here, they are Americans first, and something-Americans second.

Apparently, we had touched a nerve. I pointed out, gently but I hoped not patronizingly, that whatever any of us might feel about the various projects of black nationalism, we are dealing here with a character in a novel—a character, I hastened to add, whose reductive brand of nationalism is ultimately undermined in the course of the narrative. It only makes sense to try to understand what he might be trying to say, and there's no reason to assume that his remarks are endorsed by the author—or by the professor who assigned the book. And now let's move on to another example of anachronism in *Mumbo Jumbo* . . .

The other students in the class—of various colors and genders, some of them born on other continents, some of them first-generation college kids from rural Pennsylvania, none of them African-American—didn't respond directly to John's outburst. They were more interested in the novel's use of anachronism, and uncertain (as so many other readers have been) about whether to take seriously the novel's various conspiracy theories about Warren Harding's death, about the demise of the Harlem Renaissance, about the role of the Freemasons in American history, and about the rise of Western culture itself. For the moment, the Republic of New Africa had been forgotten once again—but John simmered throughout the rest of the hour, clearly upset that no one had addressed his comment.

I've dealt with students like John before and I'm sure I'll see them again, no matter what class I'm teaching. But that semester was different; it was the fall of 2001, and students' nerves and political opinions were especially raw. I negotiated any number of delicate exchanges that semester, many of which were indirectly related to the events of September 11. And in the years since, as conservative students and pundits have begun to mount campaigns against what they perceive as liberal "bias" in American universities, I've had many occasions to wonder whether I've always dealt with students like John in the best possible way. Although I'm a fairly opinionated and outspoken liberal-progressive writer outside the classroom, I keep most of my political opinions to myself when I enter the classroom, and only very rarely do I encounter an undergraduate student who's familiar with my writings for *Dissent* or the *Nation* or major-city newspapers. Nor do I pry into my students' personal beliefs; ordinarily, I neither know nor care where my students stand on abortion, the minimum wage, genocide in Rwanda or Sudan, war in Iraq, the regressive Social Security tax, or the policies of the World Bank. But this time I thought I should engage John more thoroughly, precisely because he sensed that the class had deliberately ignored him, and (as I learned later) he assumed that I was antagonistic to him as well.

So after class that day, I talked to John at some length as we wandered through the noontime campus swarms. He was insistent that membership in the American community requires one to subordinate his or her ethnic or national origin, and that he himself wanted to be understood not as an American of Russian or Polish or German "extraction," but simply as an American among other Americans. And he was just sick and tired of African-Americans refusing to do the same.

I replied by telling John something like this: "Your position has a long and distinguished history in debates over immigration and national identity. It's part of the current critique of multiculturalism, and to a point I have some sympathy with it, because I don't think that social contracts should be based on cultural homogeneity." Deep breath. "That said," I went on, "I have to point out that the terms under which people of African descent might be accepted as Americans, in 1820 or 1920 or whenever, have been radically different from the terms under which your ancestors, whoever they were, could be accepted as Americans. You're right to insist that you shouldn't be defined by your ancestry, but, unfortunately, most African-Americans—who, by the way, fought and died for integration for many generations—didn't have that option. And it shouldn't be all that surprising that, when African-Americans finally *did* have the option of integrating into the larger national community, some of them were profoundly ambivalent about the prospect."

I didn't press the point that Reed's novel is itself profoundly ambivalent about that profound ambivalence; I thought that we were now on terrain that had little to do with the textual details of *Mumbo Jumbo*, and I was simply trying to come to an understanding with a student who clearly felt very strongly about one of the social issues raised in class. We parted amicably, and I thought that though he wasn't about to agree with me on this one, we had, at least, made our arguments intelligible to each other. And I thought that as a professor, I had an obligation—both a professional obligation and a "liberal" one, that is, liberal in the tradition of John Stuart Mill—to make some kind of reasonable accommodation for the airing of opinions that may differ not only from my own but also from the views of most of my other students.

But the dynamic of the class had been changed. From that day forward, John spoke up often, sometimes loudly, sometimes out of turn. He had begun to conceive of himself as the only countervailing conservative voice in a classroom full of liberal-left think-alikes, and he occasionally spoke as if he were entitled to reply to every other student's comment—in a class of seventeen. He was forceful, intelligent, and articulate. Sometimes he was witty, and he was knowledgeable about science fiction; his expertise was always welcome, because I'd assigned the class three strikingly disparate examples of the genre (by Philip K. Dick, Ursula LeGuin, and William Gibson). Often, however, he was obstreperous and out of bounds.

His obstreperousness presented me with not one problem but two. It would have been a relatively simple matter to put the brakes on—to speak to him, in class or afterward, in such a way as to let him know that he was not, in fact, entitled to comment on every other student's comment. But I did not want to contribute to his growing sense of lonely opposition. The layout of the classroom itself didn't help matters. Ordinarily, small seminars are held around seminar tables, so that all students can speak to one another and to me simultaneously; but in this long and shallow room (three rows deep, eight or nine seats wide), all the seats faced the front desk, and when John would speak from the back row, I would sometimes be treated to a silent chorus of eye-rolling among students in the first two rows. I had to be careful not to endorse any such eye-rolling by look or gesture, yet at the same time I did not want to glare at the eye-rolling students in such a way as to let John know that they were blowing him off. His sixteen classmates were not, in fact, a unified left-liberal bloc; some of them were recognizably left of center, but not all. In the weeks after September 11, my students sounded off on an extraordinary range of questions, including the question of whether that day marked the death of postmodernism, as the *New York Times*'s Edward Rothstein had suggested (in an essay I distributed to the class a few days after its publication).[3] As a result, I knew more about my students' politics than I ordinarily do, and they learned more about mine than they ordinarily would have. I knew my class contained a handful of people adamantly opposed to military action against the Taliban in Afghanistan (in most cases, that put them to the left of me, though I believe a couple of my students opposed war on religious grounds and could not be easily pegged as left or right), a handful of people who wanted to redraw the Middle East from scratch in the manner of Paul Wolfowitz, and a handful of people who called themselves libertarians but whose politics didn't go much beyond keep-your-laws-off-my-bong.

Actually, some students agreed with John about one thing or another but were simply annoyed that he was taking up so much class time. They began sending me e-mail messages and speaking to me privately about how they did not want John to set the parameters for class discussion. One student complained that she was wasting time trying to think of things that John wouldn't reply to; another said that he found anti-porn feminism obnoxious, just as John did, but couldn't stand it when people dismissed feminism so sweepingly as to render suspect other people's more careful critiques (his own, for example). If I directly asked John to cool it, then he would undoubtedly feel silenced and I would be in the position of validating what was perhaps, for him, a stifling liberal hegemony over classroom speech; if I failed to restrain him, I would in effect be allowing him to dominate the class, thereby silencing the other students who'd taken the time to speak to me about the problem.

For the remaining weeks of the semester, I tried to split the difference. John spoke more often than any other student, but I did not recognize him every time he asked; when students criticized his remarks, implicitly or explicitly, I did not validate their criticisms but I did try to let them speak in rough proportion to their numbers. On the class listserv, I aimed for a similar compromise—at one particularly tense point, I wrote to the other sixteen students to ask them not to reply to every single one of John's dismissive comments about the syllabus or his fellow students' contributions to the weekly listserv discussions. For a while, order was restored.

ONE OF THE FLAWS in my approach was that it left John completely unaware of how much the rest of the class and I were doing to accommodate him—to ensure that he would continue to contribute to our discussions, in class and online, and to ensure among ourselves that his contributions would not become the focal point of discussion. (That second imperative was practically self-negating, insofar as the sentence "Don't pay so much attention to John" necessarily pays attention to John.) I'll admit that John's obliviousness to his classmates' complaints—and to my behind-the-scenes attempts to rein in those complaints—afforded me a few moments of aggravation, in which I gave in to the temptation to think of myself as the preternaturally patient professor who stays up late at night trying to figure out ways of making sure that Every Voice Is Heard. Gradually, then, another flaw in my approach revealed itself to me: I was increasingly thinking of John as a problem to be *managed* somehow. By mid-semester, then, I decided to treat John as I would any other talkative, engaging student; I would learn more about him and the various predispositions, tastes, enthusiasms, and aversions he brought to class. I knew as much about five or six of my other students—enough to know that one was a passionate civil libertarian profoundly shaken by the attacks of September 11, another was smitten to the core by the work of James Joyce, another was fluent in German and found it easier to read post-Nietzschean German philosophy in the original, another was a promising poet from a blink-and-you'll-miss-it small town in the mountains, another was a prizewinning fiction writer who wanted to work in publishing after graduation, and so on. What was up with John?

One thing I found puzzling was that although he held a good deal of the syllabus in contempt—informing the listserv that Thomas Pynchon's *The Crying of Lot 49* is full of "the sort of prose that gives writers a bad name" and opening his comment on Ishmael Reed by writing, "Dear Sir: Please translate your novel *Mumbo Jumbo* into something resembling English. Thank you. P.S. Grammar can be your friend if you are kind to it"—he was a cyberpunk fan, and cyberpunk is not normally a genre in which one finds well-crafted prose or well-rounded characters. At one point, I found myself telling John that his complaints about postmodern novels, from the convolutions of Pynchon to the plotlessness of DeLillo's *White Noise*, were common to many readers of contemporary American fiction, but that few of those readers would then proceed, as he did, to name William Gibson's *Neuromancer* as their favorite item on the syllabus. Insofar as his dislike for Pynchon, Reed, and DeLillo wasn't rooted, as it is for so many readers, in a preference for plausible characters and/or the high seriousness of George Eliot or William Faulkner, I wasn't sure what to make of it—nor did I understand why he'd signed up for a course called "postmodernism and American fiction" in the first place. Another student told me she'd taken the course because it had three science fiction books on the syllabus, and she was merely tolerating the rest of the material. Perhaps John's motivations were similar; at any rate, I made a mental note not to emphasize science fiction quite so much in the future if it was attracting students who didn't like reading anything else.

I also learned a thing or two—but only a thing or two—about why race was such a volatile topic for John. Penn State had weathered an exceptionally unpleasant spring in 2001, just before I arrived on campus; dozens of students had received anonymous racist letters and e-mail messages, and the leader of the Black Student Caucus had received direct death threats. In May of that year, the *Chronicle of Higher Education* reported on the incidents and Penn State's attempt to defuse the crisis and address the concerns— more accurately, the outrage—of minority students and faculty:

> Trouble began in mid-April, when Daryl Lang, a reporter who covers diversity issues for the student newspaper, *The Collegian*, received a letter filled with profanity and racial slurs. The letter instructed Mr. Lang to forward an enclosed letter to LaKeisha Wolf, president of the university's Black Caucus. The letter to Ms. Wolf contained direct death threats. "I could have killed you 10 times by now," the letter reads. "This is a white academy in a white town—in a white country and by god it's going to stay that way, nigger bitch."[4]

Many students rallied in sympathy with the Black Caucus and Penn State's African-American students, who make up a paltry 4 percent of the overall student population, forming what they called a "village" in the student center. But most students, I heard from various sources, had no idea what was going on. And, sure enough, there were also those who insisted that the protestors were overplaying their hand, and one professor, a Christian conservative in the education school, even went so far as to suggest that the death threats were a hoax and that the campus was in fact facing "a Tawana Brawley situation," referring to the young black New York woman who in 1987 baselessly charged that she had been assaulted and raped by a group of white men. John informed me, in one of our after-class conversations, that he had had some kind of run-in with one of the African-American campus demonstrators that spring, in which he emphatically told the demonstrator he was not a racist.

It was not hard to imagine that whatever took place between John and the demonstrator might have been quite ugly, and I could also imagine (extending the principle of charity) that the demonstrator might possibly have given John some reason to feel defensive, angry, or even threatened. Yet I couldn't shake the feeling that, although John and students like him might occasionally feel wary or uncomfortable in some areas of campus (and perhaps in classes like mine), they aren't in any real danger. Every once in a while, in the wake of the 2000–01 demonstration (even to this day), the local campus conservatives like to point to all the things they think the Penn State administration does for black students; one recent flier complained that there is a Paul Robeson Center on the campus (and Robeson was a Communist!), whereas the campus conservatives have to meet in a classroom. After I finished shaking my head at the sheer foolishness of the complaint—did these kids really think that the HUB–Paul Robeson Center, which is simply a student-union building used by absolutely everyone at Penn State, was established as the headquarters of a black-activist organization?—I wondered just how many of my conservative white students, if given the chance, would prefer to be black at Penn State, black in the United States.

I didn't fault John for bringing his predispositions, tastes, enthusiasms, and aversions into our classroom. Nor did I mind the fact that his political and cultural beliefs informed his response to the material. I did think—and still think—that he sometimes used the novels as springboards for political editorializing, and that his response to Abdul Hamid in *Mumbo Jumbo* was a fairly clear example of how not to do literary criticism. Still, I can't deny that I quite often invite students to comment on the broader social or cultural implications of the literary works they read; avoiding broader social and cultural questions seems to me to be yet another example of how not to do literary criticism. So it's not as if I would ever chastise a student for suggesting, for example, that Hamid's speech about Mormonism is, just possibly, a tad snide and unfair, just as I would not chastise a student who objected to Reed's portrayal of the nationalist Hamid as something of a huckster and a hypocrite.

Besides, there was a still larger issue at stake, inasmuch as some of John's comments were clearly directed specifically to me: to what extent should my own beliefs be an explicit part of my teaching? This is not a rhetorical question. It is something I weigh every time I walk into the classroom, regardless of the rapport I have or have not established with a group of students. Literature professors have exceptionally wide range in this regard, since their subject matter covers most of the known world from history to psychology to physics, and in some cases (such as science fiction, including the cyberpunk variety) features of worlds not yet known to history or psychology or physics. Mimesis, after all, is a staggeringly capacious thing: literature is capable of addressing every conceivable personal, social, cultural, and political question humans have posed to themselves since the invention of written language, as well as depicting forms of language, behavior, and social organization that do not exist outside of the imaginative worlds created by written language. So when people tell me I should focus my teaching on "literature" rather than on personal, social, cultural, or political questions, I always stop to ask them what, exactly, they imagine literature to be about.

Even if I were not working in literary study, with its capaciousness and its uncontainable mimesis, I cannot begin to imagine what it would be like to be a teacher without beliefs, or what it would be like to be a teacher whose beliefs about the world did not inform his work and his very demeanor. And yet one of my beliefs is this:

the classroom is an intimate, quasi-public, quasi-private space, and it would be an abuse of my position if I were to treat my students as captive audiences who need to be educated about the rightness of affirmative action or the wrongness of Republican fiscal policy. I would be selling students short if my classes did not reflect some of my beliefs about literary theory or feminism or postmodernism or multiculturalism, since I have spent my entire adult life studying such things and am familiar with a wide range of opinions about them, quite apart from my own; just as I am duty-bound to make this argument or that under my own name when it is relevant to the material, so too am I duty-bound to inform students of some of the most cogent critiques of the positions I favor. But it is not my job to change students' minds about this policy or that, this person or that, by the end of the semester. I can hope to affect the way my students apprehend the world, and I especially hope to affect the way they approach the possibility that some forms of interpretive disagreement may not in fact be negotiable. But when I hear leftist professors here and there arguing that their students watch six hours of Fox News every day and that it's therefore their job to expose them to the "other side" for an hour, I tend to imagine that their classes sound, to some students, more like a seventh hour of Fox News than the voice of liberation. It is a skewed notion of dissent to think that one's classroom should be deployed as the counterweight to conservatism in the rest of the culture; it is a poor conception of rhetoric that leads a professor to speak as if everyone in the room agrees with him or her; and it is a curious form of pedagogy to conduct oneself as if one's lectures could simply and suddenly cause the scales to fall from the eyes of a roomful of Republican undergraduates.

Good teaching involves all kinds of ventriloquism. Sometimes I speak in my own voice; sometimes I refer students to a general consensus (Faulkner's career goes downhill after *Go Down, Moses*) or a generally accepted set of historical facts (there was almost no market for African-American fiction before the era of the Harlem Renaissance); and sometimes I present interpretations I disagree with or actively dislike in order to present lesser-known sides of a ten-sided question, or simply to stir things up. Like liberal New York University professor Siva Vaidhyanathan, I often find myself being a classroom contrarian in the hope that it will make my students sharper. "Most often," Vaidhyanathan writes,

> at liberal places like Wesleyan, the University of Wisconsin, and New York University, I find myself playing devil's advocate. I take positions for the sake of challenging lazy lefty thought. I have voiced approval of Starbucks, Barnes and Noble, and Wal-Mart and made the occasional hemp-clothing-wearing student defend her criticisms of them. I have asked pointed questions that indicate support for television and Web censorship. I have argued against peer-to-peer file sharing. In a course on multiculturalism in which every student had inchoate positive feelings about pluralism, I spent the entire semester breaking it down and exposing its weaknesses. I tried to turn feelings into thoughts and encouraged them to abandon some opinions and strengthen others. Somebody had to do it.[5]

Yes, somebody has to do it. And for most teachers, it's all in a day's work.

LATE IN THE SEMESTER, we read Richard Powers's 1988 novel, *Prisoner's Dilemma*. Part of it is set during World War II and involves a character's fantasia about how Walt Disney turns out to be an American of Japanese ancestry. Appalled by the 1942 federal order to intern Japanese-Americans living in the United States, Disney manages to get two of his employees out of the camps so that they can help him work on a top-secret film project, which will not only win this war but prevent all future wars. I noted that Powers is asking whether it is right to fight a totalitarian enemy by employing totalitarian tactics, and I pointed to passages in which he adduces the internment camps as examples of the game-theory problem known as the prisoner's dilemma (hence the title of the novel).[6] In the prisoner's dilemma, two prisoners are prevented from communicating with each other, and each is given the following options: if you confess and the other guy follows suit, you both get ten years; if you keep quiet and the other guy does the same, you both get two years; if you keep quiet and the other guy squeals, you get the chair and he goes free. At first, each prisoner thinks, well, this is simple enough; I should keep quiet, and the other guy should keep quiet. But then the problem appears to him in another way: if I keep quiet, I get two years or I get the chair; if I squeal, I go free or I get ten years. Clearly, then, I do better when I squeal. And since the other prisoner reasons the same way, they each get ten years, or five times the sentence they'd have gotten if they had kept quiet. You can play with the parameters, but that's the classic version. Almost invariably, prisoners choose to confess, even though mutual trust in the other's steadfastness is clearly the way to go if they want to (a) stay alive and (b) keep their jail time to a minimum. Powers's point is that a world without mutual trust would be a world of unending world war; as the novel unfolds, the prisoner's dilemma becomes a metaphor not only for the Japanese-American internment camps but also for the postwar nuclear era of mutually assured destruction, and for one family's attempt to come to terms with the legacy of that era.

Because it was the fall of 2001, internment camps were a hot topic. The two previous times I had taught the novel, in 1995 and 1999, my students had never heard about the imprisonment of Japanese-Americans during World War II, or about the confiscation of their property. But after the debates about the Patriot Act and the detainees in Guantánamo, almost everyone in the class had heard about the World War II camps. Realizing, then, that every-

thing we said in class about World War II would have sharp resonance for the world after September 11, I mentioned that Powers
has been criticized for apparently suggesting a kind of moral
equivalence between Nazi concentration camps and US internment camps—since the latter, however outrageous and indefensible they were in a putatively democratic nation, were not part of a
program of genocide. *Prisoner's Dilemma* refers at one point to
"roundups far more hideously evil than the local one," thus distin-
guishing between the Holocaust and the Japanese-American
internment, but this has not deflected criticism of Powers on that
score. So I asked the class what they thought of the critique.

John wasn't having any of it. There's no moral equivalence here
at all; Powers is out of his mind, and even Powers's critics have gone
wrong in implicitly agreeing to parse out the different forms of
moral wrong at stake—because, and let's get this much straight, the
internment camps were justified. Far from being outrageous and
indefensible, they were a reasonable security precaution in a desperate time and, furthermore, the detainees were treated quite well.

At that point, I have to admit, I was flummoxed. I've never lost
my composure in a classroom, but I was so stunned that I almost
blurted out, "You've got to be kidding." Even if I had, though, I'm
not sure John would have heard me, because the entire classroom
was immediately in a minor uproar. Everyone from the pacifists to
the drug-law libertarians to the undecideds chimed in at once to
criticize—to say, collectively and incoherently, OK, pal, this time
you've gone too far. "You know nothing about the Japanese who
were imprisoned." "You know nothing about the Constitution."
"You're forgetting that the United States actually issued an apology
to the internees, as well as financial reparations," students said. For
a few seconds, it looked and sounded as if John's classmates wanted
to argue him right out of the room.

So, instead of blurting, I whistled. Loud. "All right. Wait a
minute." The following silence was punctuated by a few low mur-

murs. "The object here isn't to pile on," I said over them. "This is, in fact, one of the things the novel wants us to debate."

"But John," I added, turning to him, "I do want to remind you that you spoke up quite forcefully, earlier this semester, on behalf of the belief that we're all Americans first, and that our national and ethnic origins shouldn't matter. Didn't the internment camps violate that principle?"

No, he said, because here we were dealing with the possibility of treason during wartime, and some Japanese-Americans had, indeed, been in touch with relatives in Japan in ways that threatened national security. Fine, I said, I believe you're quite mistaken about that, and I will be happy to direct you to sources that will challenge you,[7] but suffice it to say for now that you reject one of the premises of the novel, somewhat more emphatically than Powers's harshest critics. Now, let's take this to the rest of the class. Does the prisoner's dilemma apply to World War II in the ways Powers suggests? John here says that the camps were justified; the threat of treason must be met with mass internment. How does Powers treat this argument?[8]

We got through the novel, of course—we didn't lose any lives, and no one was injured. It was only literary criticism, after all. But the class had been completely derailed. John was confirmed in his isolation and sense of opposition, his classmates took to even more severe eye-rolling and head-shaking at his remarks, and, by December, when we got to Colson Whitehead's 1999 novel *The Intuitionist*, a whimsical allegory about race relations and the history of elevator inspection,[9] John was complaining that there were no good white characters in the novel. By that point, even I had had enough, and I told him, via e-mail, that his complaint was not only unwarranted on its face but thoroughly beside the point. In this class, I said, we are not in the business of pursuing reductive identity-politics enterprises like looking for "positive images" in literature, regardless of what group images we might be talking about.

When the semester was over, I wondered whether John's story was the stuff of which right-wing legends are made. Would he remember the seminar as the class in which his right to free speech and debate was trampled by politically correct groupthink, even though he spoke more often than any other single student? He couldn't possibly contend that I'd graded him on the political content of his remarks, because he had received an A for the course. But there was no question that he felt embattled, that he didn't see any contradictions in his argument about the internment camps, and that he had begun to develop an aggressive-defensive "I'm not a racist, but these people . . ." mode of speaking about not only black literary characters but black writers and critics as well. In the last couple of weeks of the term, I found myself speaking to him almost solicitously, as if to say, "You know, if you understand so little about how some of your remarks might be taken by members of racial minorities, and yet you say so much about them, you could be in for some rough times. You might want to read a manual on tact."

But who am I to say such things? For all I know, John might be able to craft a life in which he can deride African-American ambivalence about integration and defend Japanese-American internment camps without ever confronting anyone who disagrees with him. More than that, he might be able to build an entire career out of saying things that I and most of my friends and colleagues would find repugnant. After all, Dinesh D'Souza wrote an entire book on what he called the "civilizational differences" between blacks and whites, defending "rational discrimination" and insisting that "the American slave *was* treated like property, which is to say, pretty well,"[10] and it didn't stop him from winning sinecures at the American Enterprise Institute and the Hoover Foundation, or from being hired by CNN in 2004 as a news analyst. And Michelle Malkin has managed to write a shameful book, *In Defense of Internment*,[11] that advances John's argument about the Japanese-American camps even though the claim that the camps were justified by political necessity has repeatedly been shot down by every reputable historian and journalist, to the point at which it verges on being one of those "interpretations" that no sane person countenances, any more than we countenance the "interpretation" that reports of the Holocaust have been wildly overblown by the international Jewish lobby. And yet, despite offering what her publisher proudly and ignorantly calls a "ringing justification" for the Japanese-American internment camps, Malkin remains a widely published syndicated columnist. Clearly, then, my standards for reasonable discourse, at least when it comes to race, are not universally shared. I can set the tone for my own classroom, but I don't have any business advising John how to talk about anything once he completes my course.

Reflecting on that course years later, I've come to see that only a small, intense class can produce the kind of dynamic we dealt with that semester—where I often felt compelled to restrain students from criticizing someone whose arguments I myself found obnoxious, and where I had to weigh carefully, seven days a week, what things I could say to students in the quasi-public, quasi-private space of the classroom, and what things I should reserve for face-to-face after-class discussions or follow-up e-mail messages. Because of the syllabus, and because of September 11, students wanted to talk after class, on off days, on e-mail, with a professor who would converse with them on all matters local and global. Few critics of academe—and even fewer critics of liberal-left professors—have any idea what kind of work that entails, which is one reason, surely, why headlines like "Conservative Student Punished by Stalinist Campus Orthodoxy" strike those of us who teach as so surreal.

Over my twenty years in teaching, I've had many conservatives in my classes. I like to imagine that I've even had one or two Stalinists, too. I've had many intelligent, articulate students who behaved as if they had a right to speak more often and at greater length than anyone else in the room; I've had versions of Reese Witherspoon's character in *Election* and Hermione Granger in the *Harry Potter* series, who knew the answers to every question ever asked; I've had my share of blurters with very little sense of social boundaries, a few of whom may genuinely have had some degree of Asperger's syndrome, with various autistic or antisocial symptoms. To all such students—indeed, to all students, those with disabilities and those without—I try to apply the standard of disability law: I make reasonable accommodation for them. Needless to say, that doesn't mean that I treat non-disabled students as disabled; it simply means that I try to take each student on his or her own terms. The beautiful thing about the standard of "reasonable accommodation" is that it is a universal imperative (everyone should be accommodated, within reason) that requires one to acknowledge individual idiosyncrasies (not every accommodation will take the same form). It offers a liberal vision of society that I find particularly appealing, both in the classroom and out. The challenge, however, lies in making reasonable accommodation for students whose standards of reasonableness are significantly different from yours. Few aspects of teaching are so difficult—and, I think, so rarely acknowledged by people who don't teach for a living.

SOME OF MY FRIENDS tell me I think too much about students like John, and that, in his case, I overaccommodated a disruptive student precisely because I was too worried about exacerbating his sense of grievance. They're probably right on both counts, but then again, I think I have plenty of reason to worry these days. Over the past five years, conservatives' complaints about American universities—long a feature of conservative culture, at least since the publication of William F. Buckley's 1951 *God and Man at Yale*—have reached a fever pitch. The predominance of liberals on college faculties is taken as proof that conservatives are actively discriminated against in hiring and tenure decisions; commentators like David

Horowitz and Stanley Kurtz are calling for direct governmental oversight of professors, programs, and even individual course reading lists; and a network of student complaint is being built, via groups such as Noindoctrination.org and Students for Academic Freedom, to allow conservative students to report on the doings and teachings of liberal professors—or, more accurately, professors who offend conservatives' political sensibilities in one way or another. It is a dicey time to be a liberal college professor. If you don't have tenure, as two-thirds of us do not,[12] you had better be very careful about what you say and to whom you say it.

I have written this book not only to offer a reply to academe's conservative critics but also to offer curious readers a look into the classroom dynamics of undergraduate courses in contemporary literature and culture, since these are some of the most widely derided and maligned courses in the literature of conservative complaint. But this book is not a string of defenses and denials. On the contrary, it is about liberal "bias" in my own teaching; it is about how classroom discussion is framed, and how I try to frame it. It is also about some of the odd fantasies people (including college students) have about college campuses, and the wrenching personal transformations that either do or don't occur on them. Finally, it is about what it's like to teach young men and women in large public universities in Pennsylvania and Illinois, in the rural middle of otherwise populous states in a complexly divided and fractious democracy. My desire is inescapably that of a veteran and inveterate teacher: I want to explain. In the course of explaining, I will undoubtedly do some special pleading, for I feel that I am working under special circumstances, at a time when both my institution and my faith in reasoned debate are challenged in unprecedented ways. I want to explain not merely because my liberal colleagues and I are under attack from an organized and ascendant conservative movement, but because I believe that liberal education is fundamental to the future of democracy in ways many of us have not fully realized. The United States is the home of the world's only experiment in mass higher education, and even those aspects of American higher education that consist of career training and narrow professional tracking nevertheless contribute to the formation of a credentialed (as opposed to a hereditary or a clerical) class of people who, ideally, should be able to understand cultural values and cultural conflict in New Guinea and in New Orleans. Even the vocational side of college education, in other words, has some cosmopolitan potential. However, this book is concerned primarily with the nonvocational aspects of American higher education—the ones that have to do with the imperative to foster rational debate regardless of its ends.

One of the things at stake on my end of the campus is the very ideal of independent intellectual inquiry, the kind of inquiry whose outcomes cannot be known in advance and cannot be measured in terms of efficiency or productivity. There is no mystery why so many conservative commentators loathe liberal campuses; it is not simply that conservatives control all three branches of government and a good deal of the mass media, and are striking out at the few areas of American cultural life they do not dominate. That much is true, but it fails to capture the truly radical nature of the conservative attacks on academe, for these are attacks not simply on the substance of liberalism (in the form of specific fiscal or social policies stemming from the Progressive Era, the New Deal, and the Great Society) but on procedural liberalism itself, on the idea that no one political faction should control every facet of a society. Radical conservatives' hatred of procedural liberalism, with its checks, balances, and guarantees that minority reports will be incorporated into the body politic, can be seen in House Republicans' rewriting of the rules of their chamber so that Democrats cannot offer amendments, propose legislation, or challenge committee chairs; in Senate Republicans' attempts to establish a similar tyranny of the majority in their chamber, by eliminating the filibuster except in "extraordinary circumstances"; in conservative pundits' defenses of a secret National Security Agency program of domestic spying authorized by the president without legislative or judicial oversight, in direct violation of the Constitution; and in the radical right's increasingly venomous and hallucinatory attacks on a judicial branch most of whose members were in fact appointed by Republicans. What animates the radical right, then, is not so much a specific liberal belief about stem-cell research here or hate-crimes legislation there, but rather the very existence of areas of political independence that do not answer directly and favorably to the state. Independent journalists, independent judges, independent filmmakers, independent professors—all are anathema to the radical right.

There are some forms of conservatism that are absolutely essential to my conception of liberalism. Because I cannot have and do not seek unanimity in political and cultural matters (I have been told that a political party made up of people who agree with me about everything could comfortably conduct its meetings in a phone booth), I believe that the liberal ideal consists in engaging my most stringent interlocutors, so long as we share an underlying commitment to open-ended rational debate. This means that I am open to all manner of reasonable challenges to my beliefs with regard to abortion, affirmative action, taxation and public-sector spending, stem-cell research, disability law, feminism, international relations, nationalism and citizenship, love, hate, war, and peace. But it also means that I inevitably come into conflict with certain kinds of conservatives who value "reason" very differently than I do, and as a result I invariably produce what one of my conservative interlocutors once called a "moral mist" in the classroom, in which (as he put it) certain positions are tacitly understood to be more virtuous than others, and students who want to argue for one of the less virtuous positions understand that they will, in effect, have to argue twice—once to make their point, and once to make the point that they are entitled to make their point.

What do I mean by "moral mist"? Just this: most conservative students should have no problem with my courses, and, in the past, my conservative students have fared just fine. (The postmodernism seminar offers them little in the way of support, however, because conservative intellectuals and artists haven't contributed much to the debates about postmodernism except to wish the whole thing into the ash heap of history.) I do not hold forth on the superiority of Keynesian to Hayekian economics, and only rarely am I moved to say anything about the creation of the social welfare state, so for the most part I don't produce the kind of moral mist that economic libertarians and conservatives would find noxious. And though I am an agnostic myself, I never speak ill of Christianity, Judaism, Islam, or any organized religion, so there is no sense in which any religious student should feel that he or she has to argue twice in my classroom. But on race and sexuality, invariably, my syllabus, my comments, and my very demeanor cannot help but cue students that some forms of social conservatism will indeed have to make their arguments twice in order to be heard. Cultural conservatives of the sort who feel oppressed because their classroom environments do not always permit them to say that homosexuality is a sin and/or a curable disease will surely find my classrooms less than ideal. Likewise, students who defend the Japanese internment camps can expect to be challenged, especially when their remarks appear to contradict remarks they've made earlier in the semester. The practice of critical thinking, after all, is not contentless; it can and does challenge unreasoning prejudice of all kinds, and without it neither the Enlightenment nor the contemporary university is thinkable. And insofar as it places additional moral burdens on certain kinds of conservatives whose opposition to homosexuality stems from deeply held religious belief, yes, this kind of critical thinking can appear to such students to be a form of prejudice in itself.

This conundrum, forged in the gap between procedural liberalism's openness to debate and substantive liberalism's opposition to

racism, sexism, and homophobia, seems to me one of the most difficult moral and intellectual quandaries any liberal teacher has to
face. In the "political correctness" debates of yesteryear, it sometimes took the form of the mind-bending charge that liberals were
the truly intolerant forces in American society, because they failed
to tolerate certain forms of intolerance that were grounded in conservative religious belief. This phrasing of the problem has befuddled more than one liberal, leaving such liberals not only befuddled
but committed to finding better (and more liberal) ways of including the voices of people whose most cherished aim is to silence us
forever. Liberals are required to foster and practice a kind of critical pluralism with regard to social and cultural disputes, but they
are not and should not be required to promote—or protect from
criticism—the views of radicals and authoritarians who construe
all forms of liberalism either as treason to the republic or as
grounds for eternal damnation. The rise of the authoritarian right
thus gives me reason to suspect the motives of conservatives who
call for governmental regulation of professorial speech; I think that
such conservatives are less interested in "fair and balanced" campuses than in campuses that can be compelled, quickly and pain-
lessly, to toe the party line. And yet, as I hope to show in the
following chapters, the rise of the authoritarian right is not merely
an academic affair. The university is one of the last remaining areas
in American life dominated by liberals—and dominated by a most
curious kind of liberal, namely, liberal intellectuals who are committed both to substantive and procedural liberalism, to a form of
pluralism and reasoned debate that does not always culminate in
liberal *conclusions*. It is no overstatement, therefore, to say that the
right's attacks on American universities are attacks on one of the
critical institutions of democracy.

In the pages that follow, I'll give you some idea of what really
goes on in my classrooms, and what kind of critical thinking I promote among my students; along the way, I'll try to show that the

right's campaigns against people like me are not only hysterically overblown, but, in fact, inimical to the ideal of a free society. First, I'll turn to the most common complaints—that the liberal tilt of university faculty amounts to discrimination against outspoken conservative students, and is itself the result of discrimination against conservative scholars.

2.   Conservative Complaints

I$_N$ J$_{ANUARY}$ 2005, O$_{HIO}$ $_{STATE}$ $_{SENATOR}$ L$_{ARRY}$ Mumper introduced an "academic bill of rights for higher education" that, as the *Columbus Dispatch* explained,

> would prohibit instructors at public or private universities from "persistently" discussing controversial issues in class or from using their classes to push political, ideological, religious or anti-religious views. . . .
>
> Mumper, a Republican, said many professors undermine the values of their students because "80 percent or so of them (professors) are Democrats, liberals or socialists or card-carrying Communists" who attempt to indoctrinate students. . . .
>
> The language of Mumper's bill comes from a 2003 booklet by conservative commentator David Horowitz that lays out how students can persuade universities to adopt the "bill of rights." The booklet says it is "dedicated to restoring academic freedom and educational values to America's institutions of higher learning."
>
> The issue has gone national.[1]

The issue had indeed gone national. By the first six months of 2005, state legislatures in California, Florida, Indiana, Louisiana, Maine, Maryland, Massachusetts, Minnesota, New York, North Carolina, Rhode Island, Tennessee, and Washington, as well as

Ohio, had seen bills bearing some resemblance to David Horowitz's "Academic Bill of Rights." Georgia and Colorado, two states
in which Horowitz had campaigned vigorously, adopted "non-
binding resolutions" in favor of the principle that conservative
students must not be intimidated or indoctrinated by their liberal
professors. In Pennsylvania, my home state, the Republican-
controlled House of Representatives voted in July 2005, largely
along party lines, to create a "select subcommittee" to investigate
individual campuses, courses, and professors; the bill stipulates that
"if an individual makes an allegation against a faculty member
claiming bias, the faculty member must be given at least 48 hours'
notice of the specifics of the allegation prior to the testimony being
given and be given an opportunity to testify at the same hearing as
the individual making the allegation."[2] McCarthyite as this sounds,
it is actually an improvement over the original bill, which offered
professors no such "opportunity" to confront their accusers.

Though many mainstream pundits and commentators consider
Horowitz a fringe figure, a former far-left ideologue turned far-
right ideologue, his Academic Bill of Rights is no joke, and has
won him audiences with sympathetic state lawmakers like Ohio's
Mumper, Minnesota's Republican state senator Michele Bachmann,
and Colorado's Republican governor Bill Owens. When Larry
Mumper introduced Senate Bill 24, he was asked how he would
interpret the clause that makes the sensible demand that "Faculty
and instructors shall not infringe the academic freedom and quality
of education of their students by persistently introducing controversial matter into the classroom or coursework that has no relation
to their subject of study and that serves no legitimate pedagogical
purpose."[3] What, a *Columbus Dispatch* reporter wondered, would
constitute "controversial matter" under this heading? "Religion
and politics, those are the main things," replied Mumper.[4] If Senate
Bill 24 were to pass in Ohio, in other words, there would be at least
one state senator who understood it as a license to challenge college

courses that dealt "persistently" with religion or politics. Bad news for political science, history, philosophy, sociology, and religion departments, but good news for people who would prefer universities devoted largely to sports and weather.

Meanwhile, in Florida, Representative Dennis Baxley insisted, upon introducing a similar bill and shepherding it through an eight-to-two party-line committee vote, that the legislation would help to combat "leftist totalitarianism" on the part of "dictator professors," by allowing students to sue professors whenever they felt their beliefs were not being "respected." At the University of Florida, the *Independent Florida Alligator* reported:

> Students who believe their professor is singling them out for "public ridicule"—for instance, when professors use the Socratic method to force students to explain their theories in class—would also be given the right to sue.
>
> "Some professors say, 'Evolution is a fact. I don't want to hear about Intelligent Design [a creationist theory], and if you don't like it, there's the door,'" Baxley said, citing one example when he thought a student should sue.[5]

For Minnesota's Senator Bachmann, similarly, the attraction of Horowitz's "bill of rights" is that it would allow the theory of evolution to be considered an artifact of "liberal bias."[6]

It is hard, no doubt, for many liberals and thoughtful conservatives to take these developments seriously. A campaign for "academic freedom" which would bar professors from dealing with religion and politics, and which seeks to give students the right to sue their biology professors for teaching the theory of evolution without giving proper "respect" to a "theory" for which there is no (and, by definition, cannot be any) scientific evidence whatsoever? How does this make any kind of sense? Most of the liberals and thoughtful conservatives I know would consider this to be a phenomenon of the fringe right wing, no more consequential than the extreme right's past campaigns against the fluoridation of drinking water and the introduction of zip codes. But then, many of the liberals and thoughtful conservatives I know are still in some form of denial about the extent to which the fringe right is now a powerful, agenda-setting presence in state legislatures (not to mention the highest levels of the federal government). And most people outside academe are thoroughly unaware of how well-organized the anti-academic right is, and how successful the Horowitz machine has been in getting its version of campus controversies represented in national media—regardless of the actual realities of the events they describe.

Three examples from 2005 should suffice to convey some sense of how the anti-academic right's campaign has operated to date. Each one involves a student claiming to have been persecuted by liberal faculty, and each one has made national news—usually by way of Fox News, on which David Horowitz is a regular visitor. The first involved a student at an unnamed Colorado college who was allegedly compelled to write an essay on why George Bush is a war criminal, and who allegedly received an F when she turned in an essay on why Saddam Hussein was a war criminal instead. Horowitz wrote about this case in his online magazine, *FrontPage .com*, on December 5, 2003;[7] the tale was repeated in various media, not only on Fox News but in the *Christian Science Monitor*, the *New York Sun*, and the *Wall Street Journal's OpinionJournal.com*. It is a cautionary tale about academic liberal bias so virulent as to punish innocent students for failing to impugn their president during a time of war. The only problem with the story is that it is false; no such essay was required, the professor in question was a registered Republican, and the student did not receive an F. Not until March 2005—more than a year after the story first broke—was the full extent of Horowitz's shenanigans revealed, by Scott Jaschik of *Inside Higher Education*:

Additional context comes from Robert Dunkley, an assistant professor of criminal justice at Northern Colorado who was identified by Horowitz as the professor involved. In an interview, Dunkley said that politics had nothing to do with the student's grade, and that the context of his course has been distorted.

For instance, Dunkley said that the course focused on the relationship between deviance and being classified as a criminal. "We talked in class about how George Washington was considered a war criminal to the British," he said. "We were going into the idea that different people define criminal behavior differently."

And in case there's any confusion, Dunkley wants it known that he does not think the father of our country was a war criminal. "I'm an American citizen and I thank God for George Washington. Without George, we wouldn't be here."

Dunkley said that he's angry about the way Horowitz and his supporters have made him an example of alleged liberal bias in academe. Dunkley said that he comes from a Republican family, is a registered Republican and considers himself politically independent, taking pride in never having voted a straight party ticket.

He said that he would have explained himself or his course to Horowitz or his backers, but was never asked. "He's cooked this whole thing up," Dunkley said.[8]

Horowitz does not admit defeat—or even error—gracefully. When confronted with this article, he countered with a column which he titled "Some of Our Facts Were Wrong; Our Point Was Right."[9] A plausible enough claim, except for the bit about the professor, the bit about the student, and the bit about the grade.

So much for Exhibit A. Exhibit B is still worse. It involves nineteen-year-old Foothill College student Ahmad al-Qloushi, a Kuwaiti-American who claimed that he received a failing grade on a term paper about the US Constitution because it was "pro-American," and who promptly appeared as a guest on Fox News's

Hannity and Colmes show on February 17, 2005.[10] Horowitz flogged this case as well; it was picked up by the Rev. Sun Myung Moon's *Washington Times*, and bandied about briefly on the Internet, partly for its obvious shock value: anti-American professor harasses Middle Eastern student who loves the United States! But it was bandied about only briefly—because once al-Qloushi's essay itself became available, the story died an undignified death. Al-Qloushi's political science professor, Joseph Woolcock, had posed the following question:

> Dye and Zeigler [authors of an American government textbook] contend that the constitution of the United States was not "ordained and established" by "the people" as we have so often been led to believe. They contend instead that it was written by a small educated and wealthy elite in America who [were] representative of powerful economic and political interests. Analyze the US constitution (original document), and show how its formulation excluded [the] majority of the people living in America at that time, and how it was dominated by America's elite interest.

Most people who have taken college-level political science courses will know that this is a standard line of inquiry with regard to the founding of the United States: on one hand, the Declaration of Independence insisted that all men were created equal, and on the other hand, the Constitution (the original document) backed away from this radical claim in favor of a far more limited conception of republican citizenship. Indeed, I can say—from my office across the quad in the English department—that if students of American political science are not introduced to the contradictions underlying the foundation of a revolutionary democratic nation that practiced slavery and restricted the vote to landowning men, they are being miseducated.

If al-Qloushi had been given an F for arguing that the Constitu-

tion represented the best compromise available at the time—a compromise between Hamiltonian and Jeffersonian conceptions of
democracy, mediated by a Madisonian insistence on the separation
of powers and a realistic assessment of what it would take to get the
Southern states to agree to something stronger than the Articles of
Confederation—then Horowitz and Fox News might have been
justified in pleading his case as an example of liberal bias. But what
al-Qloushi actually wrote was this (I will not cite the essay in full—
it is available online—but I will give you some idea of its quality):

> I completely disagree with Dye and Zeigler's contention that the
> founding father had ONLY their best interests at heart and that that
> the constitution of the United States was a progressive document for
> its time compared to the aristocratic monarchies of Western Europe
> (excluding Britain). The American constitution worried monarchs in
> Europe. The right for men to choose their own representatives was
> unheard of in the rest of the world. Yet in a young country which
> freed itself from the shackles of the greatest empire of the time. The
> founding fathers were stalwart heroes who led the brave young men
> of this great land and in order to establish a democracy maybe not a
> direct or perfect democracy but one that guarantees the freedom of
> its citizens. . . .
>
> The United States constitution might have excluded the majority
> of people at the time. But it progressed and America like every nation
> in the world progressed and became a greater nation the constitution
> is now a document held in great esteem by Americans the Founding
> Fathers of America are greatly enshrined in dollar bills and the
> American people are proud of their country and history. . . .
>
> It is the American constitution that helps the American govern-
> ment to solve its problems in legal ways and in ways that will bring
> true American justice and resolve. The American foundation was
> built by the American constitution and the Founding Fathers and
> nothing can destroy these foundations.

"Terrorist attacks can shake the foundations of our biggest buildings, but they cannot touch the foundation of America. These acts shatter steel, but they cannot dent the steel of American resolve."

President George W Bush. . . .

If the constitution was so negative then how did the United States the most powerful nation in the world today. If it was so negative how did the Soviet Union collapse in the Cold War? The United States constitution is a great document which for its time was extremely progressive and the evidence to the that is the United States' accomplishments to date.

Quotes By
Thomas Jefferson
George W Bush

After the essay became available on the Internet, most conservative academics immediately distanced themselves from it; one conservative professor/blogger gave it a low D, and another gave it an F. The essay has the germ of a plausible thesis—that the Constitution was progressive for its time but required reinterpretation and amendment to adapt to evolving conceptions of human freedoms—but is terribly written and largely tangential to the question at issue. But one thing is uncontroversial: it is not a college-level essay.

Now, stop and contemplate the political dispensation under which an essay like this is submitted as evidence of liberal bias in the university. Remember, as you wonder at this state of affairs, that American conservatives have been complaining—plausibly enough, in some cases—for the past three decades about the sorry state of undergraduate writing and the alleged prevalence of "feel-good" forms of pedagogy which seek to bolster students' self-esteem even when the students in question are incapable of composing a decent sentence in English. And then marvel, if you will, at the phenomenon of a conservative culture of complaint—not a fringe or marginal culture, but a culture that extends to national media networks like Fox News—that takes an essay like al-Qloushi's not as evidence of the shoddy quality of undergraduate writing but as evidence of the persecution of conservative students by leftist professors. For any teacher who has ever encountered an incompetent essay of any kind, the elevation of al-Qloushi to the status of Conservative Student Hero is a profound testimony to the intellectual vacuity of the anti-academic right—and the intellectual bankruptcy of the right-wing media apparatus for which such tales of oppression and atrocity are now the stock in trade.

And yet just as Exhibit B exceeds Exhibit A, so in turn is it exceeded by Exhibit C. In May 2005, Wells College student Nicole Krogman issued a press release that read as follows:[11]

> Wells senior Nicole Krogman is the Co-Chairman of the Wells College Republicans and an editor of the Cornell American, a conservative publication at nearby Cornell University. She is the most high-profile conservative student at Wells.
>
> In her final semester at Wells, Krogman undertook a non-credit bearing independent study tutorial with Professor Linda Lohn, Chair of Wells' American Studies Department.
>
> There was minimal communication between Krogman and Lohn during the course of the semester. Suddenly, on April 5th, rather than hearing from Lohn, Krogman received notice from the college's "Community Court," a quasi-judicial body composed of students and faculty. She was informed that her tutorial project had to be completed within seven days, failing which she would be held "in contempt of court." Given the extensive nature of the work involved and the rush of end-of-semester assignments, it was not possible for Krogman to complete the project on such a short deadline.
>
> Thereafter, the Community Court found Krogman in contempt of court, and suspended her for the remainder of the spring semester.....
>
> Ironically, Krogman was charged with "contempt" on April 15th,

just one day after the "Republican Coming Out Day" that she and others in her college Republican club had organized, a day dedicated to encouraging "closet Republicans" on campus to reveal their political orientation in the face of the college's prevailing liberal culture. It was also the day that, at the invitation of the Wells Republicans, conservative commentator Star Parker spoke on campus.

Within days, sure enough, Ms. Krogman was a guest on *Hannity and Colmes.* Moreover, she got a critical boost from Morton Blackwell of the right-wing Leadership Institute, the outfit responsible not only for training countless conservative pundits and politicians but for distributing those famous purple Band-Aids at the Republican National Convention, in symbolic mockery of John Kerry's Purple Hearts. Blackwell issued a separate press release with a slightly different story:

Once again, leftist professors and college administrators are attacking a conservative student days before graduation.

This travesty of justice is occurring at Wells College in upstate New York.

Nicole Krogman, [*sic*] wrote an article for Onyx, a campus newspaper at Wells College. Nicole used some of the language from this article in another article she wrote in the Cornell American, where she works as an editor.

Nicole told my staff that school officials "suspended" her from the school. They charged her with plagiarism for the absurd reason that she did not cite herself as the author of the article that she wrote for the Cornell American.

Nicole is a senior at Wells College. She expected to graduate this month. Now she can't. Wells College does not graduate students in the winter. As a result of the attacks by the left, she cannot graduate until next spring.

Even worse, because the school forced her out of her classes so late in the semester, she cannot get any portion of her tuition refunded. What malicious people you and I are fighting on campus.

What malicious people, indeed. But what's this about poor Nicole not citing herself? Well, actually, according to the *Syracuse Post–Standard*, the plagiarism charge against Ms. Krogman was a bit more serious than that:

> Appearing on Fox News Channel's "Hannity & Colmes" show, Nicole Krogman said that her suspension is rooted in a "ridiculous" allegation of plagiarism concerning a piece she wrote for the Onyx, the campus newspaper, in November 2004.
>
> That 21-paragraph article contained one original paragraph. Of the 1,149 words in the piece, 90 were her own. The rest was copied straight from the words of four other authors, who were not credited in print.

Here's where the story gets interesting. The course that Ms. Krogman didn't complete on time was a course in journalism ethics, to which she had been assigned by a student-faculty court as a result of her plagiarism. And it's not clear that Ms. Krogman learned anything in that course, for, as one liberal blogger discovered after spending a few minutes with Google, her column for the May 7, 2005, issue of the *Cornell American* consisted almost entirely of passages lifted from uncredited sources. Apparently, professors who frown on practices like these are now legitimate targets for right-wing smear campaigns. Such professors are, after all, "malicious people."

Perhaps, as this book goes to press, the right-wing smear machine will manage to come up with a more plausible example of liberal professors haranguing and punishing conservative students. But that machine has been in place for some time now, ever since Reed Irvine founded Accuracy in Academia in 1985, searching assiduously for evidence that liberal professors persecute and penalize conservative students, and this is the best they've come up with so far: a couple of rank incompetents topped off by a serial plagiarist, out of a potential victim pool of sixteen million undergraduates nationwide. Recently, they've moved the search to the Internet; since 2003, Horowitz's subsidiary outfit, Students for Academic Freedom (whose motto is "You can't get a good education if they're only telling you half the story"), has been soliciting testimony from students in the form of an online "Academic Student Abuse Center." On this website, students can (and do) complain about everything from their professors' irrelevant political monologues to the ubiquity of the homosexual agenda. Reading the postings on the Abuse Center leaves me with the impression that on rare occasions, a tiny handful of my colleagues really do harangue their students by going on explicitly political tangents, though it is not clear what the results of these monologues might be other than a classroom full of annoyed or bored students. But for the most part, the evidence provided on the SAF website is as self-undermining as anything I've described so far:

> This complaint applies to the discriminating nature of grading of my English teacher. She knows I'm an advancer of conservative ideas b/c I where a "W" t-shirt to class on sometimes. Ever since the 1st day of class when I wore my "W" shirt she has treated me cold and been discriminating in grading my essays. On the last one, I wrote about how family values in the books weve read aren't good. I know the paper was pretty much great because I spell checked it and proofred it twice. I got an D– just because the professor hates families and thinks its okay to be gay. — Ohio State, English, 2/9/05

> We were then required to watch an immoral Seinfeld episode dealing with masturbation, an exercise with little sociological value. She then gave a lecture on "moral relativity," which she defined very

closely with "cultural relativism." — St. Louis University, Sociology, 2/13/05

Talked about flags as symbols of states and argued that new Iraqi flag was not a result of a transparent and fair process. Argued AS FACT that new flag had similar colors to Israeli flag and that this could be problematic. Claimed AS FACT that other Arab societies had red, green and black in their flags. Very biased. Had no visual proof of this. *Action Taken:* I will fact check and complain to administration. He has an English accent but claims to be an American. — St. Michael's College, Human Geography, 4/30/04[12]

This aspect of the conservative critique of universities would be laughable, if only right-wing state legislators weren't taking it so seriously. In Ohio, for instance, it only took one student's account of persecution to get Larry Mumper to introduce his Horowitzian bill to the state senate; according to the *Columbus Dispatch*, "Mumper said he's been investigating the issue for months and has heard of an Ohio student who said she was discriminated against because she supported Bush for president."[13] This does not strike me as overwhelming evidence for Mumper's major premise, which was that "I see students coming out having gone in without any ideological leanings one way or another, coming out with an indoctrination of a lot of left-wing issues."[14] What *I* see, by contrast, is that conservative students are now encouraged to complain about their grades and their professors for any and all reasons, attributing their less-than-desirable grades not to their own ignorance (about flags or moral relativism or the correct spelling of "proofread") but to pervasive liberal bias. It is as if a nationwide whining network has been established for the least prepared and least capable students in the class. If I were a conservative intellectual with qualms about the liberal tilt of academe, I would be embarrassed at the evidence provided by students like these.

But then, if I were a conservative intellectual, I would also be embarrassed by some of the students who have decided to target liberal faculty in more aggressive ways. For example, at Santa Rosa Junior College in the spring semester of 2005, the president of that campus's College Republicans posted, on the office doors of ten faculty members, red stars accompanied by a copy of a state education code section—itself an artifact of the McCarthy era—prohibiting the teaching of Communism with the "intent to indoctrinate" students. Local press coverage of the event revealed that the Horowitz-inspired student who posted the stars had not meant to "attack" anyone, but merely to "start a discussion":

> [P]olitical science major Molly McPherson of Rohnert Park said she had only intended to start a discussion about the personal politics of SRJC humanities instructors by posting the stars. . . .
>
> The red stars were not intended as a personal attack on individual instructors, she said. "I regret that it was taken that way."[15]

McPherson, despite her youth, already had the routine down cold: a provocative, neo-Nazi publicity stunt (with stars, no less), followed by a protestation of innocence, and capped off with the standard non-apology apology: not "I regret posting red stars on the office doors of faculty members in order to intimidate them," but merely "I regret that it was taken that way." Perhaps this is what the new right-wing student culture will look and sound like: in some cultures, people "begin discussion" by raising a point or simply saying hello; in this culture, people "begin discussion" with a little anonymous threat here and follow-up slander there.

AT THIS POINT, reasonable people might wonder what in the world these students are thinking, and how in the world people like Horowitz, Blackwell, Hannity, and company imagine that they can get away with passing off nonsense like this as serious evidence of liberal bias. The answer is that for right-wing activists like these, the assault on academe doesn't have anything to do with actual academic protocols and practices; it's simply another political game, to be played by the rules they apply to every other kind of political game. They have enjoyed great success in national politics by making up stuff about John Kerry's war record, accusing John McCain of fathering a black child out of wedlock, and attributing to Al Gore any number of things he never said, and they think of their attack on liberal professors in the same terms—with the critical proviso, of course, that most liberal professors are even slower and less effective respondents to smear campaigns than were Kerry, McCain, and Gore.

Thus, for certain right-wing culture warriors it is not sufficient to note that there are far more liberals on college faculties, as a percentage of the faculty population, than there are liberals in the country as a whole, as a percentage of the general population. One recent, reliable, comprehensive survey of our political attitudes, conducted by the Higher Education Research Institute and covering 55,521 faculty members from 416 institutions, showed that from 1989 to 2001–02, the percentage of faculty members identifying themselves as either "liberal" or "far left" grew from 42 to 48 percent; the percentage describing themselves as "conservative" or "far right" held steady at 18 percent; and the group identifying itself as "middle of the road" shrank from 40 to 34 percent. The survey noted that "movement toward 'liberal' or 'far left' political identification over the last 12 years has been especially strong among women faculty: from 45 percent to 54 percent. . . . In 2001, 21 percent of male professors and 14 percent of female professors defined their political views as either 'conservative' or 'far right.'" In the general population, by contrast, a 2005 Harris poll showed that 18 percent of Americans describe themselves as liberal, 36 percent call themselves conservative, and 41 percent are "middle of the road."

Interestingly, those data have held firm for decades; moderates have remained at 40 or 41 percent, conservatives have varied between 32 and 38 percent, and liberals have remained at 18 percent since the Vietnam War.[16]

There's really no question, then, that campuses are teeming with liberal faculty, especially when campuses are compared with the rest of the country. That 48–18 differential is pretty significant. Strangely, however, those numbers are just not exciting or dramatic enough for most right-wing culture warriors, so they've gone and made up some new numbers more to their liking, in order to portray campuses as places where decent hardworking conservatives can't so much as get their feet in the door. In 2002 Horowitz teamed up with Karl Zinsmeister of the American Enterprise Institute, whose monthly magazine, *American Enterprise*, devoted the cover story of its September issue to a survey that apparently showed that liberals outnumber conservatives on college faculties by a ratio of eleven to one.[17] The study was quickly picked up by George Will and *U.S. News and World Report*'s John Leo, as well as by conservative professors like Mark Bauerlein of Emory University's English department who, in 2004, opened an essay in the *Chronicle of Higher Education* by writing, "Conservatives on college campuses scored a tactical hit when the American Enterprise Institute's magazine published a survey of voter registration among humanities and social-science faculty members several years ago. More than nine out of 10 professors belonged to the Democratic or Green party, an imbalance that contradicted many liberal academics' protestations that diversity and pluralism abound in higher education."[18] Conservatives may in fact have scored a tactical hit, but it bears pointing out that the study is severely skewed. As Martin Plissner wrote in the *American Prospect*, a liberal magazine, Horowitz and Zinsmeister "sent student volunteers to boards of election to search out the party registrations of 1,843 college teachers at 21 institutions." And though a liberal–conservative ratio of over eleven to one is stark, Plissner notes that these eleven-to-one dice are loaded:

> In the University of Texas sample, for example, 28 of the 94 teachers came from women's studies—not exactly a highlight of any school's core curriculum or a likely cross section of its faculty. At the same time, none of the 94 was from the university's huge schools of engineering, business, law or medicine—or from any of the sciences. At Cornell University, it's the same story: 166 L's by the *AE* bar graphs, and only 6 R's. But not one faculty member in the entire sample taught in the engineering, business, medicine or law schools, or in any of the sciences. Thirty-three, on the other hand, were in women's studies—more than any subject, save for English.
>
> The methodology employed is similarly slapdash at the other chosen campuses. Harvard's faculty of more than 2,000 is represented by 52 members from just three academic disciplines, all in the social sciences. More than half of the University of California, Los Angeles sample comes from just two disciplines: history and, once again, women's studies.[19]

My colleagues in the Department of Statistics call this kind of thing Cherry-Picking 101. Apparently, a comprehensive study of over 55,000 faculty members' self-descriptions, revealing that liberals outnumber conservatives by a ratio of 2.67 to 1 (48 to 18 percent) at over four hundred institutions, is just not good enough for these people. No, they have to go and look up the party registrations of 1,800 faculty members at twenty-one institutions, because the data are tastier when the data are cooked.

When it comes to cooking data, Horowitz is the Iron Chef. Not content with exaggerating hysterically about the presence of liberals on the faculty, Horowitz has also advanced the bizarre theory that liberals utterly dominate the world of commencement speeches; in September 2003, he published on *FrontPage.com* the results of a survey which showed that "99% of graduation day speakers called themselves liberals, Democrats, or Green Party Members." The survey was conducted by Horowitz's Center for the Study of Popular Culture; it covered thirty-two of the United States's 1,500 four-year colleges (mainly places like Wellesley, Oberlin, Swarthmore, Wesleyan, Berkeley, and Cornell—famously liberal campuses where both students and faculty tend toward what one might call the vegan–anti-globalization–*Vagina Monologues* cultural left), and it listed people like Ted Koppel, Tom Brokaw, Scott Turow, Cokie Roberts, Peter Jennings, Claire Shipman, Christopher Reeve, and Lowell Weicker as "liberals" while listing Alan Greenspan and Helmut Kohl as "neutral." Greenspan and Kohl are, of course, openly partisan figures, whereas most of the journalists and celebrities listed by Horowitz as "liberals" are invited to speak not because they are liberals but because they are journalists and celebrities. (Oddly, even in this heavily weighted scheme of things, liberals, Democrats, and Greens do not actually get 99 percent of the speaking engagements; Horowitz here claims that the left–right ratio is a mere ten or fifteen to one.) The results of the "survey" appear on Horowitz's website under the heading "One Last, Leftist Lecture," and are accompanied by a picture of the Demon Lady herself, Hillary Clinton, dressed in cap and gown.[20] That's the campus according to Horowitz: leftist indoctrination at the hands of Hillary Clinton, Cokie Roberts, and Claire Shipman—and in a commencement address, no less. In the world of right-wing fundraising, I suppose this is all well and good; many of Horowitz's readers are, after all, possessed of the notion that television news anchors like Koppel and bestselling novelists like Turow are in cahoots with academic leftists, and, for them, Hillary is the appropriate icon for a Two Minutes of Hate followed by a generous donation to *FrontPage.com*.

A Horowitzian fixation on the political leanings of commencement speakers is a faintly comic affair, worthy of Jack D. Ripper in

Dr. Strangelove. But when a right-wing attack machine wants to crush a liberal academic who ventures into the public sphere, the results can be quite ugly. The most egregious example is probably Abigail Thernstrom's 1993 hit job on Lani Guinier, who had been nominated by Bill Clinton to serve as the head of the Justice Department's civil rights division; in the pages of the *New Republic*, Thernstrom mischaracterized Guinier's work horribly,[21] eventually helping to persuade the never-steadfast Clinton to withdraw her nomination before she had been debated by the Senate. Thernstrom did not attack alone; she was merely finishing a job that began at the *Wall Street Journal* (in an essay by Clint Bolick, whom Thernstrom had alerted to Guinier's appointment in the first place). But for academic readers, who tend to abide by scholarly protocols of citation, possibly the most remarkable aspect of the *New Republic* essay was Thernstrom's random use of quotation marks, which gave the impression that Thernstrom was citing Guinier when in fact she was simply making things up:

> [I]n Guinier's world, black constituents can lack representation even if their elected officials are black. If the officeholders are not "community-based," "culturally rooted" and politically and psychologically "authentic," then they're "tokens"—contaminated by white support. Thus neither Virginia Governor Douglas Wilder nor Andrew Young counts as a "black advocate"; they are too "assimilated" into the political mainstream. The authentic black has a "distinctive voice" and a level of group consciousness incompatible with white enthusiasm.

What Guinier actually argued, of course, was that any winner-take-all voting system can be rigged or gerrymandered so as to disenfranchise 49 percent of its constituents, and in a series of law review essays she proposed a range of alternative voting systems, from cumulative voting to proportional representation, to offset what James Madison sagely called the tyranny of the majority. The interesting thing about Guinier's ideas is that they empower any minority in any district; contrary to what Thernstrom would have you believe, it's not always about African-American voters electing "authentic" African-American representatives. As Guinier notes in her book *Lift Every Voice*, the Illinois House of Representatives was elected by proportional representation until 1980, and as a result Republicans could actually get elected by (and therefore would occasionally feel obligated to) the people of the city of Chicago. But Abigail Thernstrom was not hired to do an academically legitimate version of political science; she was hired to hit Guinier, and she got the job done. When she was asked what lesson academic critics should learn from the tactics with which she took down Guinier, she gave a reporter two words of advice: "Grow up."[22]

That's the way things are done in Washington, as grown-ups like Thernstrom are aware. But academe, for all its faults, tends to frown on tactics like these; when people publish essays and books in which they plagiarize the work of others or make factually inaccurate claims, their scholarship is rigorously reviewed and their careers are put in jeopardy, as former Emory University historian Michael Bellesiles can testify.[23] We don't catch every last scoundrel and malefactor, to be sure, but we have an anti-scoundrel and anti-malefactor policy in place when it comes to the claims we make in public. Students like Nicole Krogman, I imagine, have been taught by their intellectual mentors in the right-wing punditocracy that it's perfectly all right to blow off old-fashioned, useless subjects like journalistic ethics, and that it's perfectly all right to make up numbers and rewrite registered Republican faculty members as vicious Bush-bashing liberals, but the practices that might eventually win her a job as a right-wing pundit would bar her from any academic department of journalism in the country. Conversely, Lani Guinier did not survive the right-wing media attack apparatus, but, because academe does not follow the rules of the right-wing media attack apparatus, Guinier eventually landed on her feet—not at the Justice Department, but at Harvard Law School, where she became the first tenured woman of color in the school's history.

The spirit animating right-wing hijinx is not entirely relativist; it is not simply a matter of grabbing any argumentative handle that happens to be lying nearby. These activists believe—insofar as their own words can be believed—that they are acting in the service of a larger truth. Just as Abigail Thernstrom honestly believed that Guinier's defeat was ultimately more important than any of the piddling factual claims that legal scholars might plausibly make about her work, so too does David Horowitz believe that the marginalization of people like David Horowitz is more important than any minute parsing of whether people like David Horowitz are in fact marginalized. I call this "the fib for truth," and I take my terms from Horowitz himself—more precisely, from his exchange with Fox News pundit Bill O'Reilly on February 1, 2005:

> O'REILLY: All right. We're talking—Nancy Rabinowitz is on the faculty at Hamilton, and. . . .
> HOROWITZ: Right.
> O'REILLY: You know—but it is to Hamilton's credit that you were invited to speak there, correct?
> HOROWITZ: Yes. Well, I—you know, the conservative kids invited me. It's a little different when you're invited as a—you know, a speaker paid by and invited by the faculty. It's not like the faculty brought me up there.

But, in fact, it *was* like the faculty had brought him up there. It was precisely as if the faculty had brought him up there; historian Maurice Isserman had invited him to speak at Hamilton College in the fall of 2002, and Horowitz had acknowledged as much on his own weblog, when, on September 18 of that year, he wrote, "Today I am at Hamilton College in Clinton NY to speak on the Sixties. It is one of the rare occasions I have been officially invited, in this case by historian Maurice Isserman with whom I have had an email correspondence for some time." And when I pointed out all of this on my own weblog, Horowitz responded on his weblog as follows: "I fibbed about my invitation to Hamilton and about my Academic Bill of Rights. . . . It was truer to say that I had to be invited by students (and the second time I went that was exactly the case) than to say the faculty there—the Kirkland project in particular, which is what we were talking about—would invite me."[24] So it was a fib, a little white lie. But it was a fib for truth, just like the story about the student from a Colorado college who had been flunked for refusing to argue that George Bush is a war criminal.

The fib for truth is on Horowitz's side, in this case. By his own report, he speaks at thirty to forty campuses per year, and his speaking fee is $5,000. That's a pretty hefty fee, by academic standards; megapundits like Sean Hannity can demand $100,000 and a private jet for their every appearance, but in my experience—which includes four years of directing a humanities institute at the University of Illinois, during which I never paid any speaker more than $3,000, regardless of his or her international reputation (and I entertained many scholars with international reputations)—the fees for public figures run roughly one to two powers of ten times the fees of ordinary academic speakers ("ordinary" here means "with the exception of a couple of academic superstars who command $10,000 or more"). Many academic departments, humanities institutes, and scholarly "speakers' series" simply cannot afford someone in Horowitz's range. But the local College Republicans can foot the bill, just as the local College Democrats can afford to bring in a celebrity like Michael Moore, because their speakers' series are subsidized by student activity fees. Unfortunately, Horowitz is obsessed with the cultural legitimacy that would (he thinks) accrue to an invitation from a faculty group as opposed to a student group. Yet his public presentations are predicated in part on his experience as a figure who is "excluded" from academe; in other words, Horowitz has somehow managed to build a sub-

sidiary career, clearing $150,000 to $200,000 in speaking fees on top
of his $310,000 salary, out of complaining—on his way from the
Georgia state legislature to Fox News to the Colorado state legislature, eking out an existence on the very margins of American society—that he isn't getting more speaking invitations from the very
faculty members he insults and slanders. And when someone like
Hamilton College's Maurice Isserman does invite him to campus,
Horowitz proceeds to deny it on national television. Obviously, the
fact that Horowitz receives few speaking invitations from faculty
members is not evidence that faculty members are overwhelmingly
leftist. It is evidence that faculty members are, despite their many
idiosyncrasies, overwhelmingly sane.

STILL, FOR ALL OUR overwhelming sanity, we do have some controversial scholars working in controversial areas of study. Scholars of
sexuality, for instance, can usually assume that a good portion of
the American citizenry is deeply hostile to their work, particularly
if their work involves gay and lesbian sexuality in any form, however mediated. The hostility isn't always as overt as that of
Alabama state representative Gerald Allen, who in April 2005 proposed a bill that would prevent Alabama's public libraries from
buying books by gay authors or involving gay characters (his original intent was to strip libraries of all such works, from Shakespeare
to Alice Walker), saying, "I don't look at it as censorship. I look at
it as protecting the hearts and souls and minds of our children."[25]
Thankfully, relatively few conservative public officials see it as
their job to protect the children of America from the heritage of
Western culture. But the homophobia confronting scholars of sexuality is there, all the same, from sea to shining sea.

Likewise, faculty in Middle Eastern studies, particularly those
who are ardently pro-Palestinian or critical of US policies in the
region, have come under fire from conservative constituencies—

albeit conservative constituencies that have little in common with those that are exercised by the idea of students reading literary works by gay and lesbian authors. It is unsurprising that Middle Eastern studies is controversial, especially after September 11, and though it is a field well outside the areas of my expertise, I have tried to follow some of the more public debates involving, on one side, scholars such as Rashid Khalidi, Joseph Massad, and Hamid Dabashi, and on the other, figures such as Daniel Pipes, Martin Kramer, Stanley Kurtz, and the organization called Campus Watch, which was established by Pipes through the Middle East Forum. In at least one way I am not a neutral observer of Campus Watch; when, in 2002, I learned that Campus Watch had created a list of Middle Eastern studies scholars in order to (in their words) target professors who "actively dissociate themselves from the United States," and that they had named twenty US colleges that "fan the flames of disinformation, incitement and ignorance" by having Middle Eastern studies programs that contain professors who are harshly critical of Israel, I wrote to them to protest what I called their Stasi-like tactics, as did over one hundred professors and graduate students across the country. In response, Campus Watch created a webpage—since discredited and taken down— which they titled "Solidarity with Apologists" (the apologists in question being the Middle Eastern studies scholars Campus Watch had now deemed to be "apologists for terrorism"), and they included my name on their short-lived blacklist. At the same time, Campus Watch insisted that their organization "fully respects the freedom of speech of those it debates while insisting on its own freedom to comment on their words and deeds."[26] I found (and still find) this claim remarkably disingenuous. It is as if Campus Watch were to say, "We respect these scholars' freedom of speech—we simply call them 'apologists for suicide bombings and militant Islam' on our website. We're not to blame if people call for their firing, imprisonment, or death."

As a result, I viewed the controversy in 2004–05 over Columbia University's Middle Eastern studies program with some ambivalence.[27] The program came under intense scrutiny both internally and externally, as a campus committee reviewed the scholarship and classroom behavior of a number of Columbia professors while local right-wing tabloids like the *New York Post* and the *New York Sun* kept up a steady drumbeat of calls for those professors' dismissal. There was no question, I thought, that professors like Khalidi and Massad were to my left on the question of Palestine, and that I could not agree with everything they had to say on the subject; but there was no question that, with regard to the principle of academic freedom, my agreement with their remarks was entirely beside the point. They were being subjected to an astonishingly vicious campaign of political and intellectual harassment, conducted not only by tabloid media but by a horde of opportunistic New York politicians and, perhaps most importantly, a right-wing pro-Israeli group called the David Project.

In April 2005, writing in the *Nation* on the Columbia controversy, Scott Sherman described Massad as "a man who traffics in absolutes": "For Pipes & Co.," Sherman suggested, "Massad is something of a gift: He is strident, dogmatic, proud, deliberately provocative and utterly uncompromising in his defense of the Palestinian struggle."[28] Massad's reply to Sherman, a few weeks later, unfortunately adopted something very much like a strident and uncompromising approach, opening with a full-bore attack on Sherman and the *Nation*:

> Even the mainstream *New York Times* showed more journalistic professionalism in its coverage of the Columbia University witchhunt when it refused to engage in the kind of baseless character assassination in which Sherman engages.
>
> Without providing a shred of evidence for his profile, Sherman describes me, among other things, as "dogmatic" and as "a man who

traffics in absolutes, a man who often infuriates even those who are sympathetic to his views." It is unclear how Sherman knows any of this. Has he spoken to all "those who are sympathetic to my views"? Did they all tell him that I often infuriate them? What are the signs of my dogmatism? How can one even begin to respond to such yellow journalism?[29]

Subsequently, in response to Sherman's remark that Massad is capable of "unleashing a steady stream of inflammatory anti-Zionist rhetoric: 'racist Jewish state' is a locution he constantly employs," Massad spent two paragraphs explaining why Israel is a racist Jewish state. Of all the charges brought against the Department of Middle East and Asian Languages and Cultures (MEALAC), and all the inflammatory innuendo circulated by New York newspapers and the David Project's mysterious film-in-progress, *Columbia Unbecoming*, the only one found to be credible was the claim that Massad lost his temper with a student, Deena Shanker, in 2002 in the course of a classroom discussion of the Israeli assault on a Palestinian refugee camp in Jenin. In his reply to Massad, Sherman quoted from the Columbia committee's report as follows:

"Upon extensive deliberation," the report noted, "the committee finds it credible that Professor Massad became angered at a question that he understood to countenance Israeli conduct of which he disapproved, and that he responded heatedly. While we have no reason to believe that Professor Massad intended to expel Ms. Shanker from the classroom . . . his rhetorical response to her query exceeded commonly accepted bounds by conveying that her question merited harsh public criticism." Quoting from *The Faculty Handbook of Columbia University*, the report went on to say that "angry criticism directed at a student in class because she disagrees, or appears to disagree, with a faculty member on a matter of substance is not consistent with the obligation 'to show respect for the rights of others to hold opinions differing from their own,' to exercise 'responsible self-discipline,' and to 'demonstrate appropriate restraint.'"

Sherman had already interviewed Ms. Shanker himself, and had argued that

> if the faculty committee determines that Shanker's account is correct, Massad's transgression, though certainly reprehensible, would hardly justify the overriding thesis of *Columbia Unbecoming*: that pro-Israel students are systematically silenced by professors in MEALAC. Shanker herself insists that MEALAC is "a really wonderful department, for the most part." She believes that Columbia's Jewish community is too religious, and she has come to value MEALAC's secularism. "I definitely feel safer in the MEALAC department as a Jew than I do at a religious Columbia Jewish event," she says.[30]

Three points seem worth stressing about this episode—the single most plausible instance of a leftist faculty member intimidating a student. One, Columbia's investigation did the right thing with regard to Massad, and the outraged claims from the Pipes–Kramer–David Project partisans that the report was a whitewash should be understood as more posturings from ideologically driven culture warriors. Two, the fact that a stridently pro-Palestinian professor teaches at Columbia is not really cause for a national (or even a regional) witchhunt. One would think—one would hope—that a putatively free society that values the free exchange of ideas could tolerate a handful of Israel's most severe critics alongside legions of Israel's most passionate defenders. And three, as Jon Wiener pointed out in the *Chronicle of Higher Education*, the tactics employed by the right to harass Massad are far more corrosive of academic freedom than any pro-Palestinian analogies between Israel and South Africa; Massad and his colleagues have received numerous death threats, while Campus Watch and the David Project have been sending "monitors" to the classes of Columbia professors in order to gauge the extent to which the university deviates from the Campus Watch position on Israel. By contrast, Wiener pointed out, when three black students complained to Harvard professor Stephan Thernstrom fifteen years earlier about "the absence of a black perspective in a lecture about slavery," the news media and conservative organizations described Thernstrom as a sacrificial victim of political correctness:

> At Columbia the issue could have been defined, in the words of Joan W. Scott of the American Association of University Professors, as "the threat to the integrity of the university by the intervention of organized outside agitators who are disrupting classes and programs for ideological purposes." Instead the issue became professors' "anti-Israel bias."
>
> At Harvard the issue could have been a professor's overreacting to students' disagreement with one of his lectures. But it came to be defined as the victimization of the professor by the forces of "left-wing McCarthyism." The key was not the nature or seriousness of the complaints, but rather the political forces outside the university that defined the issues at stake.[31]

The political forces outside the university, as we professors have learned time and time again in such matters, are considerably stronger than anyone inside the university.

That's why we're so skeptical about recent critiques of Middle Eastern studies programs, even when those critiques contain more than a grain of truth; we suspect that what our critics really want is direct control over such programs. Indeed, just as Horowitz would have state universities regulated by state legislatures, so too would Pipes, Kramer, and Kurtz place international studies programs under federal supervision. Such programs are currently funded under Title VI of the Higher Education Act of 1958, and are called

"Title VI programs" for short; they cover not only the Middle East
but every area of the globe. Partly because Kurtz, in his testimony
before the House of Representatives in 2003,[32] insisted (following
the lead of Kramer's 2001 book, *Ivory Towers on Sand*) that international studies programs are dominated by pro-Palestinian faculty
hostile to America and influenced largely by the work of Edward
Said, the House unanimously passed House Resolution 3077 in
October of that year. The bill's original language empowered an
advisory board (made up of seven members, three of whom would
be appointed by the secretary of education, two of whom would be
appointed by the Speaker of the House, and two of whom would
be appointed by the president pro tempore of the Senate) to "annu-
ally monitor, apprise, and evaluate the activities of grant recipi-
ents." That extraordinarily sweeping language sent a chill through
most of the scholars who read it, for it covers not just your local
pro-Palestinian scholar but everyone working in any international
studies program involving any group of people living on any one of
the inhabited continents, and it does not define the term "activities"—leaving the door wide open for federal surveillance of whatever activities such an advisory board would deem worthy of its
attention.

That section of the bill was amended along the way. When it was
passed, HR 3077 spoke more innocuously, as Stephen Burd reported
in 2003, of directing the advisory board to "'monitor, apprise, and
evaluate a sample of activities' supported by Title VI, with the goal
of 'providing recommendations for improvement of the programs'"; the bill was not acted upon by the Senate in 2004, and the
Senate passed an altogether different reauthorization of the Higher
Education Act in 2005, which (according to Burd) "included a pro-
vision requiring the colleges that participate in foreign-language
and area-studies programs, which are supported under Title VI of
the Higher Education Act, to guarantee that their projects offer
'diverse and balanced perspectives.'"[33] Nevertheless, I think many

professors have reason to distrust the intentions of HR 3077's chief supporters; as Martin Kramer wrote in a 2003 essay, "Why We Don't Need More Students Majoring in Middle Eastern Studies,"

> At the best universities, students who major in Middle Eastern studies do learn languages, but they also get indoctrinated by a professoriate that is dead-set against the exercise of American power against anyone for any reason. This sort of preparation is more likely to produce a human shield than a proconsul. Middle Eastern studies in America, as presently constituted, are worse than useless to the defense of American interests. The U.S. government's decision, after 9/11, to double the number of scholarships in Muslim languages will only mean that in the next crisis, there will be even more "experts" urging us to stay home, lest we enrage the "Arab street."
>
> The United States doesn't need a lot of new grads to explain "why they hate us." What it needs are people who are so persuaded of its mission in the world that they are prepared to undergo some hardship and risk to advance it. I happen to think that calling that mission "empire" just gets in the way. But whatever the mission is called, its bearers have to be persuaded that it is the worthiest of causes. That demands cultural self-esteem and self-mastery—the true purpose of an elite education. It doesn't require a working knowledge of Arabic.[34]

Kramer is right, of course; if you're interested in establishing American university graduates as proconsuls in Iraq or Syria, knowledge of Arabic is superfluous. Still, it is strange to hear right-wing partisans speak so glowingly of "cultural self-esteem" as the "true purpose of an elite education." It seems like only yesterday that they were mocking African-American students and faculty for talking about bolstering the self-esteem of American minority groups. And it seems to me that they had it right the first time; the true purpose of an elite education is not the fostering of cultural self-esteem and the hardening of the conviction that one's nation has a unique mission in the world. The true purpose of education is to try to foster in students a kind of critical cosmopolitanism, such that they learn, among other things, to question any notion that one's nation or tribe is favored by God or destiny. Not every form of education seeks to realize this "true purpose," I admit. Come to think of it, there is a word for educational institutions that foster students' cultural self-esteem and sense of self-mastery, and that graduate a cohort of people who are so persuaded of their mission in the world that they are prepared to undergo some hardship and risk to advance it. We call them madrassas.

IN MY OWN TEACHING, I am not nearly so vulnerable as is a controversial Middle Eastern Studies scholar or an outspoken gay or lesbian professor. When my classrooms touch on controversial matters, the professor at the front desk is a tenured, loud-whistling, hockey-playing heterosexual white guy who usually tries to take potentially incendiary remarks and redirect them to the material at hand. In the spring 2004 African-American literature class in which one of my students drew an analogy between abortion and Sethe's murder of her youngest child in Toni Morrison's 1987 novel *Beloved*, for instance, I simply remarked that many people would resist the idea that a nine-month-old child has the same moral status as a fetus, and many people would insist otherwise, and that in Alice Walker's 1976 novel *Meridian*, by contrast, the title character has an abortion and meets with incomprehension from her immediate family, who point out that black women have labored for many decades to bear children that they could call their own only to have Meridian spurn that legacy by choosing to terminate her pregnancy and then to request a tubal ligation. The debate about abortion, I pointed out, has a different resonance altogether for generations of African-American women who, like Sethe, were piercingly aware of the antebellum law that the child follows the condition of the mother; and the debate about the status of the black family in America has resonated for the century and a half since Margaret Garner—the woman on whom Morrison based *Beloved*—killed her young child so that she would not grow up a slave. But, I said, replaying the abortion debate in this classroom, in this context, will take us away from the specific ethical dilemma with which Morrison presents us: is it right to kill an infant in order to save her from a life of slavery? (No character in the novel, except Sethe, believes that it is.) When such questions come up in my classroom, I do not feel threatened by my students in any sense, and though (thanks to my activities outside class, as a writer and blogger) I have earned myself a couple of dogged cyberstalkers who post negative reviews of my teaching and my published works on various websites, I have never, to my knowledge, encountered a student or an auditor who was taking my class for the purpose of monitoring the political content of my courses.

As I have discovered over the past twenty years, matters are altogether different in classes that involve loud, emphatic white male undergraduates making a point of letting young black or Latina women (teaching assistants, nontenured adjuncts, and assistant professors, especially) know that they aren't going to stand for any of their feminist or reverse-racist bullshit; in a couple of cases I'm familiar with, the women in question felt physically threatened by their students in ways I have never experienced. Women and minority professors who espouse "liberal" beliefs (even when they involve simple statements of historical fact, like the fraudulence of the Gulf of Tonkin Resolution or the segregation of US troops during World War II) can come under fire—from students, parents, legislators, and campus administrators—in ways that straight white guys like me usually do not. I stress the vulnerability of gay and lesbian teachers primarily because there are numerous vocal conservatives—such as Indiana University law professor Eric Rasmusen—who have argued publicly that gay men and lesbians should not be permitted to teach at all.[35] I have no doubt that conservative students are sometimes made uncomfortable by liberal professors. And though you're not likely to hear this from David Horowitz or George Will, I can assure you that there are many teachers (especially teachers without tenure, even more especially teachers on one-year renewable contracts) who are made uncomfortable by their conservative students as well.

One such teacher is Ann Marie B. Bahr, who teaches philosophy and religion at South Dakota State University. She describes herself as anything but a firebrand: "In graduate school I was more religiously and socially conservative than most of my fellow students," she writes. "But although I have had my differences with liberals, I never felt that they forbade me to express an informed professional opinion. The chilling effect of today's conservative watchdogs is a much more serious matter." In a May 2005 essay in the *Chronicle of Higher Education*, Professor Bahr described that chilling effect in detail: "Last semester I had my first significant falling-out with students, inspired—I have no doubt—by David Horowitz and his crusade against liberal bias in academe." Her students' "falling-out" could more aptly be described as a massive opting-out, since, in one of her courses, Ms. Bahr's antagonists chose simply to avoid her class rather than attend it:

Some of the students in my course on "Religion in American Culture" were upset that George M. Marsden's *Religion and American Culture* (2nd ed., Harcourt, 2001) and Randall Balmer's *Mine Eyes Have Seen the Glory: A Journey Into the Evangelical Subculture in America* (3rd ed., Oxford University Press, 2000) were on the reading list. They felt that those two books were biased against evangelicals.

Marsden is a highly respected evangelical scholar, and Balmer's work on evangelicals has also been highly acclaimed. Although his religious affiliation is not as clear as Marsden's, I had never before heard complaints that he has been unfair to the evangelicals about whom he writes. I would have thought that the two scholars had impeccable credentials for inclusion in my course, but I now suspect that the objective, scholarly tone of the books upset my students.

I had also assigned some online readings about Christian Identity, a white-supremacist movement that considers Jews and anyone who is not white to belong to inferior races; believes that anything—e.g., feminism and homosexuality—not in accordance with traditional gender roles is sinful; and claims to be based on the Bible. Those readings were part of a series of items about Protestant, Catholic, Nation of Islam, American Indian, and other visions of America.

In the session that I had set aside for discussion of the Christian Identity readings, a student asked me if I would have included them had I known how many students believed in the movement. I had not expected many, if any, of my students to be affiliated with Christian Identity, so I had not prepared a response to that question. I think I said something to the effect that I did not fear for my life from the group because I was a white person who was neither a feminist nor a lesbian. (There have been reports of violence associated with Christian Identity.)

About two-thirds of my students did not return to class after that day, which was around the midpoint of the semester, except to take exams. Because I never had an opportunity to discuss the matter with the students who left, I don't know if they were members of Christian Identity, or if they simply believed that a movement that claimed to be based on the Bible could not be wrong. I had never had a large-scale problem with attendance before.[36]

In one sense, Professor Bahr is markedly more liberal than I am; if two-thirds of my students in any course were to refuse to attend half the scheduled classes except for exams, I would flunk them. That there are students who balk at encountering opinions with which they disagree—regardless of whether they are endorsed by the professor—is striking enough, but it's all the more striking if you know that George Marsden is also the author of *The Soul of the American University: From Protestant Establishment to Established Nonbelief,* a stringent (and, to my mind, mistaken) critique of the secularism of American universities.[37] In other words, Ann Marie Bahr's students weren't being force-fed maximum-strength doses of Charles Darwin, Madalyn Murray O'Hair, and Noam Chomsky; they were being asked to read the work of a well-respected scholar who regrets that universities have fallen away from their original calling, namely, to educate the clerisy. No matter; the objective, scholarly tone of his book upset Bahr's students.

Professor Bahr is not sanguine about her prospects as a teacher. After recounting another episode in which students closed themselves off to her class after they asked to discuss homosexuality and the Bible (it wasn't originally on her syllabus, "which was already crowded thanks to the requirements placed on general-education courses by the state Board of Regents, piled on top of the disciplinary imperative of explaining academic methods of studying the Bible and applying them to the New Testament") and then got the sense that Bahr was going to agree with a Reformed Church minister who "explained why there is plenty of room for debate on the question of how Christians should respond to their homosexual brethren," Bahr concludes her essay on a sour note:

> It seems that I must now bow to political or popular pressure because the ultimate judges of my professional expertise will not be my scholarly peers, but the public. And while members of the public and students may be able to judge many aspects of my teaching (that is why we have student evaluations of professors), they cannot judge whether I am teaching according to the best standards of the discipline.

Politics has always played a role on our campuses, but we are now experiencing a new form of political intrusion in academic life, and it is extremely dangerous. It has a direct impact on academic freedom because it threatens professors—with the loss of the usual presumption that they are experts in their subject matter, or even with the loss of employment, if they do not agree with popular opinions.

That is too high a price for me to pay to keep my job, and I have resolved never again to bow to religious or political pressure in the classroom. In the future I will send students to the Internet to view authors' credentials. When I next teach the New Testament, I will use the disagreement between Gagnon and myself to demonstrate that scholarly debate—unlike political debate, in which each side is expected to be partisan—is a way of systematically testing the beliefs of both sides, and that my job is to critically assess all the arguments, from within my area of expertise.

Like many other academics, I have dedicated my life to the faithful transmission of the truth as best I can discern it. It makes me sick to my stomach to think of falsifying the truth, or even sacrificing my right to have an informed professional opinion.

Bahr does not draw any larger conclusion from her experience, but I think it's implicit nonetheless: undergraduates who will not remain in class to hear interpretations they consider offensive are not to be construed as heroic dissenters from liberal orthodoxy. Likewise, students like Nicole Krogman, who attempt to pass off other writers' right-wing broadsides as their own right-wing broadsides, are not to be lauded and decorated for their lonely opposition to malicious leftist faculty. We are dealing here not with campus freedom-fighters but with bad students—that is, with students who reject from the outset most of what "learning" is supposed to entail.

Yet in another sense, a nonacademic sense, they are very good students indeed. They have learned well the lessons taught by Horowitz, who urges campus conservatives to construe themselves as victims of liberal intolerance and to appropriate the words of the civil rights movement; they have learned from gay and lesbian students how to appropriate the term "coming out," as in Conservative Coming Out Day, as if campus conservatives regularly face the kind of stigmatization and harassment that led to the beating death of Matthew Shepard. Occasionally the "aggrieved minority" gambit backfires, as it did at Penn State in late 2003 when, just after "Conservative Coming Out Day," it was discovered that Brian Battaglia, the president of the Penn State College Republicans, had posted on his website the pictures of his Halloween party, among which were photos of a guest in blackface (former Undergraduate Student Government senator Jason Covener, mocking Takkeem Morgan, the vice president of the USG) and an unidentified student in a hood, over the caption, "He took a break from cross burning to drink a cold one." Quite apart from the routineness and the ubiquity of the blackface-and-hood phenomenon—it happens so often on Halloween that it is almost as if some outspoken campus conservatives cannot help themselves—there was the embarrassment of prominent College Republicans being outed as racists within days of their "coming out."[38] Battaglia and the College Republicans responded—and this, too, has become routine— by construing campus criticism of his pictures as censorship, suggesting that they had as little understanding of the First Amendment (which pertains to the prior restraint of speech, not to the protection of speech from criticism) as they did of the history of gay and lesbian Americans whose coming out truly imperiled their lives.

And yet, despite the best efforts of Christian Identity here and the College Republicans there, on balance, campuses are usually liberal places. More specifically, campuses are liberal in the same sense that NPR and PBS are liberal when compared to the rest of the American media, and we are despised by the American right for roughly the same reasons. Like the much-reviled public media, we actually have lots of conservatives running around, and some of them are our most prominent and politically powerful colleagues. During the twelve years I taught at the University of Illinois, three of the most important professors in the state were Richard Posner, the conservative law professor at the University of Chicago; Chicago's Richard Epstein, the influential libertarian economist whose work on "takings" and eminent domain became part of federal law;[39] and Ronald Rotunda, the University of Illinois law professor who, in the late 1990s, helped congressional Republicans frame their impeachment case against President Clinton. Similarly, PBS—a reputedly liberal redoubt—has *Wall $treet Week*, Ben Wattenberg's *Think Tank*, Tucker Carlson, and Tony Brown, alongside the reliably multicultural *Sesame Street* and *Postcards from Buster*, the latter of which earned a denunciation from US Secretary of Education Margaret Spellings in early 2005 for promoting the "homosexual agenda" when Buster visited Vermont and came into contact with a lesbian couple living in a civil union.[40]

To say that universities are liberal like PBS, then, is to say that universities are left of the mainstream *in the aggregate*, even though much of the campus devotes itself to the basic research and development and technology transfer—be it in nanotech, supercomputing, agribusiness, or military contracts—that most conservatives heartily endorse.[41] The campus culture at Penn State is, for example, significantly more liberal, especially on "social issues," than the surrounding upper-Alleghenies district; for a fifty-mile radius around State College, there isn't a single Democratic stronghold, not even an old-school union town, in the midst of solidly white, solidly rural, solidly Christian, solidly impoverished central Pennsylvania. And yet Penn State is second only to MIT in federal research funding from the Department of Defense; it has had a fifty-eight-year association with the US Navy for secret research, and boasts a Marine Corps Research Unit on the campus itself. Surely, both after 9/11 and before, some of this work must be vital to national security, so I do not oppose all of it in knee-jerk campus-lefty fashion; then again,

I can say very little for or against it, because I am not privy to any of it. But I can say this much: Department of Defense research is part of any major university's bloodstream and revenue stream, and it is rarely acknowledged when right-wing culture warriors take to their keyboards to denounce the anti-capitalist, anti-globalization, anti-humanist, anti-American campus left.

We campus liberals, meanwhile, often think of ourselves as inhabiting a kind of tenuous archipelago strung across the rural regions of the country; we're not all clustered in Berkeley or Cambridge, and only rarely do our campus towns resemble the progressive Valhallas of Madison, Wisconsin, or Ann Arbor, Michigan, where the recycling laws, like the espresso, are strong and widely appreciated. In State College, Pennsylvania; Urbana–Champaign, Illinois; Cedar Rapids, Iowa; West Lafayette, Indiana; Gainesville, Florida; Columbia, Missouri; Mount Pleasant, Michigan; Norman, Oklahoma; and Laramie, Wyoming, we talk of Strindberg and Stravinsky with our colleagues while our neighbors in the outlying county march against abortion and gay rights. In all such locales, the campus culture is like unto a flame in an oil can, with faculty and liberal students huddled like hobos in fingerless gloves trying to catch a little warmth in the night. And yet those campus towns, however isolated and anomalous they may be, will keep that liberal flame going for some time to come, for three reasons: one, because the disciplines of the liberal arts really do promote critical thinking and independent inquiry; two, because the cosmopolitan character of large campuses, which is due partly to the presence of foreign students from every continent, makes even rural State College a place with two fine Indian restaurants, a Korean deli, and a Viet-Thai restaurant, a place where Urdu and Spanish and Korean may be heard even in the local pizza joint, and where the heterogeneity of the students and faculty stands in stark contrast to the homogeneity of the population in the surrounding counties; and three, because even amid one of the most significant Christian fundamentalist revivals in the long history of American Christian revivalism, campuses are relatively secular places to live and work. Short of an outright military or fundamentalist takeover of the country, they will very likely remain that way for the foreseeable future—as I'll suggest in more detail in the next chapter.

3. In the Liberal Faculty Lounge

I N LATE NOVEMBER 2004, JUST AFTER THE REELEC-
tion of George Bush, *Washington Post* columnist George Will
turned his attention to the two-year-old Horowitz–Zinsmeister
survey of professors' political leanings, not to express outrage at the
news that liberals dominate academe but to profess boredom about
the "news" that liberals dominate academe:

> The great secret is out: liberals dominate campuses. Coming soon:
> "Moon Implicated in Tides, Studies Find."
>
> One study of 1,000 professors finds that Democrats outnumber
> Republicans at least seven to one in the humanities and social sci-
> ences. That imbalance, more than double what it was three decades
> ago, is intensifying because younger professors are more uniformly
> liberal than the older cohort that is retiring.[1]

Ho-hum, dog bites man . . . but wait! It turned out that Will was
not actually bored by this old news. He hadn't really put all that
vitriolic Horowitzian outrage behind him. On the contrary, he was
just as furious as is Horowitz; he simply has more control over his
writing—as he demonstrated in the conclusion of his column,
which offered the High Church version of Horowitz's rabble-
rousing prose:

Many campuses are intellectual versions of one-party nations—except such nations usually have the merit, such as it is, of candor about their ideological monopolies. In contrast, American campuses have more insistently proclaimed their commitment to diversity as they have become more intellectually monochrome.

They do indeed cultivate diversity—in race, skin color, ethnicity, sexual preference. In everything but thought.

The column that opens with a genteel yawn, then, closes with this barbaric yawp: American campuses are on a lower level than that of axis-of-evil regimes like North Korea or Iran, because at least those regimes are *honest* about their ideological monopolies.

A few months later, in March 2005, George Mason University professor of communications Robert Lichter (together with Stanley Rothman and Neil Nevitte, professors of political science at Smith College and the University of Toronto, respectively) released yet another survey, which Howard Kurtz quickly trumpeted in the *Washington Post*:

> College faculties, long assumed to be a liberal bastion, lean further to the left than even the most conspiratorial conservatives might have imagined, a new study says.
>
> By their own description, 72 percent of those teaching at American universities and colleges are liberal and 15 percent are conservative, says the study being published this week. The imbalance is almost as striking in partisan terms, with 50 percent of the faculty members surveyed identifying themselves as Democrats and 11 percent as Republicans.
>
> The disparity is even more pronounced at the most elite schools, where, according to the study, 87 percent of faculty are liberal and 13 percent are conservative.

Because of the heightened liberal–conservative disparity at elite schools, Rothman claimed that the study—based on data about

1,643 full-time faculty at 183 four-year schools—provided positive proof that conservative scholars face discrimination in hiring:

> Rothman sees the findings as evidence of "possible discrimination" against conservatives in hiring and promotion. Even after factoring in levels of achievement, as measured by published work and organization memberships, "the most likely conclusion" is that "being conservative counts against you," he said. "It doesn't surprise me, because I've observed it happening."[2]

Lichter sounded the same note, saying, "This is the richest lure of information on faculty ideology in 20 years. And this is the first study that statistically proves bias [against conservatives] in the hiring and promotion of faculty members."[3]

Neither statement is true. Whatever a "lure" of information might be, the Lichter–Rothman–Nevitte study is based on an astonishingly smaller data sample than that of the Higher Education Research Institute. Nor do Lichter et al. take into account the percentage of conservatives applying for academic jobs or being reviewed for tenure, at elite institutions or elsewhere, so they have no evidentiary basis for claiming discrimination simply on the basis of underrepresentation. Indeed, despite the bluster, Lichter, Rothman, and Nevitte offered no data whatsoever on the number of conservative job applicants who were turned down for academic jobs because of systemic liberal bias.

"Bias"-watchers know that Lichter and his associates have a long history of coming up with strange findings that just happen to correlate precisely with the obsessions of their funders, such as the far-right Scaife Foundation. Lichter is especially notable for finding liberal bias everywhere in American media, not only in PBS programming (in a 1988 study that excluded from consideration William F. Buckley's *Firing Line* and Morton Kondracke's *American Interests*, and business programs like Louis Rukeyser's *Wall $treet*

Week) but even in mass-media coverage of the first Gulf War. According to research conducted by Lichter and his wife, Linda, most American coverage of the war in 1991 was critical of the United States. If that's not the way you remember things, well, that's probably because you're not as skilled at statistics as the Lichters are. As Fairness and Accuracy in Reporting pointed out in 1992,

> The Lichters' tendency to generalize from a narrow sliver of data is the main way that their studies end up supporting their preconceived conclusions of left bias. Take the Center's report on Gulf War coverage (*Media Monitor*, 4/91) and its widely cited claim that "nearly three out of five sources (59 percent) criticized U.S. government policies during the [Gulf] War." This, of course, is not 59 percent of all 5,915 sources, but of those 249 sources (4.2 percent) who in the Lichters' judgment stated an explicit position. This leaves only 148 sources, or 2.5 percent of all sources, who made explicit criticisms of U.S. policy (from the left, right or center).
>
> On what basis can you generalize from the 4 percent of sources who supposedly expressed overt opinions to the 96 percent who didn't? Doing so results in absurd claims, such as, "Surprisingly, the U.S. government fared little better than its Iraqi counterpart in the soundbite battle." That would be surprising, considering that 44 percent of total news sources were from the U.S. government, according to the Center's own research.[4]

But it would not be surprising coming from former American Enterprise Institute fellow Lichter, who issued his peculiar report on media coverage of the Gulf War because, as he noted with alarm at an Accuracy in Media conference in April 1991, "I see a trend toward journalists seeing themselves as citizens of the world rather than patriotic Americans."

Is it any wonder that liberal professors distrust the studies conducted by Lichter, Rothman, Nevitte, Horowitz, and Zinsmeister?

They sound to us like people who could discover leftist bias in cook-books that advise readers to season liberally. We don't deny that we outnumber conservatives, and we admit that we have a near monop-oly on departments in the arts and humanities. But why would con-servatives take this as prima facie evidence of active discrimination?

It turns out that there's something more serious and insidious going on here, and that—once again—race is an issue, even though African-American scholars make up only 5 percent of all college professors nationwide (and half of those scholars teach at historically black institutions).[5] For much of the conservative complaint about "underrepresentation" is drawn disingenuously from the legal dis-course of affirmative action; in the *American Enterprise* issue that announced the findings of the Horowitz–Zinsmeister study, attor-ney Kenneth Lee, a member of the far-right Federalist Society for Law and Public Policy Studies, made the case in so many words. "The simple logic underlying much of contemporary civil-rights law," said Lee, "applies equally to conservative Republicans, who appear to face clear practices of discrimination in American acade-mia that are statistically even starker than previous blackballings by race."[6] Even starker than previous blackballings by race: according to Lee, conservative scholars have it worse than did African-Americans under segregation and Jim Crow. (This would mean, I imagine, that on some campuses there are fewer than zero conserva-tives.) It is a fantastic and deeply offensive claim in and of itself, but it becomes all the more offensive if you go back and look at the his-tory of conservatives' opposition to affirmative-action programs in American higher education.

In his recently published history of affirmative action, *The Pur-suit of Fairness*, Terry H. Anderson points out that when universi-ties first became subject to affirmative-action policies, schools like City College of New York "exemplified the problem; the English Department had 104 faculty members, but just 15 were females, and only one was tenured." The conservative defense of this gender disparity, at the time, was that there was no reason to expect that the gender or racial composition of college faculties should mirror that of the general population. At Berkeley, for instance, political scientist Paul Seabury joined a group to protest affirmative-action policies in faculty hiring, the Committee on Academic Nondiscrimination and Integrity; as Anderson recounts, Seabury insisted that it was

> ridiculous to recruit faculty based not on scholarship but on "statistically under-represented" groups: "Blacks, Irish, Italians, Greeks, Poles, and all other Slavic groups (including Slovaks, Slovens, Serbs, Czechs, and Croatians) are under-represented," he declared, and so are Catholics, and even Republicans. His department had only "two Republicans in a department of thirty-eight. . . . Yet I doubt that even Nixon's HEW crusaders for equality of results would tread into this minefield of blatant inequality."[7]

Seabury thus applied a reductio ad absurdum to the idea of under-representation, and mocked the idea that anyone would apply the principles of affirmative action to the "minefield" of faculty party affiliation. How far we have come in only one generation! Once upon a time, even the conservative critics of affirmative action ridiculed the idea of gerrymandering university departments so that the political sensibilities of their faculty members matched that of the general population more accurately. Today, however, this program is an explicit and increasingly popular item on the conservative agenda.

Imagine what the world would be like if this logic were applied to other professions—say, to special education teachers, human rights attorneys, and playwrights. In a 2005 essay, arts critic Terry Teachout wrote, "I've seen, read, and heard about enough contemporary American and British plays to know that the political point of view of most of their authors is well to the left of center. . . . Of the two hundred-odd new plays I've seen in my two years as a working critic, not one could be described as embodying a specifically right-wing political perspective, nor do I know any New York–based playwrights or actors who are openly conservative."[8] Teachout is right; the theater industry is simply crawling with liberals. However, because Teachout is a thoughtful and judicious conservative, as well as a serious critic of the arts, he did not proceed from this observation to decry "bias" in the theater industry and to petition the New York State Assembly to oversee the production of more "balanced" plays in New York in the interest of creating greater "ideological diversity" in contemporary theater.

What's true of playwrights and actors is true of many professors in the liberal arts—particularly in fields that deal with literature, visual arts, and theater. This much should be obvious. So let's stop nitpicking with all the cherry-pickers. Let's start instead from the premise that liberal professors outnumber conservative professors by a substantial margin, and that some fields, like English, are as well-stocked with liberals as any off-Broadway revival of *Torch Song Trilogy*. And let's be generous and take at face value a completely unmoored claim, Ohio state senator Larry Mumper's statement that "80 percent or so" of professors are "Democrats, liberals or socialists or card-carrying Communists."[9] And let's not bother with petty details, like whether those Communists are actually carrying cards like Visa and Discover. It's time to ask the obvious question: why should this be so?

If you listen to Mumper, who has been listening to people like David Horowitz, it's due to explicit, intentional anti-conservative discrimination: "Our colleges and universities are still filled with some of the '60s and '70s profs that were the anti-American group," said Mumper in January 2005. "They've gotten control of how to give people tenure and so the colleges continue to move in this direction." But this is far too simple an explanation. Yes, universities are full of people who were hired in the 1960s and 1970s but actually the vast majority of them are unimpeachably pro-American, and they don't go around trying to fire conservatives; it's not as if there are hordes of conservative junior scholars who, when they come up for tenure, are being cut off at the knees by biased liberal tenure and promotion committees. If you'd like to believe otherwise, I invite you to try. Begin with graduate school. In my field, where roughly 15,000 PhDs have been granted since I earned my degree in 1989,[10] you'd have to believe that there are literally thousands of politically conservative PhD candidates in the field of English language and literature out there. You'd have to believe that liberals like me have tried to head them off at the pass all these years, by telling them that graduate school involves anywhere from five to ten years of rigorous study culminating in the production of a book-length work of original research, and that when they complete their doctorate while living hand-to-mouth on stipends or taking out student loans, they get to go on the academic job market with the knowledge that they have about an even-money chance of landing a tenure-track job and making somewhere in the 40K range.[11] And you'd have to believe that despite all the discouraging words they'd heard from liberals like me, these bright, promising twentysomething conservatives have clogged our graduate programs to the point at which we've simply had to institute hiring quotas to keep them from joining the professorial ranks and eventually overrunning us.

The really curious question, I think, is why the junior scholars and the graduate students are just as liberal—or, as George Will suggests, "more uniformly liberal"—than most of their senior colleagues who were hired thirty or forty years ago. Underlying that curious question is still another, more fundamental question: why does academe appear to be so desirable a location for ambitious young liberals, progressives, and leftists?

People who know little about academe believe they know the answer: it's a cushy job with terrific job security, and so of course your nanny-state liberals and your card-carrying socialists and Communists would gravitate toward it. After all, it provides a refuge from the free-market, at-will-employment economy against which so many progressives and leftists inveigh, and it allows lazy liberals to earn a good living at the expense of hardworking taxpayers and parents while working only a couple of hours a week haranguing their students with the lecture notes they haven't revised since May 1968—and then, of course, vacationing in France and other anti-American climes in the summer.

The belief that we work a couple of hours a week is sheer nonsense; faculty work time isn't reducible to classroom time, any more than you can measure a lawyer's work by the amount of time spent in a courtroom, or a journalist's work by the amount of time spent actually typing stories. My own job—even with a low, two-courses-per-semester teaching assignment at Illinois and a three-courses-per-year assignment at Penn State—requires an average of fifty to sixty hours a week, almost year round, in reading, researching, writing, course preparation, and grading, and all manner of tedious, draining, and (nonetheless) important departmental and professional committee work.[12] What makes my job more attractive than most is the fact that I have considerable leeway in deciding *which* fifty or sixty hours I will work each week. I also have a great deal of autonomy about how I'll work those hours; academe has a very loose dress code, which means that I don't have to wear suits, ties, and dress shirts unless I want to, just as I don't have to wear the color-coordinated company shirt and hat I was issued in 1988, when I was supporting myself by delivering pizza (while writing my dissertation and copyediting for two scholarly journals in my spare time). So I'm spared the distinctive uniforms of both the high- and low-wage sectors of the economy. Likewise, although I report my faculty activities every year to my department head and work in a vertical system where the chain of command runs clearly from the department head to the college dean to the university provost to the university president, I am subject to none of the intrusive managerial oversight that characterizes so many American workplaces: I suffer no time clocks, no drug tests, no psychological evaluations, no restrictions on facial hair or piercings. On the other hand, the fields that tend to house the greatest percentage of liberals—and, perhaps relatedly, the greatest percentage of women—tend to be the lowest-paying fields in the university; professors in the arts and humanities make significantly less than their counterparts in law, medicine, and finance, in part because universities don't have to compete with the private sector in order to lure literature professors to campus. And because it takes so long to complete a doctorate in the humanities, most assistant professors don't start making a decent wage until they're in their thirties. Still, for the fortunate few who get tenure-track jobs, the wages *are* decent, and the workplace autonomy is priceless.

There's no doubt that the hope of tenure is a powerful attraction. It was certainly among my considerations when, in 1983, I applied to graduate school in English literature knowing that I would have to finance the whole venture myself, that I had a pretty slim chance of finishing a PhD by the end of the 1980s (if indeed the University of Virginia allowed me to proceed past the MA in the first place), and that even after I'd earned a doctorate I had only an even-money chance of landing a tenure-track job. In 1983, assistant professors of English were making $22,000 a year;[13] that year, the first-year corporate lawyers for whom I worked as a word processor in the midtown offices of Simpson, Thacher, and Bartlett were making over $70,000. I honestly thought, when I applied to graduate school in literature, that I was effectively taking a vow of poverty—and for the next ten years, I was. I wound up having to pay off $12,000 in student loans when I earned my PhD at the age of twenty-eight, but I knew I had the consolation of working in a sector of the economy where I would not be suddenly "terminated" without cause in my forties or asked to train my "outsourced" replacement in my fifties.

Personally, I wouldn't trade tenure for a higher-paying but less secure job. But the astonishing thing about the people who teach in universities these days is that so very few of them have tenure. Two-thirds of us have no form of job security whatsoever; your average university is replete with "adjuncts," "instructors," "lecturers," "visiting teaching associates," and (less euphemistically) "fixed-term appointees" who teach four or five courses per term and who simply do not have the academic freedom promised in the 1940 Statement of Principles of the American Association of University Professors. They can be challenged, harassed, and reported to the press or to the legislature by any student or administrator who has the will and the resources to pursue them, and they know that their reappointment depends on (a) the annual department budget, (b) their institution's enrollment figures, which may or may not have an effect on (a), and/or (c) the quality of their student evaluations from the previous semester.

The use of adjuncts, instructors, and part-time "freeway flyers" (who teach a variety of courses at more than one campus) is most prevalent in the humanities; faculty in the sciences sometimes have similarly exploitative work arrangements, but they have very different teaching schedules (that depend on, among other things, their ability to secure grants from public or private sources) and a variety of "postdoctoral" positions for young researchers that don't correspond to the "adjunct" and "visiting" positions in English or history. For instance, the science postdocs don't always wind up teaching introductory service courses, the way the English adjuncts and graduate students do; more often, they work in labs. Many of the disciplines in the applied sciences (and the social sciences, such as psychology) rely on the system of grants and private sponsorships, which means not only that the working conditions of graduate students in those fields depends largely on the ability of their faculty supervisors to secure funding for the projects on which students work as assistants, but also that the faculty themselves are often valued more for their skill at grantsmanship and their revenue-producing potential than for their teaching. Still, the part-timers in every field, and of every political persuasion, are exceptionally vulnerable; in the fall of 2004, for instance, DePaul University suspended adjunct professor Thomas Klocek after he argued with pro-Palestinian students at a student activities fair. Susanne Dumbleton, dean of the School for New Learning, wrote to the *DePaulia* in October 2004, "The students' perspective was dishonored and their freedom demeaned. Individuals were deeply insulted. . . . Our college acted immediately by removing the instructor from the classroom."[14] Yet the students in question were not in Klocek's class, and his remarks on Israel and Palestine had nothing to do with any classroom on DePaul's campus. Though he had taught at DePaul for fourteen years, Klocek was an adjunct and had no more job protection than the cashier at Burger King. Certainly any ideal of academic freedom that covers controversial pro-Palestinian scholars at Columbia should cover critics of pro-Palestinian students at DePaul.[15]

The lesson is obvious, and chilling: if you're an "adjunct" or an "instructor" or a "graduate teaching assistant," it's not in your interest to make waves, politically speaking.[16] The presence of those easily disposable teachers on the campus has nothing to do with the anti-American 1960s generation controlling the tenure apparatus, and everything to do with the extraordinary weakness of college faculty when it comes to basic labor issues that affect the professional status of their colleagues. How weak are we? Weaker than tissue paper. For over a decade now, colleges have been hiring three new fixed-term, part-time, adjunct faculty for every tenure-track position on the books.[17] At large research universities, the first-year writing course is likely to be staffed almost entirely by people who are not on the tenure track. Think of what that means: thousands of eighteen-year-olds on every campus filing into required sections of freshman composition, where they are asked to produce research papers and various kinds of argumentative and persuasive writing—and where they are taught and graded by people with little or no job protection. For some students, those freshman comp courses represent the only classes in which they are asked to write persuasive essays, and/or the only small, under-twenty-five-student classes they'll have all term. The students come from every kind of background; their social and political opinions are all over the map; and some of them, being eighteen years old, have strikingly little tact when it comes to self-expression.

Composition teachers have spoken to me often about this phenomenon, asking me how they should handle the student whose paper on "someone I admire" turned out to be a paean to his summer-job supervisor who was unafraid to call Mexicans lazy, greasy wetbacks to their faces; or the student who, after reading Judy Syfers's famous satirical essay, "Why I Want a Wife,"[18] tearfully complained that the course material was attacking his own marriage; or the students who, in response to an assignment to write a business letter promoting an imaginary new product, chose to submit to their young female teaching assistant a proposal for a "pocket vagina." When you realize that introductory writing classes can be highly volatile places, putting very young students together with precariously employed instructors, you have to marvel that there are so few unpleasant encounters in such courses.

But you also have to marvel at the fact that so few college courses require substantive writing from undergraduates, and that so many academic departments seem to regard "writing-intensive instruction" as the preserve of the humanities (or, worse, of English alone), as if the disciplines of economics, psychology, and sociology have all progressed beyond writing and can now be taught largely or entirely by means of Scan-Tron multiple choice tests, which are graded by computers. And when you look at the overall employment picture in universities—Freshman Composition being only the most vulnerable area, where the hiring of short-term instructors depends literally on enrollment numbers that often don't come into focus until two weeks before the start of the term—you also have to marvel that so many smart, dedicated young scholars continue to flood into academic fields in which their chances of landing a good tenure-track job are so slim.

Robert Brandon, chair of the philosophy department at Duke University, briefly made national news in 2004 when he cheekily suggested that professors tend to be liberal because liberals tend to be smarter than conservatives:

> "We try to hire the best, smartest people available," Brandon said of his philosophy hires. "If, as John Stuart Mill said, stupid people are generally conservative, then there are lots of conservatives we will never hire.
>
> "Mill's analysis may go some way towards explaining the power of the Republican party in our society and the relative scarcity of Republicans in academia. Players in the NBA tend to be taller than average. There is a good reason for this. Members of academia tend to be a bit smarter than average. There is a good reason for this too."[19]

I have nothing against hiring intelligent people, of course, and I don't mind a little self-flattery from my liberal colleagues now and then, either. But when you look at the career choices that budding twentysomething intellectuals are making, with the liberals heading off to graduate school in English and philosophy and the conservatives working in think tanks, media conglomerates, legal foundations, and congressional offices, you're tempted to conclude that liberals dominate academic fields because they're simply not very smart about the way the world works.

WRITING TWO DECADES AGO, University of North Carolina English professor John McGowan surveyed the 1986 Modern Language Association convention and wondered what all this anxious, self-conscious leftism was doing at a Modern Language Association convention:

> I asked a friend over breakfast in the Marriott's coffee shop why anyone who truly wanted to promote a feminist or Marxist revolution would ever make the decision to become an English professor. Surely there are more direct avenues to such an end. I suspect that most of us got into the literature business first and acquired our political commitments later; now we were rather sloppily trying to make the two fit.
>
> My friend replied that we all had modernist adolescences; modernism habitually portrayed itself as revolutionary and liberating, and to some extent it was those things. After all, he and I had read Joyce, Lawrence, Eliot, and Conrad as teen-agers and had used them, like we used rock music, to escape the suburbs in which we grew up. Only now, with postmodernism's assault on such modernist certainties, did the gap between art and radical politics yawn so wide, and the current theatrics were a response to the horrible suspicion that art was as completely co-opted as everything else. Besides, he added, look around. What other alternatives are there for the political radical; where else can you imagine a tolerable life for yourself? We may have—we certainly seem to have—uneasy consciences about our political correctness, but what other sphere offers a better opportunity for integrity? I had to admit that he had described my bind perfectly—and with a kindness that put my impatient hostilities to shame.[20]

McGowan's account of this literary version of suburban adolescent rebellion rings true to me—and to the lives of many of my friends in academe. Yet the description does not fit me to a T; I grew up in Flushing, Queens, with parents who knew a great deal about modern literature and relatively little about rock and roll, and I happened to acquire most of my political sensibilities at exactly the same mid-adolescent moment that I fell in love with serious literature. But these quibbles aside, I think McGowan provides the most persuasive answer to the "supply" side of the liberals-in-the-liberal-arts question: take the edgy appeal of the avant-garde since the mid-nineteenth century, combine it with a passion for rock and roll and a desire to be true to oneself (a most unpostmodern notion) and to do no harm (a very *pre*-postmodern notion), and you've got all the ingredients of a budding young literary intellectual in the late twentieth century.

Well, not quite all the ingredients. I've left the most obvious one for last: for I was inspired by my reading of serious literature not to become a writer of poetry or fiction, but to become a critic and teacher. How exactly did *that* happen? Chiefly, I think, because I was enthralled by seeing talented critics at work, on the page and in the classroom. The critics and teachers I admired in my youth were the ones who showed me not only what they could do with literary works, but also what the works themselves could do when read closely with a fierce and unrelenting intelligence. As a high-school student and as an undergraduate, I would leave my literature classes or finish reading critical essays with the sense that someone had lent me new and finer instruments for apprehending the world—or that, in Kenneth Burke's famous phrase, I had been given better equipment for living. This, I think, is part of what people mean when they say that criticism helps you "get more out of" your reading; at least, it's what I think they mean when they tell me, "I read Philip Roth's *The Plot Against America* recently, but I suppose you got more out of it than I did." What my teachers did, in showing me how to "get more out of" literary works, was to show me how those works *work*. They didn't reduce literature to ideological or political positions, and they didn't stand around gushing about literature's exquisite beauty, either. They simply directed my attention to the passages and tropes and crafty devices that go into complex literary works—and all complex human utterances. You might say that good literary criticism does what Russian formalist Viktor Shklovsky claims for literature itself: it "lays bare the device," and, in laying bare the device, or showing how the work itself lays bare the device, it renews perception and makes us attend to the tangible and emotional and social details of the created world. In Shklovsky's phrase, it "defamiliarizes" the world; it "makes the stone stony."[21]

This is, for the most part, a modernist/avant-garde account of literature and criticism. There are more conservative routes to literary study, routes that have nothing to do with modernism or the desire to leave the suburbs. I knew a few graduate students, back in the day, who were drawn to the neoclassical Augustan era of the early eighteenth century and were deeply motivated by the desire to return to the classical unities and forms of order, leaving behind all this superficial, ironic postmodern dreck; I knew a few graduate students who believed with Matthew Arnold that literature must be the secular religion that saves us from the depredations of contemporary culture; I also knew a few graduate students who immersed themselves in the very early periods of English literature partly out of a conviction that prior to the Reformation people knew what was really important, namely, the fate of your eternal soul. But I could count those students using my fingers and toes—in a graduate program of three hundred.

These days, I often think my field is so pervasively liberal-left that smart young conservatives will shun it altogether. I know there are still some conservatives out there who truly love the arts and humanities—"old school" arts and humanities, usually, more Augustan than modern, more Chaucerian than Kafkaesque, but I'll settle for what I can get and, besides, some of those old schools were pretty good. Arts-and-humanities conservatives may be a dying breed, as conservatism in America becomes more and more associated with the know-nothing, Tom DeLay wing of the Republican Party; as University of Texas philosophy professor Brian Leiter wrote in November 2004, "Perhaps . . . the ratio of Democratic voters to Republican voters in the academy has increased over time because the Republican party has gone increasingly bonkers, such that educated and informed people by and large can't stomach it any more?"[22] But when they disappear from the earth altogether, along with conservative American economists who believe in honest budgets and honest business practices (an endangered species) and conservative American environmentalists who respect scientific evidence (already extinct), I know that I will miss them terribly. Or, to put this another way, I often wish I had more conservative colleagues in literary study.

I'm serious about this. I don't mind in the least having substantial political disagreements with colleagues, just so long as they're smart colleagues who hit the rhetorical ball back over the net with gusto and topspin. I already have plenty of these on the left, even though Horowitz and company would have you believe that a department of Democrats is somehow a department in which everyone agrees with one another. But when all the substantial intellectual disagreements in a discipline are arguments among leftists and liberals, the premises of argument are inevitably skewed—especially in those lefter-than-thou circles in which the most "oppositional" position claims for itself the greatest moral authority. And when an entire department or an entire field of inquiry produces a uniform moral mist, it's no wonder that after a while it will attract only those aspirants who like breathing the air. The sheer length of graduate programs in English is no help, either, as Louis Menand pointed out in a recent essay. "The median time to degree (if your degree happens to be in English) is 9.8 years," Menand wrote, and "that figure does not include stop time, when students take a leave of absence." Menand argues that "the obscene length of time to degree" has a stultifying effect on the entire profession:

> Time to degree is a problem not only because of the embarrassing labor practices it is associated with. It is also an intellectual problem.

The obstacles to professional success are so high at the portal that students are largely self-sorted before they get there. They already talk the talk in class, and their main goal in graduate school is to learn how to talk it at conferences. And the obstacles at the other end, the placement and tenure anxieties, don't exactly encourage iconoclasm. Time to degree, job placement, and the tenure rate virtually guarantee a culture of conformity. The profession is not reproducing itself so much as cloning itself. One sign that this is happening is that there appears to be little change in dissertation topics in the last ten years. Everyone seems to be writing the same dissertation, and with a tool kit that has not altered much since 1990.[23]

Likewise, in his November 2004 *Chronicle of Higher Education* essay, "Liberal Groupthink Is Anti-Intellectual," Mark Bauerlein argued that the liberal mist is so pervasive in some fields that conservatives are gradually weeded out in the course of their studies:

> while the lack of conservative minds on college campuses is increasingly indisputable, the question remains: Why?
>
> The obvious answer, at least in the humanities and social sciences, is that academics shun conservative values and traditions, so their curricula and hiring practices discourage non-leftists from pursuing academic careers. What allows them to do that, while at the same time they deny it, is that the bias takes a subtle form. Although I've met several conservative intellectuals in the last year who would love an academic post but have given up after years of trying, outright blackballing is rare. The disparate outcome emerges through an indirect filtering process that runs from graduate school to tenure and beyond.[24]

While I remain skeptical that there are substantial numbers of conservatives seriously interested in the liberal arts, slowly but inexorably being eliminated by our indirect filtering processes, I have spoken to a number of conservative faculty and graduate students in literary study in recent years and they have all sounded one theme: in their daily rounds in the workplace, they know they must negotiate the fact that almost every one of their colleagues assumes that all of *their* colleagues are liberal in one way or another. Theirs is, without question, the position of minorities in a majority culture, even if the injustice done to them—colleagues speaking casually in meetings and corridors as if there were no conservatives within earshot—is hardly one of the most severe or profound injustices human beings have perpetrated on one another.

Not until May 2005 did a young conservative—Ross Douthat, the author of a biting memoir of undergraduate life at Harvard[25]—step up and suggest that conservatives have only themselves to blame for the dearth of conservatives in academe. Writing in the *New Republic*, Douthat dismissed Horowitz's Academic Bill of Rights as ineffectual:

> even the most controversial of Horowitz's proposed "rights"—the provision in the Bill requiring professors to "make their students aware of serious scholarly viewpoints other than their own"—wouldn't have much effect on classroom life, because it's precisely the *lack* of serious conservative scholarship that's the problem for the right to begin with. (This is particularly true within those disciplines typically singled out by conservatives as most in need of political diversifying. How many "serious scholarly viewpoints" put forward by conservatives are you likely to find in, say, an anthropology or a comparative literature department?) There are, of course, many talented conservative academics languishing in think tanks or second-tier colleges—but not *that* many. Even if the Bill of Rights brought them all flooding through the university gates, you could empty every right-leaning think tank a dozen times over, and you still wouldn't have enough professors to bring political balance to the faculties of the Ivy League alone. . . .

No, what the right really needs are numbers—not an Academic Bill of Rights but a slew of academic converts, a generation of like-minded graduate students who can integrate upward into the higher echelons of the university, and eventually transform it.[26]

Douthat draws an analogy between such a Young Conservative movement and the New Left of the 1960s, but a more precise analogy would be to second-wave feminists, who had a deeply contentious relationship both to the New Left and to the academic disciplines they tried, with substantial success, to transform. No one can honestly say that universities welcomed the academic wing of the feminist movement in the 1970s, and the first large cohort of women who were tenured in fields such as comparative literature and anthropology knows this better than anyone. Whatever slings and arrows academic conservative scholars are suffering now, I doubt very much that they compare to the kind of resistance most feminist scholars faced a generation ago; I wonder, for example, what the lone tenured female faculty member in City College's early-1970s' English department thinks about the conservative complaint today. And yet, feminism began to have an impact on literary criticism in the early 1980s,[27] and it became widely acknowledged as a major subfield of study within the next decade. Academe is still an unfriendly environment for women (let alone for feminists) in many disciplines,[28] and to this day women are significantly *over*represented in the profession's lowest echelons.[29] But nevertheless, the demographic difference between the professoriate in 1971 and in 2006 is stark, and it should give aspiring conservatives a benchmark; it is indeed possible to change the intellectual course of scholarly fields, and if conservatives are serious about doing so, they should expect that it will take about a generation or so. *If* they are serious.

Quite apart from the question of whether conservatives are willing to undertake something like feminism's long march through one small wing of the academic institution, there's another question that I face every year, as a teacher and a mentor: do I really want to encourage another generation of liberal students to apply to graduate school in literature? Exactly how does this advance the causes of liberalism? Personally, I wish liberals and progressives had less of a presence in literature departments and more of a presence in legislatures. In recent years, when promising, politically active liberal students have come to me to talk about their plans for graduate school in English, I've told them that we already have all the liberals we need in English, and that if they truly want to have some impact on the world they should consider law schools, international relations programs, or public policy institutes. They may have to undertake a long march through institutions more conservative than mine, but surely this will be good for them—and for liberalism.

The most interesting—and, I think, most insightful—aspect of Mark Bauerlein's version of the conservative complaint is its insistence that a field's domination by liberal-left thought is bad not only for the field in question but also for liberal-left thought:

> The phenomenon that I have described is not so much a political matter as a social dynamic; any political position that dominates an institution without dissent deteriorates into smugness, complacency, and blindness. The solution is an intellectual climate in which the worst tendencies of group psychology are neutralized.
>
> That doesn't mean establishing affirmative action for conservative scholars or encouraging greater market forces in education—which violate conservative values as much as they do liberal values. Rather, it calls for academics to recognize that a one-party campus is bad for the intellectual health of everyone. Groupthink is an anti-intellectual condition, ironically seductive in that the more one feels at ease with compatriots, the more one's mind narrows. The great liberal John Stuart Mill identified its insulating effect as a failure of imagination:

"They have never thrown themselves into the mental condition of those who think differently from them." With adversaries so few and opposing ideas so disposable, a reverse advantage sets in. The majority expands its power throughout the institution, but its thinking grows routine and parochial. The minority is excluded, but its thinking is tested and toughened. Being the lone dissenter in a colloquy, one learns to acquire sure facts, crisp arguments, and a thick skin.

But we can't open the university to conservative ideas and persons by outside command. That would poison the atmosphere and jeopardize the ideals of free inquiry. Leftist bias evolved within the protocols of academic practice (though not without intimidation), and conservative challenges should evolve in the same way. There are no administrative or professional reasons to bring conservatism into academe, to be sure, but there are good intellectual and social reasons for doing so.

Those reasons are, in brief: One, a wider spectrum of opinion accords with the claims of diversity. Two, facing real antagonists strengthens one's own position. Three, to earn a public role in American society, professors must engage the full range of public opinion.

There's much to admire in Bauerlein's brief for conservatives. Indeed, it is (as Bauerlein makes clear in his citation of Mill) classically liberal: the university should indeed be an argument culture, as Gerald Graff has long argued,[30] and arguments are strongest when they engage with the strongest possible opposing arguments. But Bauerlein's essay doesn't always practice what it preaches. His accounts of some academic subfields, for instance, are at once tendentious and glib: "the quasi-Marxist outlook of cultural studies rules out those who espouse capitalism," he writes, as if cultural studies theorists favor planned economies (they are much more often criticized, as in the work of Thomas Frank,[31] for being unwitting advocates of libertarian capitalism); "if you disapprove of affirmative action, forget pursuing a degree in African-American

studies," he continues, as if the study of African-American literature, history, and culture turns on the one social policy that American conservatives think of first when they think of black people
and universities; and finally, most laughably, "if you think that the
nuclear family proves the best unit of social well-being, stay away
from women's studies."

People who espouse serious argument should not descend to
caricature,[32] and Bauerlein's characterization of women's studies—
a field in which my wife works, even as she helps to maintain the
nuclear family to which I belong—is one step away from the claim
that "womyn's studies" would simply prefer a world without men.
But if we are to stay on a higher plane, then it should suffice to
point out that Bauerlein draws his examples exclusively from fields
dominated by liberals and yet speaks freely of the "one-party *campus*" (my emphasis) as if the campus consisted entirely of departments of education, cultural studies, African-American studies,
and women's studies. This is a Horowitz–Zinsmeister tactic, and
should not be taken at face value. And as for those last two fields,
Bauerlein's argument proceeds as if its author were unaware that
conservatives opposed the creation of women's studies and African-
American studies and widely oppose their existence even today.
Perhaps, to borrow a page from Ross Douthat's argument, when
conservatives grant the right of these fields to exist, their intellectual contributions to them will become more cogent; until then, it
remains unclear how scholarly disciplines associated with women
and African-Americans will become intellectually stronger by hiring people who claim to want to abolish the disciplines altogether.

Bauerlein's account of group psychology is as meritorious as his
emphasis on substantive argument, but his chief example is as suspect as his characterization of women's studies. He argues, following Cass Sunstein, a professor of political science and jurisprudence
at the University of Chicago, that the "Law of Group Polarization
. . . predicts that when like-minded people deliberate as an orga-

nized group, the general opinion shifts toward extreme versions of their common beliefs." I have indeed seen this occur—not in individual departments, where the faculty usually cannot agree on whether to offer introductory undergraduate surveys or whether to serve vegetarian entrées at a reception, but in conferences and conventions, where one or two radical voices quickly manage to drag an entire roomful of otherwise sensible people right off the cliff. It happens every so often, for example, at the Delegate Assembly of the Modern Language Association, on which I have served for many years, and at which I have had ample opportunity for exasperation and bewilderment. Then again, it's precisely because I serve on the assembly that I can spot what's wrong with Bauerlein's account of that body:

> The annual resolutions of the Modern Language Association's Delegate Assembly, for example, ring with indignation over practices that enjoy popular acceptance. Last year, charging that in wartime, governments use language to "misrepresent policies" and "stigmatize dissent," one resolution urged faculty members to conduct "critical analysis of war talk . . . as appropriate, in classrooms." However high-minded the delegates felt as they tallied the vote, which passed 122 to 8 without discussion, to outsiders the resolution seemed merely a license for more proselytizing.

Bauerlein's misrepresentation of that resolution is subtle but important. It did not "urge faculty members to conduct" critical analysis of war talk; rather, it proposed "that the Modern Language Association supports its members in conducting critical analysis of war talk, in public forums and, as appropriate, in classrooms." Plainly, no one is being urged to talk in any way they don't want to, about the war or anything else. Rather, the resolution is nothing more— or less—than a post-9/11 restatement of the principle of academic freedom, and one would hope that an "insider" like Bauerlein would have more sympathy with it, more awareness of the degree to which it enjoys "popular acceptance," and greater willingness to promote that popular acceptance.

Moreover, Bauerlein does not mention the fate of the other anti-war resolution proposed to the 2003 MLA Delegate Assembly—a resolution calling for "the withdrawal of troops from Afghanistan and Iraq and reallocation of funds to reverse inattention to, and grave deficits in, funding of education and other human services." From 2002 to 2005 I served on both the Delegate Assembly Organizing Committee and the MLA Executive Council, to which this resolution came in February 2004, and I concurred with a majority of council members that the resolution fell outside the mission of the Association, which is "to promote study, criticism, and research in the more and less commonly taught modern languages and their literatures and to further the common interests of teachers of these subjects." In other words, the council agreed with the Delegate Assembly that we have the right, as a nonprofit academic association, to uphold the freedom of speech of our members, but we do not have the authority to call for the withdrawal of troops—or, for that matter, for their redeployment to North Korea, should the mood strike us. The MLA is not quite as nutty as Bauerlein would have you believe.

Nor are my colleagues as monolithic and single-minded as the phrase "one-party campus" would suggest. I have substantial differences and disagreements with liberal faculty members all the time, which suggests that there are many important intellectual issues for which one's political party affiliation is simply irrelevant. An anthropology department stocked with registered Democrats can still be a contentious, unruly, even dysfunctional department, as can an economics department stocked with registered Republicans. No faculty-meeting debate—about the direction of the graduate program, about the finalists for a new assistant professorship, about a new initiative from the dean's office—gets resolved when someone stands up and says, "People, people—why are we arguing about the staffing of undergraduate courses and the desirability of hiring a new nineteenth-century scholar? Surely we can all find common ground in hating George Bush."

It's not as if I'm a passive bystander in all this, either; there are some aspects of "liberal" faculty culture I can't stand. One such aspect can be summed up in the phrase "I consider myself a liberal but . . ." I've encountered the "I consider myself a liberal, but" phenomenon so often in academe that I hardly bother to remark on it anymore, but I'll mention an example or five here: the registered-Democrat faculty member who complained that a local "shop with cops" program, in which young children in poverty go Christmas shopping with city police, was teaching African-American kids to expect a lifetime of handouts (a problem to which the white children in poverty were apparently immune); the registered-Democrat faculty member who told an accomplished female undergraduate that she shouldn't bother thinking about graduate or professional schools since she was inevitably going to settle down and marry; the registered-Democrat faculty member who told an African-American undergraduate not to get a master's degree in education lest he wind up teaching his "ghetto slang" to children in public schools; the registered-Democrat department chair who told a Jewish member of his faculty that his people were prone to complaining; the registered-Democrat member of a search committee who advised against hiring a young gay scholar on the grounds that he would wind up cruising for sex in the streets of their small Southern town. These examples, of course, do not exhaust the ways in which "liberal" faculty members can be illiberal. I've come across innumerable "liberal" faculty members who have no trouble exploiting their teaching assistants and research assistants—and who have no sympathy whatsoever with graduate teaching assistants trying to unionize in order to negotiate for raises, grievance procedures, and medical benefits. There seems to be, on some campuses and in some departments, an aura of genteel, almost patrician liberalism that always makes me think of a song written by my friend and former bandmate Larry Gallagher (now a San Francisco-based singer-songwriter), "I'm Sorry for What My People Did to Your People," one of whose verses goes:

I'm sorry for what my people did to your people
It was a nasty job
Please note the change of attitude
On the bumper of my Saab.

Then there's the campus wing of the far left, the Ward Churchills who pop up every so often making outrageously stupid and/or morally obtuse remarks, thereby providing Bill O'Reilly, Rush Limbaugh, and David Horowitz with yet another scandal and another recruiting device. There's no question that we have a few of them on the academic left, and this is where my analogy between academe and NPR or PBS (in the previous chapter) breaks down: you just don't find anyone on the public airwaves likening the victims of September 11 to "little Eichmanns," as did Churchill, or saying, as University of New Mexico history professor Richard Berthold did on the day of the attack, "Anyone who can blow up the Pentagon has my vote." There's a critical difference between Berthold and Churchill, however, quite apart from the fact that Berthold's remark immediately made national news and Churchill's short essay, "Some People Push Back: On the Justice of Roosting Chickens" didn't draw fire until early 2005: namely, that Berthold apologized for his foolish remark, calling it "the worst attempt at an incredibly stupid joke,"[33] whereas Churchill has offered only the explanation that he meant the "'little Eichmanns' characterization" to apply "only to those [World Trade Center workers] described as 'technicians.' Thus, it was obviously not directed to the children, janitors, food service workers, firemen and random passers-by."[34]

What's even more remarkable than this assignation of profound moral culpability to the very people (other than children, janitors, etc.) who were killed by the attacks of 9/11,[35] to my mind, are the rigorous parsings of Churchill's "explanation" by the faction I call the Monty Python left. These are the people who doggedly insist that Churchill was not "justifying" or "celebrating" the attack, but simply pointing out that it was one example of the inevitable "blow-back" from atrocities and odious alliances assignable to American foreign policy in the Middle East. The blowback argument, by itself, is an intellectually legitimate argument; there is no doubt that the United States funded the Afghan mujahideen in their struggle against the Soviet Union in the 1980s, just as there is no question that US support for Israel has generated a great deal of anti-American sentiment in the Arab world. The question remains, however, as to how much of that anti-American sentiment is "legiti-mate" in the sense that it should be approved by the American left, for surely not all of it can be, and the question remains as to whether our funding of the Afghan mujahideen twenty years ago should be considered sufficient cause for September 11—since it is also possi-ble to argue, as has Paul Berman, that we funded bin Laden and then he attacked us, and there's ingratitude for you.[36]

Indeed, the larger issue of the extent to which US foreign policy was an enabling condition—which is very different from being a direct cause—of al-Qaeda is an entirely serious matter, and any serious attempt to address it should also take into account the his-tory of Wahhabist fundamentalism and so-called political Islam, the origins of which (in the Muslim Brotherhood) had little to do with US policies. But Ward Churchill was doing nothing of the kind; he was not asking why well-educated, middle-class Egyptian and Saudi young men were hijacking civilian aircraft and flying them into office buildings in New York and Washington even though the people of Nicaragua, Chile, Vietnam, or the Cherokee

Nation have far more pressing grievances against the US, and he most certainly was not asking about the "root causes" of Islamist radicalism. Rather, he was likening the World Trade Center dead to one of the architects of the Holocaust. And then, in his wake, along comes the Monty Python left, whose credibility is confined to obscure corners on a bunch of campuses and a string of fringe organizations in major cities, and they tell themselves that it's important not to "distance ourselves" from Ward Churchill's remarks, especially now that he's explained that the dead members of the working class, the dead passersby, and the dead kids were all right by us; it's only the dead who were supposedly aiding and abetting the project of American empire who deserve our condemnation. As I waded through these defenses and parsings in the early months of 2005, they began to resemble a black-comedy skit gone wrong. I imagine the skit running something like this:

What about the cheesemakers in the WTC restaurants? Are they exempt, along with the janitors and firemen? No, the cheesemakers were far from innocent—as were the WTC dairy producers in general. They may have been "very little Eichmanns" as opposed to "little Eichmanns," but they were nonetheless comparable on some scale to the technicians of the Holocaust.

What about the accounting department on the eighty-second floor of the south tower? Were they guilty? Yes, the accounting department was as guilty as sin. The eighty-second floor was an especially imperialist floor, even if the photocopy room could more accurately be described as "quasi-crypto-imperialist" rather than nakedly "neo-imperialist."

Ward Churchill's far-left defenders didn't get quite so absurd as this, but they came close. And I think they came close partly because of the law of group polarization, eloquently bearing out Sunstein in this respect. When Churchill's remarks became national news in 2005, most liberals (myself included) responded by saying, well, such sentiments are truly repellent, but there is no question that they are covered by the principle of academic freedom; academic freedom means nothing if it does not protect remarks that most people find repellent, whether we're talking about Ward Churchill's desire to blame some of the WTC dead for 9/11 or Canadian professor J. Philippe Rushton's belief in the genetic superiority of the white race. A smattering of academics far to my left, however, realized quickly that if they came out in support of academic freedom while marking their distance from Churchill's essay, they would be—gasp!—agreeing with liberals. In a rigorous enterprise of self-differentiation, therefore (and I watched this happening over a couple of days on a couple of left-wing listservs), they decided that because the "academic freedom" defense was a "liberal" position, they needed to *go further* and defend the specific content of the "little Eichmanns" line. No doubt a very tiny few of those people sincerely believed that the employees of Cantor Fitzgerald (but not the food service workers or the firefighters, etc.) deserved, somehow, to die that day. But most of them, I am now convinced, took this vile position chiefly in order to distinguish themselves from the mere "liberals" to their right.

It is quite true, as Churchill and many others have argued, that American accounts of global conflicts treat American lives as more worthy of consideration than Iraqi or Nicaraguan or Vietnamese lives. But it is quite another thing to claim that the World Trade Center victims who worked in global finance are somehow complicit with atrocities like that of the Holocaust. No liberal, no progressive, no leftist is required to defend such a claim; for that matter, none of us will ever know how many trenchant critics of American foreign policy were killed in the twin towers that day.

Writing in 1970, long after he had abandoned Marxism for a distinguished place on the American intellectual right, Sidney Hook argued that tenure guaranteed a scholar's "right to heresy":

The qualified teacher, whose qualifications may be inferred from his acquisition of tenure, has the right honestly to reach, and hold, and proclaim any conclusion in the field of his competence. In other words, academic freedom carries with it the *right to heresy* as well as the right to restate and defend the traditional views. This takes in considerable ground. If a teacher in honest pursuit of an inquiry or argument comes to a conclusion that appears fascist or communist or racist or what-not in the eyes of others, once he has been certified as professionally competent in the eyes of his peers, then those who believe in academic freedom must defend his right to be wrong—if they consider him wrong—whatever their orthodoxy may be.[37]

Read against the sounds of the chorus of conservative commentators and politicians calling for Churchill's firing, this is a remarkable passage; what's especially remarkable about it is that Hook used this rationale to defend a young Marxist named Eugene Genovese, a professor of history at Rutgers University, who in 1965 had then made public his support of the Viet Cong—and, as Hook notes, had become immediately infamous for doing so, because New Jersey's Democratic governor, Richard Hughes, rightly refused to fire Genovese on the grounds of aiding and abetting the enemy and the Republican gubernatorial candidate Wayne Dumont, "focused his entire campaign on the issue of Genovese's right to teach." Perhaps there's a lesson here for the good people of the state of Colorado, many of whom called on Governor Bill Owens to have Churchill fired for his remarks. But the cogency of the lesson depends in part on the legitimacy of tenure, and on our willingness to come to terms with the fact that so few college professors working today actually have tenure.

David Horowitz, to his credit, did not join that conservative chorus as it demanded the firing of Churchill; on the contrary, at first he unambiguously upheld Churchill's right to teach. This is, perhaps, a sign of Horowitz's recognition that academic freedom covers even the most noxious heresies when they stem from honest pursuit of an inquiry or argument (and grotesque as it may sound to some ears, the question of whether there can be such a thing as "collective guilt" among the citizens of a superpower is indeed an inquiry). Or, perhaps, it is a sign that Horowitz—who is, above all else, a master organizer and mobilizer—knows very well how efficiently and effortlessly academic far-leftists like Churchill do his work for him.

IN THE PRECEDING PAGES I may have made it sound as if campus life is continually vexing, what with the faux liberals and the Monty Python characters. We also have our occasional cranks, our poseurs, our bloviators, our pedants, and a couple of those people who are just impossible to work with, but in this respect we're very much like any other workplace—except for the pedants, who are relatively more numerous on campus than off.

But the fact remains that I respect and admire the majority of my colleagues. There are many with whom I have never discussed politics; I know them only by their scholarship or their teaching or their service on committees—and I always have a high opinion of colleagues who conduct committee meetings briskly, getting directly to the heart of the matter about the departmental bylaws or graduate admissions standards. Moreover, because I've served on so many personnel, executive, and supervisory committees, I've been in a position to read the work and peruse the teaching records of colleagues in subfields quite distant from mine, and I'm often amazed at the quality of their research and writing. Thanks to some of that tedious committee work I do, I'm well aware that I'm surrounded by coworkers who just happen to be extraordinary teachers, and whose daily work in the classroom inspires students to read more widely and deeply than they had previously thought imaginable.

I am always dismayed, though, by parochialism, whether it

involves students who have never questioned the assumptions of their families and immediate communities, or faculty members who think that their little dispute with a gaggle of colleagues down the hall is the most important crisis in American higher education. Over the past two decades, we humanists have sometimes managed to give curious onlookers the impression that we think the most important struggle on the planet involves the divide between Traditional Scholars and Contemporary Theorists. In my twenty years in English departments, I've watched many squabbles between the old guard and the young Turks, and I've participated enthusiastically in many of them, usually on behalf of the latter. English is not, despite its reputation, uniquely fractious; in my eight years of involvement with humanities institutes, I've had ringside seats for fights between Latin Americanists and Iberianists in Spanish departments, digital media designers and oil painters in art departments, cultural theorists and archaeologists in anthropology departments, and analytic and Continental philosophers in philosophy departments. Each of these arguments is important in its own right, and involves strongly held intellectual commitments that have deep roots in the academic disciplines of the past few centuries; it's simply not always true that the debates, as Wallace Sayre once phrased it, are so fierce because the stakes are so low. Still, I've often come away from these debates wishing that these people would realize that the most vocal and stringent critics of American universities couldn't care less about the difference between traditional art history as practiced by Edwin Panofsky and eclectic postmodern art history as practiced by James Elkins. Sooner or later, I want to tell them, the right-wing state legislator is going to show up at the campus gates, flanked by his staff and a couple of hundred irate parents and local residents, demanding to know why "secular humanism" is so prevalent in American universities. Thus challenged, about half my colleagues will reply, "But we're not humanists—we're anti-humanists and post-humanists," whereupon the legislator and his posse will proceed to mow 'em all down, snarling, "We don't care what kind of humanists you are."

There are, I think, three morals to be drawn from this fictional scenario at the campus gates. One, in most arts and humanities departments, the old guard and the young Turks, the Latin Americanists and the Iberianists, the digital media designers and the oil painters, the cultural theorists and the archaeologists, and the analytic and Continental philosophers will all go to the polls in November and vote overwhelmingly (but not unanimously) Democratic. Two, while this state of affairs suggests to the nation's right-wing culture warriors that arts and humanities departments must be overhauled and injected with massive infusions of Republicans, it suggests to me that the voting records of my colleagues are actually one of the most trivial features of our departmental deliberations. Our voting records matter when we're discussing politics at dinner parties, yes, when so many of us casually assume that there can't possibly be anyone seated at the table who would confess to being an admirer of Ronald Reagan, but they do not matter in the least when we're discussing the undergraduate curriculum, the graduate program, the future of the honors college, the rigorousness of the writing requirement, the senior-year capstone course, or any of the other things that make up the actual diurnal work of running an academic department. Curricular disputes are especially unpredictable in this regard; it is not uncommon to find the department's gay, ponytailed, hemp-wearing poet insist that today's students simply must be grounded in a series of required "core" courses in British literary history, whereas the lone suit-and-tie Rockefeller Republican is arguing that the English major should have no requirements whatsoever. And three, when we take a wider view of the campus and include the disciplines of economics, physics, psychology, health and human development, architectural engineering, criminal justice, business management, molecular biochemistry, and kinesiology, we'll remember—as well we should—that the courses of study in such fields, all of which are critical to the modern American research university, are commonly (and deliberately) ignored by the most strident conservative critics of American higher education. If you try to imagine professors of business, professors of health sciences, professors of physics, and professors of landscape architecture marching and teaching in lockstep to some monolithic liberal ideology, you'll see what I mean. The fact that conservative critics of faculty "bias" reduce all such intellectual and disciplinary disputes to the question of whether a faculty member votes Democratic tells us much about the blinkered worldview of culture-war conservatives, but very little about what actually goes on in actual college departments.

Despite all these petty annoyances and vexations, there's no question that I now have the best job I've ever had. I love the workplace autonomy, and, as a person and a parent, I deeply appreciate the irregularity of the long-but-irregular hours. Most of all, though, I love being surrounded by colleagues who are smart, deeply learned (not the same thing), and utterly dedicated to their jobs as teachers. Every once in a while I look over at other, more lucrative and prestigious wings of the campus, or further afield to my college classmates who went into law, and I notice that their working conditions are even better than mine, particularly when it comes to the grainy details. For example, I am writing this passage in my English department office, a cheerless, gray cinderblock affair in which I cannot even hang a picture of my family (the cinderblock resists all such sentimental gestures), and in which I cannot work during much of the summer because my building does not have air-conditioning. "We work," says one of my more distinguished colleagues, "in squalor." Yet, from another angle, the undeniable ugliness and inadequacy of my department building is beside the point, and my distinguished colleague is exaggerating terribly, as if he had no idea of what real workplace squalor entails. For why should I measure my job by the standard of whether I enjoy working in my office, when it permits me so much latitude to work outside my office? Why should I complain that my office is too hot in the summer, when I have no obligation to go to my office in the summer? Besides, my office may be ugly, and downright inhospitable in August, but it is not significantly uglier than your average workspace cubicle, and it is about three times as large as your average cubicle.

My office, and the building in which it is located, seems to me a physical symbol of many of the contradictions of my job. My department is a department of liberals, sure enough, but (despite the title of this chapter) we actually have no faculty lounge, and there is nothing in our building to suggest that we are an elite of any kind. Similarly, we may have exceptional latitude, personally and professionally, when we design our courses and plan our semesters, but we have very little clout when we tell upper-level administrators that our graduate students work in tiny, partitioned cubicles that not only depress some of our current graduate students but scare away some of our prospective graduate students. As Chris Bush, a Cotsen–Behrman Fellow in the Princeton Society of Fellows, points out, these contradictions are but material examples of the larger contradictions that define our place in the world:

> Most Americans seem both to think very little of literature professors and to expect the world of them. . . . Today's professor is both elitist and mired in pop culture dreck. S/he is politically correct—but irrelevant to contemporary concerns. The professoriate is impotent, but corrupting the nation's youth on a mass scale. Americans want the Humanities to be practical, training students to face real problems in the real world. But they also want the Humanities to discuss works of art as works of art, without the distractions of politics, history, race, class, gender or other such hooey. At the same time, literature should teach moral values. And parents should feel they are getting their money's worth. Failure to meet not only any, but all of the above cri-

teria results in moral decay—and in not being "relevant," which professors aren't supposed to care about anyway, unless they're not.[38]

This description resonates with me. I am, after all, something of an
elitist (I prefer good students to slackers, smart job candidates to
mediocre ones), and I am definitely mired in pop culture dreck.
Perhaps it is only fitting that my job is so envied and despised at the
same time. As I've said, much of the envy is not misplaced; I really
do have wonderful working conditions, even amidst the general
erosion of the professoriate. Then again, you probably wouldn't
want my actual office, particularly in August. And when it comes
to being despised, I see no reason why people who despise secular
liberal humanists generally wouldn't despise me too.

Of course, much of my work is done neither in my office nor in
my study at home, but in classrooms. Before I proceed to explain
what goes on in those classrooms, I should probably explain—
briefly—what kind of teacher my students have understood me to
be. Gauging from my students' and my peers' evaluations over the
past twenty years, I'm not one of those renowned, charismatic,
widely successful teachers who win awards and change lives. I'm in
the next tier down: a good teacher, often a very good teacher, but
not a truly dazzling teacher. My former students speak to me
warmly in coffee shops and restaurants; some have kept in touch
for years. My official student evaluations are good evaluations, on
balance; most students find that I lead lively discussions, respond in
depth to their oral and written comments, and am willing to entertain any plausible interpretation of any literary work that comes
before us. I don't worry too much about the instructor-evaluation
numbers themselves (for the record, 4.45 out of 5 at Illinois, 6.3 out
of 7 at Penn State); I agree with my colleagues who argue that
overemphasizing the numerical quanta plays into a consumerist
logic in which students are recast as customers, and teaching evaluations become customer-satisfaction surveys in which the customer

is always right. But I read my narrative evaluations very carefully, and so far mine have tended to reinforce the statistical quanta much more often than not. So why do I place myself in the second tier of literature professors? Mainly because the first tier, many of whom I have witnessed in action and one of whom happens to be my wife, consists of stunningly, jaw-droppingly talented teachers. They engage students of all kinds, from the clove-cigarette-smoking riot grrrl with the Doc Martens and the multiple piercings to the beefy backward-baseball-cap fellow whose T-shirt says "COLLEGE" just like Bluto's in *Animal House*. They earn stellar evaluations regardless of whether they're teaching highly specialized electives or general introductions, large lectures or small seminars, and they spark student enthusiasm for every kind of subject, from "Women and the Avant-Garde" to "The Impact of Agricultural Price Supports on Developing Nations." As for me, I'm the next best thing, which isn't too shabby as such things go.

So much for what students think of me. In the next chapter I'll tell you what I think of them—of some of the students in my classes, and some of the students who would never dream of venturing into my classes.

4.   Students In and Out of Class

I LIKE MOST OF MY STUDENTS. SOME OF THEM ARE inspiring: occasionally, over the course of a semester, I learn that they are juggling part-time jobs, complicated family dramas, long-distance relationships, or chronic illnesses—and no, I don't hear these things only when papers are due, because I rarely give extensions on papers, and I say as much on every syllabus. I feel for such students, partly because when I was an undergraduate I also juggled part-time jobs and complicated family dramas, and, when I did, the thing I usually dropped in all that juggling was rigorous class participation. I took incompletes, I dropped courses, I scrambled at the last minute—and only managed to finish semesters in good shape, with good grades, about half the time. I performed much better in graduate school, but then I was older and wiser in graduate school, and more distant from complicated family dramas. Having worked part-time, up to twenty hours a week, all through college and graduate school, I know that many of my students are working just as hard, in class and out: a student with even a moderate workload of fifteen hours at a job, fifteen hours of classes, and twenty hours of homework is putting in a full week's work and ten hours of overtime.

Not every college student in the United States is working overtime, of course. My friends at small liberal arts colleges tell me of dealing with massively entitled students who drive cars far more expensive than anything in the faculty parking lot, and who look upon their classes in the humanities as amusing or annoying little pit stops on their paths toward world domination. My friends at smaller state schools—the places that the late great North Carolina State basketball coach Jim Valvano once termed "directional schools," because they usually include a point of the compass in their name—tell me of trying to teach thoroughly disengaged students who have never encountered a work of literature written before 1900, and will almost surely never do so again after college. I've seen versions of these kinds of students myself: kids from the wealthier suburbs for whom the relatively low tuition of a public school poses no problem for their parents' finances, and who arrive on campus in a phalanx of Jeep Grand Cherokees; kids from all over whose major interest on campus seems to lie in figuring out how to combine one bar's All You Can Eat Wings Night with a competing bar's Special Massive Alcohol Consumption Night. (Much of what you've heard about binge drinking on campus, unfortunately, is true. Some of the most lethal forms of student drinking could be eliminated if we restored eighteen as the legal drinking age, but because this idea is both humane and pragmatic it will never be enacted.) But for the most part, I've been quite fortunate. The overwhelming majority of students in my classes truly want to be there, and aren't simply going through the motions; most of them, even in the lower-level survey classes, do their work diligently and do it reasonably well. About a third of them do better than "reasonably well," and four to six of them, in every class of thirty-six or forty, manage to impress or astonish me.

Because I've spent my entire career at large public universities, I've seen a rough cross-section of America, ages eighteen to twenty-five—better-heeled and better-educated than the median, but not so exclusive a cohort as you'll find in the Ivies or the Seven Sisters, nor so idiosyncratic a bunch as you'll find at Antioch or Carnegie Mellon or the Rhode Island School of Design. Students at Illinois and

Penn State are drawn in part from the suburban collar counties surrounding Chicago and Philadelphia, but both schools also educate an appreciable number of young adults from depressed areas, rural and urban, who—even in the year 2006, more than sixty years after the GI Bill and almost forty years after the desegregation of higher education—arrive on campus as the first member of the family to attend college. Many of them are trying on new (and newly independent) identities; some of that admissions-brochure rhetoric is true, and some students do experience their college years as intellectually and personally formative periods in their lives. This aspect of college life is overemphasized, I think; I have seen students try on new ideas and new appearances, but rarely have I witnessed fullblown road-to-Damascus conversion experiences of any kind. (As a gay colleague once remarked to me, conservatives invest him with all kinds of power, fearing that professors like him will lead heterosexual young men "astray"; "honestly," he said, "I just wish I had the power to persuade them to do all the reading.") Overall, my students have been a generally pleasant lot, but not so pleasant as to avoid disagreeing with me or with each other from time to time.

No doubt some of my good fortune in having a cohort of pleasant-but-serious students has to do with the fact that my classes are composed chiefly of English majors, and English majors at schools like Illinois and Penn State tend to take the world of ideas somewhat more seriously than business and accounting majors. This isn't to say that students who attend college chiefly to earn professional credentials for employment aren't smart or studious; it's merely to point out the obvious, namely, that most of the English majors on campuses like mine are a self-selecting bunch who usually decide to pursue a major in the humanities because they truly love the subject matter. Just over 4 percent of American undergraduates choose to major in English. In recent years, this figure has led many critics of the humanities (usually those who believe that the humanities have been corrupted or compromised by the advent of critical theory) to speak of a precipitous decline in enrollments. Well, there has been a decline since 1970, but that's only because the late 1960s witnessed an unprecedented spike in English enrollments; in 1950, 4 percent of American undergraduates majored in English, and in 1980 that figure was 3.5 percent (it is now 4.11). In other words, apart from that late-1960s' surge that no one has yet been able to explain, English enrollments have hovered between the 3 and 5 percent mark for more than half a century. In 1970 they hit 7 percent. Those were the glory days.[1]

Much of what you've heard about American undergraduates isn't true about English majors. For example, the 2002 National Survey of Student Engagement found that "only 12 percent of last year's freshmen at four-year residential colleges reported spending 26 or more hours per week preparing for classes, while the majority, 63 percent, said they spend 15 or fewer hours on class preparation"; the 2004 survey added that 40 percent of first-year students and 25 percent of seniors "never discussed ideas from their classes or readings" with a professor outside of class.[2] There's simply no way a good English major—or even a decent English major—can cruise through college like that. I assign works of fiction on the assumption that 150 pages per week constitutes a reasonable workload of about six to seven hours on average; if students are taking five courses like mine, they're being asked to do thirty to thirty-five hours of work per week. But, you say, perhaps my students aren't doing the reading? Well, as I tell them, if you're not doing the reading you have no business being an English major, and certainly no business being in my class. The reading *is* the class; skipping the reading in a literature class is like taking a physics course but blowing off the equations part. And when I tell this to students, I add that my survey courses are always over-enrolled, and that there are always five or six people on the waiting list (that's not because I'm so popular, it's because American literature is so popular); anyone who's not doing the work, in one of my classes, is very likely taking the spot of someone who would have done the work if I'd waived the enrollment limit and allowed him or her to take the class.

Most of my students do most of the reading. How do I know? Loath as I am to admit it, I have begun giving quizzes. I've told students that quizzes in literature classes make college feel like high school with ashtrays, but I've also told them that, over the years, I've found that some students don't blow off the reading so much as put off the reading, thinking they can catch up with a few intense weeks of work at some point in the semester. Since so many of the meta-lessons of college are really extended drills in time management (that is, long after students have forgotten the details of our discussions of *The Rise of Silas Lapham* and the perils of their intermediate physics course, they'll still know how to juggle five different deadlines, each of which is approaching at a different speed), it's critical that they learn to pace themselves at the outset.

I take attendance, and I have an attendance policy, though I am reasonably willing to accommodate students who are going through complicated family dramas or chronic illnesses. I assign a range of possible paper topics to the lower-level classes. I don't ask students to explain why George Bush is a war criminal, but I do pose speculative questions like this:

> It's been said that *Their Eyes Were Watching God* is a story about how Janie Crawford, after two tries and twenty years, finally marries the right man. But it's also been said that the novel has a funny way of getting rid of Janie's men, and that all of Janie's relationships with men are flawed. Why doesn't the novel end with Janie and Tea Cake living happily ever after?

In the upper-level courses, however, I demand that students devise their own topics, since I think that's a far more appropriate task for juniors and seniors than simply replying to professors' questions. I distribute a short, 1,200-word handout that lays out my expecta-

tions for the physical and intellectual presentation of papers; it has
unduly intimidated a few students in the past (one told me she
thought I would edit her paper to smithereens), but most students
find it useful. It contains a few general guidelines, such as "Assume
a hypothetical readership of people who have already read the
book" (this obviates the need for plot summary), and a few words
about the difference between a thesis and a topic: a thesis is an
argument *about* a topic, and if it's not possible, in principle, to disagree with your thesis, then your thesis simply isn't specific (or
important) enough. Accordingly, I tell students that it often helps
to develop a thesis by imagining other readers who might disagree
with it. What, I ask them, do you want to tell us about the book in
question, and why should we believe you? Is there another way to
read the book, a way you find mistaken, partial, or downright
unsavory? Do you want to make sure we aren't persuaded by that
other way, with all the consequences it might entail, whatever those
might be? My most important criterion is that of plausibility; I
want to see how judiciously and carefully students cite the text in
order to bear out their assertions or to direct their hypothetical
readers' attention to what they think are a text's crucial passages.
Finally, I ask them not to restate their thesis in their concluding
paragraph or paragraphs, but to use their conclusions to address a
particularly knotty problem in the text or to suggest the broader
implications of their line of inquiry. I tell students straightfor-
wardly that I tend to be especially impressed by papers that ask
themselves the simple but profound question, so what? If we see
the novel this way, what does that tell us about X? Why should we
bother to argue this kind of point in the first place? And finally, I
suggest that a short piece of literary criticism should leave its reader
wanting to reread the text it discusses, having induced the reader to
mutter to himself or herself, "Hmm, I didn't catch that on the first
time through. Let me go back and see if this makes better sense of
the text for me."

Not every student clears this bar. Some are content to churn out papers in whose arguments they invest relatively little of themselves, and some don't bother to try to imagine hypothetical readers at all, let alone hypothetical readers who might disagree with them about the ending of *Their Eyes Were Watching God*. But those are my ground rules, and my responses to (and impressions of) individual students are a function of the degree to which students meet or exceed those ground rules. The students who exceed them spectacularly are the students I will never forget. I know I will never see or hear from the majority of my undergraduate students after their class with me, but the students whose lives or minds were affected by one of my courses in 1987 or 1993 or 1999 have kept in touch with me ever since; reciprocally, some of these are students whose work has affected my life and my mind in some way. In this respect, the truism seems to be true: students get out of their courses as much as they put in, and one of the reasons for this is that professors respond in kind. When we come across bright, promising students who are clearly giving us their best efforts and engaging deeply with the course material, we like to encourage those students as much as we can—and we'll usually meet them with an enthusiasm and depth of engagement equivalent to theirs.

My ground rules for class discussion are straightforward as well, though I announce them informally rather than in a handout. When I declare the classroom to be a safe space (though I know it's a pedagogical cliché) for all remarks that are well-grounded in the texts—which, lately, I have done at the outset of every semester—it doesn't mean that the space will actually *be* safe: for many students, gay, straight, conservative, liberal, every contribution to class discussion carries some risks, because they're trying out ideas in a public forum. But it does mean that students will not be humiliated, by me or by anyone else. They may be criticized or disagreed with or challenged, but they will not be humiliated. This is not a trivial matter; the possibilities for embarrassment and abjection are innumerable. I always think of a student in one of my first courses, a young man with a stutter whose silence in the classroom was—as I learned in my first student conference with him—saturated with fear of humiliation and exposure. I told him I would never compel him to contribute to discussion, but that, if he so desired, he should go right ahead, and I would set the tone in such a way as to forestall any impatience or outright mockery from his peers. He worked up his courage later that term and made a very nice observation about Henry Roth's *Call It Sleep*—considerable courage, because his stutter tended to become more severe when he was nervous. And then there was the African-American student—a promising concert violinist, a diligent reader, and a young man with Asperger's and no sense of self-presentation—who insistently raised his hand to make the same point three times in a row in the course of a discussion of James Baldwin's *Go Tell It on the Mountain* while his classmates nervously shifted in their seats. As he looked around the room, beginning to launch into a fourth rendition of his observation about the Grimes family, I asked him to hold that thought a moment and speak to me about it at greater length after class, and in the meantime to allow one of his fellow students to chip in; his classmates responded, that day and in all future classes, by giving him a little more time and space to make his remarks before amplifying or replying to them.

One semester I decided to teach a series of novels under the rubric of multiculturalism, but with a twist; I decided to ask students what ideas about culture are usually expressed in defenses of (or attacks on) multiculturalism. In response to one student's question about whether I was going to stress unity or difference in American history, I replied that I found much of the multiculturalism debate tedious and unproductive; one side speaks of a melting pot, where everything gets boiled into some kind of alloy, and the other side speaks of a glorious mosaic, in which cultures are discrete pieces of tile separated by a kind of social grout. But both sides assume, among other things, that a culture is a single, undifferentiated entity, and that it is (a) expressed in phenomena like burritos, San Gennaro festivals, arranged weddings, kimchee, polyrhythmic music, extended families, and Oktoberfest, and (b) an all-purpose explanatory schema that accounts for the behavior of individuals, the history of entire nations, and the failure of corporate mergers (as when we hear that Acme did not get along with Amalgamated because they had different office cultures). Moreover, whenever we use "culture" as a synonym for "ethnicity," we tend to overlook the question of whether the United States itself has something like a national culture, even if it consists of things like tailgate parties, reality television, and roadside diners cheek-by-jowl with fast-food franchises.[3] So I told my class that I would not assume that any of these novels simply "expresses" one or another of the cultures of the United States. On the contrary, I left open—that is, I left to my students—the question of how fiction plays a part in establishing or expressing cultural phenomena. I also left open some other pertinent questions: Does the United States have an institutional "high" culture as well as an energetic "mass" culture? If so, what are the relations between the culture of which we speak when we think of things like experimental composers and art-house films, and the culture of which we speak when we think of things like *Baywatch* and *The Bachelor*? How can we compare these, in turn, with the more anthropological meaning of "culture" we invoke whenever we speak of social practices that are specific to regions or ethnicities? And, last but not least, how do these various senses of "culture" inflect the novels we're reading—and in what kind of culture(s) do these novels participate?[4]

I don't expect my students to leave my class burning with the desire to form a more perfect union, but I do hope that, in courses like this, they'll learn a few things about the United States and its literature, and that they'll think in more subtle and supple ways about culture as a result. I also hope that my students—particularly in the survey courses—will become better writers. I help them with their prose wherever and whenever I can, offering them the standard English-professor fare of careful line-editing combined with a single-spaced half-page or so of general remarks about the success of their arguments, but I'm sometimes stunned at the weakness of their writing—and at the (related) fact that they're asked to do so little writing in their classes outside the English department. I wish they had more of an ear for poetry, and more of every available sense, tactile or intellectual, for some of the weirder and more exploratory forms that literature can take. In recent years I've read—for pleasure, in my spare time—mildly surreal novels like Paul Auster's *Mr. Vertigo* or thoroughly surreal novels like Flann O'Brien's *The Third Policeman*, and I've reminded myself that things like these are a large part of the reason I fell in love with literature in the first place. To paraphrase the sometimes surreal Emily Dickinson, when I read works like these I feel physically as if the top of my head were taken off—I know that this is literature. But my occasional attempts to leaven the American literature survey with works that abandon social mimesis, even to the slightest extent (*Mr. Vertigo* may be a surreal novel about human levitation, but it also narrates a recognizable twentieth-century United States in which even Dizzy Dean makes an appearance), have met with chilly receptions. Nabokov's *Pale Fire*, for example, is undoubtedly one of the funniest and most poignant novels-that-combine-a-thousand-line-poem-in-heroic-couplets-and-extended-insane-commentary (structured as a kind of hall of mirrors, no less), but my students just don't get it. Colson Whitehead's *The Intuitionist* might provide its readers with a thoroughly clever take on the discourse of racial "uplift" in a narrative of the career of the first black female elevator inspector in a city that resembles the postmodern-yet-1940s' Gotham City of Tim Burton's *Batman*, but my students can't believe the setting; they can't sympathize with the protagonist; they're not interested. Works like these, or Djuna Barnes's *Night-*

wood and Jean Toomer's *Cane*, I find, appeal only to a small subset
of the class; it's a subset I care deeply about, because it consists of
students who will continue to read widely and with sustained intellectual curiosity long after they've left my classroom. It's a subset
that will become the market for Serious Writing, consisting as it
does of Serious Readers. But it's a small subset of the nation's readers (and of my classes), nonetheless.

When it comes to poetry, I've made more concessions than I care
to admit. In my first course at Illinois I assigned Hart Crane's mag-
isterial modern epic, *The Bridge*. That was a mistake. (I taught it
again five years later, this time with a great deal more preparation,
determined to let my students know ahead of time that they were
in for a long, bumpy ride with one of American modernism's most
challenging, uneven, and lyrically gifted poets.) I even assigned
Wallace Stevens's "An Ordinary Evening in New Haven" and
"Notes Toward a Supreme Fiction" in that first class, only gradually scaling back to Stevens's shorter poems before realizing with
dismay that, for my average survey class, the standard Stevens lyric
was as incomprehensible as a postcard from the volcano. I eventually settled on Robert Frost, via Richard Poirier's reading of Frost
as a modernist who camouflaged his abiding concern with ideas of
order by couching it in an idiom so resolutely regional and vernacular that you'd think you were just listening to a wizened old New
Englander telling you that yep, good fences make good neighbors,
and I am done with apple-picking now.[5] I've taught Langston
Hughes as well, only to find that students like him because they
think he's plain and straightforward—even in *Montage of a Dream
Deferred*. Generally, poets (even widely accessible writers like Rita
Dove) seem to be met with varying degrees of tolerance or exasperation, depending on how clear they make themselves, as if clarity of
expression is the criterion that distinguishes good poetry from bad.
Over the years, accordingly, I've found myself drifting more and
more to the surveys of fiction, thinking that if I'm teaching stu-

dents who haven't had extensive experience with modern poetry or experimental literature, I'm better off with literary works that involve recognizable plots and recognizable characters. But this is a concession, and I have to admit as much. My only alternative is to offer highly specialized courses that attract fewer students, and while that might be more intellectually satisfying in some ways, it, too, amounts to a concession—or, perhaps, to a partial refusal of the challenge of teaching to broader and more varied groups of students.

When I first arrived at Penn State, I had the bright idea of asking my students, as they filled out index cards on the first day of class, not only to give me their names, majors, and e-mail addresses but also to tell me something about the campus that I might like to know as a new arrival. The results were surprisingly revealing; it was as if I'd conducted a survey of student habits and attitudes by means of three-by-five index cards. The responses ranged from one young man's "Wednesdays 49 cent cheeseburgers at Sports Café, Margarita Madness @ Chili's $1 margaritas and lagers until 12, Thursdays $4.75 pitchers of Captain and Coke at Crowbar—if you can't reach me at home you know where to find me" to two students' enthusiastic plugs for the student-run No Refund Theater. One student cautioned me that if I had seasonal affective disorder, I should be prepared for central Pennsylvania winters, which are long and very gray; another advised me to keep an eye out for the Pennsylvania Special Olympics Summer Games, which are held every June at Penn State. She had coached Centre County's basketball team; I told her I have a son with Down syndrome who loves to play the game, and that I hope that he will be a Special Olympian someday. Another student informed me that she was a member of Penn State's equestrian team and that they had been in the top ten since 1970; still another advised me to check out the hockey team, the Icers, to which I replied that I am in fact an academic advisor to the team. Many warned me that Penn State was huge and impersonal, but that they had found ways to negotiate the various mazes without getting lost.

One senior sent me a complex message that seemed simultaneously a gesture of frustration with her fellow students and a suggestion that I shouldn't expect too much from my classes: "Recently when I was bartending downtown, a customer told me that no one chooses to go to a large university such as PSU to learn, insinuating that in a town with over 50 bars and restaurants and upwards of 40,000 young adults, partying was priority #1. My experience as a bartender has made me begin to believe this." Privately, I told that student she probably wasn't seeing her peers at their very best, and that I was sure they would put a better face forward in my classroom than they do during Margarita Madness. Publicly, I told the class that many of them had mentioned the sheer size of Penn State and the prevalence of the party culture, but that I had not arrived from Princeton or Oberlin; things were much the same at Illinois. So I told them what I used to tell students at Illinois: large public universities can indeed be faceless, impersonal places if you let them, and they will always provide plenty of work for beer distributors and bartenders. But they're also large enough to contain many little Oberlins here and there if you know how to find them; the faculty are smart and dedicated, and the literature we're reading in this class isn't any less challenging or rewarding than it would be if we were reading it at Harvard. If you so desire, you can put a face on your faceless college by getting to know some of your professors and going to a couple of lectures or exhibits now and then.

I added that students in the liberal arts at large public universities seem to me especially concerned about the image of their schools as endless tailgate parties for tens of thousands of guests, but they could, if they wanted, think of themselves as being among the exceptions to the general rule. Liberal arts majors usually wind up in smaller classes, with more intensive faculty–student interactions, than anyone save for the artists and musicians taking tiny studio classes. They tend not to be obsessed with their grades or their career prospects; they tend to talk about ideas outside of class and think seriously about teaching for a living or pursuing advanced study in graduate school. They tend to be especially sensitive about the large-and-faceless aspects of college life because they place a higher value on face-to-face instruction, as well they should. One of the signal virtues of liberal arts education is that it bucks the trends of the corporate "multiversity," and puts faith instead in ancient, "inefficient" forms of teaching like lecture and discussion and independent study. Professors who teach large introductory courses filled with hundreds of students, or professors who teach courses in metallurgy or finance, may never confront an individual student's deeply (or lightly) held beliefs about abortion or feminism or race or terrorism or God, but in smaller classrooms in the humanities, students' beliefs are part of the very fabric of the class. Indeed, this is one of the things that draws students to arts and humanities courses despite the fact that so many of their parents, friends, relatives, elected representatives, and newspaper editorialists tell them that a degree in the liberal arts is a waste of time. And if my class size is reasonable, forty or fewer, I promise students that I will have learned their names by the end of the third week of class. I used to be able to learn their names within two weeks, but life was simpler then, and I was a younger man.

Outside the classroom, I have very general impressions of students' lives on campus—while, at the same time, profoundly distrusting professors (and dapper seventy-something novelists) who speak as if they know all about students' lives, spiritual strivings, personal habits, and complicated family dramas. When I come across campus novels like Tom Wolfe's *I Am Charlotte Simmons*, I realize with relief that I know nothing about how my students "hook up," and I don't want to know, any more than I want to run into one of my students in the middle of Margarita Madness. Likewise, I know next to nothing about what kind of "diversity train-ing" goes on in freshman and resident-assistant orientation, though I have read of one exercise—the "privilege walk," in which stu-dents are lined up on a basketball court and asked to take one step forward or one step back for each measure of "privilege" they have enjoyed in their lives.[6] This sounds to me like a well-meaning and thoroughly hamhanded enterprise, one that many students will meet with eye-rolling or grimaces that one associates with the met-ing out of castor oil. Similarly, the well-meaning "disabled for a day" idea that has swept many campuses—in which students use a wheelchair to "see what those people have to put up with"—has been criticized by some disability activists for its potential to pro-voke either sentimental pity or horror. On the other hand, "dis-abled for a day" exercises can usefully call attention to poor campus design and inaccessible buildings, and any device that brings these things to the attention of the general public is truly performing a public service.

I'm not opposed to all forms of diversity training, as so many conservatives and libertarians seem to be; I remember vividly one of my black neighbors in Champaign, Illinois, a supermarket man-ager who'd worked in Georgia and Montana before coming to the prairie, telling me how hard it was to deal with an all-white staff most of whom had never had a black supervisor. He ran (among other things) the supermarket chain's version of diversity training, and he was quite emphatic and convincing on the subject. I know that some campuses can be, and have been, cold and forbidding places for racial minorities, and I know that some conservatives are so obsessed with affirmative action that they have an inordinately hard time seeing this—or seeing how their "affirmative action" bake sales, in which lower prices are set for students of color (corre-sponding, in some conservatives' worldviews, to the lower admis-sions standards for minority students), amount to a personal insult to every black and Hispanic student on campus. But I see fairly little of students' daily interactions with each other in the dorms, the fraternities, the student clubs, and the lounges, and I cannot pronounce on the status of the project of fostering racial harmony at Penn State. What campus news comes to me is usually the news that comes to everybody else, whether it's the story about College Republicans donning blackface and hoods on Halloween or a story about a minority student being crushed to death by bouncers at a local bar.[7] I do not like extrapolating from such incidents, just as I am constitutionally incapable of drawing sweeping social conclusions from the sight of a bunch of black students sitting together in a cafeteria or a classroom.

I can, however, say a few general things about the four major political groupings I see among students: conservatives, liberals, leftists, and libertarians (who, for reasons I'll explain in a moment, tend to lean far more to the right than to the left these days). Liberals first: they tend to be civic-minded, well-informed, and inclined toward careers in education, law, or public service. They're likely to come up to me after class and ask about alternative rock or proportional representation (one student at Illinois kept up a running conversation with me on PR for three years), and they tend to sport somewhat more piercings than the average student body. Some of them sound to me like highly focused policy-wonk shock troops for the Feingold Wing of the Democratic Party, and some sound more nebulous, more like sensibilities-in-formation that might become, in ten years, either self-righteous correct-coffee-drinking moralists or selfless workers in refugee camps. Another bunch, further off to the left, finds figures like Noam Chomsky so persuasive when it comes to American wickedness at home and abroad—not capriciously, either, for that wickedness is often real enough—that they become utterly indiscriminate about "dissent," valuing even its most counterproductive forms. While I admire these students for informing themselves about the history of Central America and East Timor, I watch with dismay as they embrace the conclusion that practically any form of "resistance" to US world hegemony is worth their support, and the conviction that if the US takes up arms in a cause, any cause, the real cause is probably unacknowledged and nefarious. This conviction has been borne out quite frequently in the past, and will undoubtedly be borne out again, but it is not axiomatic, and it disturbs me to find young people identifying with "the left" in such a way as to suspend their critical judgment about leftists who do take it as axiomatic. The wholly uncritical Chomsky fans seem to me to have abdicated some of the tasks of critical thinking in precisely the same way that the wholly uncritical Bush worshippers have done, and I wish the campus left, especially, could be a domain without gurus and icons—a domain of ideas, where every citizen is obligated to scrutinize every idea on its merits.

For related reasons, I do not understand the Michael Moore phenomenon among College Democrats. I also do not understand the Michael Moore phenomenon among College Republicans; when Moore was invited to speak at Penn State in 2004, the protests from conservative students, alumni, and commentators were loud and strenuous, and most of them complained about Penn State using tuition and state money to fund a partisan political speaker. But Moore was not paid by any tuition or state money; he was paid from the student activity fee, the same source of funding for recent speakers such as Phyllis Schlafly, Ann Coulter, and George H. W. Bush. I have no respect for conservatives who have double standards for such things, and who protest a "political" speaker only when the speaker does not share their politics. (One hyperventilating conservative attorney, David T. Hardy, went so far as to sue Penn State, claiming that Moore's visit violated federal election law.)[8] I am more concerned with the Moore phenomenon among young Democrats, because I consider Moore an erratic standard-bearer for a useful left, on campus or off. While I often enjoy his street theater and his dogged determination to afflict the powerful, I have not been able to watch *Bowling for Columbine* or *Fahrenheit 9/11* without undergoing extended moments of severe head-shaking. The latter film manages to suggest—but is too skittish to press the claim in any coherent way—that the removal of the Taliban and the destruction of al-Qaeda training camps in Afghanistan were secretly motivated by the American oil industry's desire to build a pipeline in the region; the earlier film twice mentions the fact that US-led NATO forces dropped bombs in Kosovo on the very day of the Columbine massacre, and the connection is left for us to divine. I surmise that the connection goes something like this: We condemned those kids for shooting up a school, but dude, we bombed an entire country that very same day! Whoa! Makes you think! The fact that the Kosovo war was precipitated by eight long years of Serbian nationalist aggression punctuated by mass rapes, ethnic cleansing, and the massacre of eight thousand at Srebrenica goes unmentioned, as does the idea that a progressive internationalist left might well go to war in order to prevent genocide (as it once did to oppose the rise of fascism in Spain). More recently, Moore has opined that the Iraqi resistance leaders are the moral equivalents of the Minutemen,[9] a claim which sounds to me like a weird version of Ronald Reagan's obscene claim that the Nicaraguan contras were the moral equivalents of our own founding fathers.

I can only guess that Moore is a celebrity among College Democrats because College Democrats are so desperate to have at least one flame-throwing master of agitprop to put up against the shrieking, insane Coulters of the right. And I can only imagine that the national Democratic Party embraced Moore in 2004 partly because it is so very clueless about the youth vote that it's hesitant to alienate any mass-cultural figure on the left who seems to have a following among "the kids."[10] But I do not see why progressives should rally behind someone whose grasp of international politics is so shaky and underinformed, any more than I can see why

Democrats should champion someone who so enthusiastically stumped for Ralph Nader in 2000. While I support the right of the College Democrats to invite Moore to campus, and while I oppose local conservatives who tried to spread the lie that his funding came out of taxpayers' pockets, I would prefer, if I had my druthers, that the student left identify less with people like Michael Moore and more with democratic leftists like Michael Harrington and Michael Walzer.

In spring 2005, I received an enthusiastic e-mail from the local peace and justice group, informing me that yet another Michael— Michael Parenti—would be coming to speak at Penn State and that he is a fierce and principled critic of the Bush administration and its neo-imperialist foreign policy. The e-mail did not add, however, that Michael Parenti is a member of the International Committee to Defend Slobodan Milošević. With regard to Kosovo, I acknowledge that it is possible for a progressive leftist to believe, in good conscience, that the war was badly fought (insofar as it consisted of high-altitude bombings) and badly justified by the Clinton administration. But I have little patience with the leftist "guilt by association" school, which likes to claim that if I'm on the same side as Madeleine Albright, the *New Republic*, and the Kosovo Liberation Army, then there is something wrong with me; their own allies include Tom DeLay, Pat Buchanan, and far-right Russian ethnic nationalists. And I have no patience whatsoever with the far, far left, which has now gone so far off the rails as to deny the occurrence of the massacre at Srebrenica and to insist that the Serbs have been the true victims in these conflicts all along.[11] Positions like Parenti's amount to a red–brown alliance between the far left and the far right, and defenses of Milošević amount to apologies for fascism and ethnic cleansing. And though this will sound paternalistic, I worry about young men and women on the campus left who rally around figures like this, because I worry that one of two things will happen to them: either they will lower their intellectual and moral standards for such figures (this is the "he may be a flame-thrower, but at least he's our flame-thrower" argument), or they will realize at some point in their lives that some people who claim to be on the left are willing to line up with Milošević in the name of anti-imperialism, and they'll conclude that the left is every bit as bonkers as Fox News and the *Wall Street Journal* editorial page would like them to believe. I do not know which scenario I dislike more intensely.

I have fewer direct contacts with deeply conservative students, but, even so, I have been able to discern three distinct branches of the campus right. The first, the one I like best, is made up of intellectually serious students who strongly believe in that traditional-conservative combination of limited government and deference to established nongovernmental authorities. What I like about them is the "intellectually serious" part. They believe in living the life of the mind; they simply have minds substantially different from mine. Should they wind up in my classes, and should they make their political beliefs known to me for some reason, I take it as my task to sharpen their instincts and send them on their way with a whole new battery of strategies for How to Engage the Left. Some of them turn out to be energetic and stimulating interlocutors precisely because they expect opposition and want to learn how to deal with it; as liberal blogger and recent college graduate Ezra Klein suggests, this can make them much more nimble and adept than their liberal peers:

> being a vocal conservative on campus is so hard (and, in all honesty, it actually is, at least at UC [Santa Cruz]) that the kids who choose to do it are necessarily better, more informed, and more committed than most of their liberal counterparts. They're also, as a result of perceived persecution, much more committed to the success of their movement. That's why so many bright conservatives exit college and dive into the politics, while so many liberals wander off to academia

or NGO's or the Peace Corps. Campus progressives generally judge their ideologies triumphant and not really requiring their constant attention, while conservatives see theirs as embattled and in desperate need of more recruits. In the real world, of course, it's actually the opposite, but nobody knows that till their paths are already set.[12]

I think Klein is right about these students, and right about the way that campus culture can envelop young progressives in a moral mist that leaves them complacent and thoroughly unprepared for the moral mist wafting through the rest of American culture. And I don't see vocally conservative students as a threat; on the contrary, insofar as they're committed to the value of ideas and the value of contestations over ideas, they are doing exactly what college students should do.

I can't say the same for the conservatives who simply can't stand to hear a bad word about George Bush. To gauge by their columns in the student paper and their complaints on student radio, they seem to have the sense—and it has been emphatically seconded by many popular pundits on the right—that any criticism of this president and his policies is tantamount to treason. When they are criticized in turn by liberals, they invoke the First Amendment in odd and ignorant ways; yes, the First Amendment prohibits the prior restraint of speech by the state, but no, the First Amendment does not shield jerks—of any political persuasion—from hostile criticism, as these kids seem to believe. I see little hope of engaging them on any substantive issue; they speak and write as if what they distrust is intellectual debate itself, and insofar as this is in fact the case, professors like me are right not to expect too much from them as potential interlocutors. There is, I believe, all the difference in the world between students who relish a good give-and-take, either with their peers or with their professors, and those who simply want never to encounter a serious liberal argument in their four years. I think this is the student section that's so upset over the fact that 90 percent of their local political science or history professors are registered Democrats; I imagine that they want a greater proportion of conservative professors not because they truly want to engage "both sides" (as if there are only two) but because they would prefer to avoid taking classes with articulate liberal and progressive professors altogether.

The third branch consists of students the like of which I never saw at Columbia University as an undergraduate (though I met plenty of the first kind there, and I'm grateful for that), but of whom I became aware at the University of Virginia: the campus wing of the religious right, the undergraduate Christian conservatives who see themselves as keeping God's word in the very midst of blasphemy and temptation. Public colleges being what they are, this group has been by far the tiniest branch of conservatives I've encountered. Indeed, until I arrived at Virginia and got a sense of the student membership of the local Maranatha Ministries, I imagined that serious Christian conservatives would avoid secular public universities altogether. It's true that many deeply religious students wind up at denominational colleges that are more to their doctrinal taste. But a tiny number of them also wind up at Virginia, Illinois, and Penn State, where they make for a curious mix with the studious intellectual conservatives and the backward-baseball-caps-for-Bush crew.

The libertarians are, for me, the most peculiar assortment in the mix. They're usually well-informed on civil liberties, abortion, gay rights, and the sheer cruelty and foolishness of America's drug laws (and no, it's not just a matter of keeping your laws off my bong). They're generally confused but nonetheless rigidly dogmatic on economic issues, having little or no understanding of what unregulated, scorched-earth capitalism actually entails and little or no concern about poverty or disability. They're quite smart now and then about the intrusive, in loco parentis style of campus management that they identify with what I call the aggressive Lutheran liberalism I encountered in the Midwest (the kind in which your public-spirited but nosy neighbors pull over your car to make sure you're wearing your seatbelt, because it's good for you) and that they consider the local version of the so-called "nanny state"; but they're reflexively and sometimes ignorantly opposed to any regulatory or redistributive scheme whatsoever, as if tainted soup, securities fraud, defective automobiles, and toxic-waste dumping will all get sorted out by the wisdom of the market and the work of many invisible hands. On affirmative action, of course, they line up squarely with the conservatives, and they are wont to pretend that there is no other issue so important, no injustice more profound, than this.

In my undergraduate days I encountered another kind of libertarian altogether, and I occasionally run across some versions of my former classmates today. These were the Ayn Rand fanatics, the founders of Objectivist Clubs, who used to approach me and say, though not quite in so many words, "Don't you understand, Michael? Can't you see? Objectivism is a philosophy for the super-intelligent! That means you and me, you know—truly, if the world were run on Objectivist principles, we would be philosopher-kings, putting our maximal freedom to the maximal possible use! Come! Join us and help spread the rule of reason!" To which I always replied, backing away slowly, that I was fine with the rule of reason and OK with the fierce secularism but really creeped out by the whole Rand cult thing, thank you very much. Not to mention those philosopher-kings' inability to think seriously about poverty or disability.

Still, I have to admit that, for some undergraduates, libertarianism appears more attractive than liberalism or leftism, and I know that this is one of the reasons I find it vexing. Part of its appeal can be attributed to the demographic, of course; you're dealing with a group of late-teens and early-twentysomethings living away from their parents for the first time, some of whom think to themselves,

"Hey, P. J. O'Rourke is so right—the government *doesn't* do thirty percent of my laundry! Taxes are such a ripoff!" But surely some of its appeal can be attributed to the unattractiveness of the campus left, which many libertarian undergraduates associate with speech codes and privilege walks (when they think of university administrations) or with sweeping, indiscriminate denunciations of every aspect of US foreign policy since 1945 (when they think of local left activists). For a significant number of intelligent undergraduates, I fear, libertarianism simply looks more coherent and attractive than anything I might want to call "liberal-left"; how, after all, can one justify progressive taxation on the grounds that democracies have a collective interest in preventing the accumulation of too much wealth and power in too few hands, while simultaneously professing a sublime agnosticism about the free marketplace of culture and ideas? How can you be interventionist on one front and noninterventionist on the other? It doesn't make sense to these students—in part because (as journalist Rick Perstein has reminded me) contemporary liberals have no clear, compelling manifesto available for popular consumption, along the lines of Milton Friedman's book and PBS series, *Free to Choose*, and in part because these students associate liberalism with a combination of progressive tax schemes and vaguely regressive, paternalistic hectoring on the cultural front, delivered by people whose job it seems to be to complain about the horrid music and stupid movies and violent video games and scandalous quasi-pornographic images and corporate brand names consumed by These Kids Today. (I believe they are wrong to oppose the progressive tax schemes and almost entirely justified in being suspicious about the hectoring.) When these students think of the American left, they think not of freedom-fighters (and not of Milošević-defenders, either) but of annoying moralists—moralists who take on the phantasmic appearance (and it *is* phantasmic) of a cross between vegan purists and the sanctimonious Joe Lieberman, and who will pass laws forbidding the consumption of cheeseburgers and the playing of Grand Theft Auto video games if you give them half a chance. And when you've got a campus whose culture combines the most aggressively self-righteous of both camps—members of the very pure personal-politics crew (satirized by *The Simpsons* in the person of the "vegan level five" who won't eat anything that casts a shadow) and members of the humane-values-are-good-for-you-and-I-will-ensure-that-you-obey-me crew, I believe you have a potentially powerful device for driving young independents and undecideds straight into the arms of the local libertarians and College Republicans.

What really makes for hideous travesties of political correctness, however, isn't this strange combination of good intentions and moral authoritarism; by itself, the mix is merely irritating. But when you've also got a campus disciplinary apparatus with all the due process guarantees of the Star Chamber, then you've got the potential for some serious mischief. I got a taste of that mischief myself, long ago, and I'm sorry to say today that I didn't realize how serious it was at the time. In the spring of 1986, when I was a third-year graduate student at the University of Virginia, I was summoned to the office of the director of composition, where I was informed that I had been cleared of charges of racism. Great news—except for the fact that I had had no idea that I had been charged with racism in the first place. I was reading frantically for my PhD preliminary oral exam at the time (while teaching an American literature survey, taking two classes, expecting a child, and working at three part-time jobs), and had actually finished Kafka's *The Trial* not long before this meeting took place, so I was able to receive this Kafkaesque piece of information in the right spirit. "You're telling me that one of my students from the fall semester"—my first semester as a teaching assistant—"accused me of racism?" Yes, the composition director said that was exactly what she was telling me. But I had been cleared. "Wait just a second," I said. "What were the grounds?" The grounds were that I had given a C to a student in my eleven o'clock first-year writing class. "But there were two black students in that class and one student of East Asian descent. I didn't give a C to any of them—so where exactly did the racism come in?" Well, I was told, the young South Asian woman who'd gotten that C claimed that I discriminated against her because she was not born in the United States. "Excuse me?" I replied. "I thought she was from northern Virginia." Yes, she was from northern Virginia. But she said she thought *I* thought she was not born in the United States.

I was stupefied. I pointed out that the student in question had turned in, for the first draft of her research paper, an essay that was nothing but a string of quotations from start to finish—properly footnoted, sure, but just a string of quotations. No thesis, no argument, no nothing. And when I asked her to revise it, she threw in an opening paragraph and then a series of perfunctory introductions to the quotations: as X pointed out, as Y said, as Z remarked, and so on. That paper deserved an F, and I gave it a D out of the foolish goodness of my heart. The student's average for the semester was C minus, and I distinctly remember that when I bubbled in the C on the grade sheet instead, I thought to myself that it was a C for Christmas and that I should have wrapped it. And then three months later I'm "cleared" of racism after someone or something "investigates" the "charge" that I gave her a punitive grade because I believed she was born outside the United States?

Yes, it appeared that I had all this about right. And the composition program conducted its investigation without consulting or informing me at any point in the proceedings—all for my "protection"? I asked. Yes, I had that part right too.

Well, I didn't know what to say, and I said so. And then I spent the next few months being furious at that student for her gall—when, of course, I should also have been furious at the twiddling bureaucrats who allowed such an investigation to go forward. I do, of course, understand why someone who knew nothing about this student's work might, at first, take seriously the possibility that her English teaching assistant had discriminated against her for some reason. Moreover, I would not want to live in a world in which student complaints—be they about professorial racism, sexual harassment, or political intimidation—are dismissed quickly and cavalierly. I was not harmed or scarred by the experience, and I have not waved it around publicly for twenty years (as some professors might), construing myself as one of the very first campus martyrs of the political-correctness era. But I do not understand the phenomenon in which self-described liberals line up behind (or, for that matter, conduct) illegitimate, closed-door proceedings like these. Quite apart from my own involvement with one of these proceedings at the very outset of my teaching career, I believe that any day on which "liberals" decide that teaching assistants need to be investigated without their knowledge and without the right to respond to their accusers is a bad day for the ideal of social justice.

I don't want to suggest, however, that the campus right is coherent about such matters; where they wield administrative power—at denominational colleges, usually—they are every bit as ready and as willing to convene kangaroo courts. Some prominent academics on the right, like libertarian Alan Charles Kors, professor of history at the University of Pennsylvania, are consistently anti-authoritarian, and will defend students' individual rights regardless of a student's specific beliefs; others, like John Silber (former president of Boston University) and the leaders of some religious colleges, argue that it is one of their rights and obligations to handle students—and, occasionally, faculty members—with old-fashioned discipline. Emblematic of the right's incoherence is the impolitic Eugene Genovese himself, who ventured forth into the culture wars of the 1990s by writing of the "new McCarthyism" at work in liberal academe and insisting that what universities needed was "a strong dose of hierarchical authority."[13] This made a certain amount of sense to those cultural conservatives for whom obedience to traditional forms of authority is a positive social good in and of itself, for anything that erodes those forms of authority threatens to fray the social fabric. But in the very same essay, Genovese also insisted that "any professor who, subject to the restraints of common sense and common decency, does not seize every opportunity to offend the sensibilities of his students is insulting and cheating them, and is no college professor at all." One strains to imagine that this remark met with the same assent from the cultural conservatives who cheered the idea of a strong dose of hierarchical authority; it would be a wonderful world, would it not, in which American cultural conservatives go around complaining that liberal and leftist professors are not sufficiently offending their conservative students' sensibilities—subject to the restraints of common sense and common decency, of course. But Genovese simply encapsulates the right's salient internal contradiction in the culture wars, as they champion conservative students' freedom of expression while calling on traditional forms of authority—trustees, legislators—to straighten out unruly liberal faculty members with a strong dose of hierarchical authority.

CAMPUSES CAN BE dangerous places: there are far too many date rapes, hazing deaths, and random assaults, most of which can be attributed to the volatile mix of hormones and alcohol roiling in every College Park and College Station. Campuses can be depressing places: the endless string of mediocre pizza-and-subs shops, slabs of off-campus student housing (cheap apartment buildings, old rental houses converted into hives), and t-shirt emporia sometimes makes college towns look like a cross between expansive, well-cultivated grounds staffed by teams of groundskeepers and a sleazy beachfront inundated by waves of nineteen-year-olds. And campuses can be exclusive places: too much of the admissions process is skewed to the wealthy and the well-connected, and the further up the food chain you go, the more predatory a culture you'll find. But the amazing and underreported thing is that the overwhelming majority of the faculty are actually doing a fine job. We're not the ones responsible for the pizza-and-subs places or the hormones-and-alcohol combustions; we're not setting admissions policies with an eye to who's had the opportunity to take SAT prep courses and hire pre-college advisors for $30,000.[14] We're just teaching as well as we can, and, in the aggregate, most of what we offer our students is world-class material. This isn't simple boosterism, either; it's borne out by the sales figures. The United States is the only country in which half the population enters college (though only half of that half manages to graduate, and we're gradually scaling back on our fitful efforts to expand the franchise to the poor), and higher education is one of the few "product lines" in which the US enjoys what could be called a trade surplus; there are far more international students on American campuses than there are American students abroad, for the simple reason that American universities are—for all their faults—quite good places to get an education.

Even America's elite conservatives know this. They may talk a good game about liberal indoctrination here and leftist domination there, but when it comes time to send their own kids to college, do you imagine for a moment that they're looking over the brochures for Olivet Nazarene University, or even the famously conservative Hillsdale College, which accepts no federal money of any kind? Do you think they're hoping their children will click onto Yorktown University.com, a revolutionary (hence "Yorktown") Internet "university" created in 2000? You may not have heard of it, but it's one of the good works accomplished by Paul Weyrich, president of the Free Congress Foundation and one of the most influential "movement conservatives," widely credited with sparking the rise of the

Reagan wing of the GOP. Writing for the website of the Free Congress Foundation, Weyrich announced the advent of Yorktown in August 2001:

> For most of the past century the United States boasted of the finest universities in the world. But as millions of students head back to school after Labor Day, they face a bleak prospect in higher education.
>
> Unfortunately, toward the end of the 20th Century, the major institutions which produced the best and the brightest began to be gripped by "political correctness," a form of cultural Marxism. Whereas the objective at the best colleges and universities used to be to teaching people how to pursue truth, this has been turned on its head now. The pursuit of truth is largely forbidden and has been replaced by an ideology which is every bit as pernicious as what the Soviets pushed down the throats of their students for seven decades.
>
> There are a few exceptions to this rule, Hillsdale College in Michigan and Christendom College in Virginia come to mind, but these, and the handful of other sound academic institutions, are but a tiny drop in the sea of political correctness. Now many students get failing grades, face disciplinary measures or, worse yet, even the long arm of the law if they challenge the current Marxist orthodoxy. . . .
>
> This is the only online university dedicated to the restoration of Western civilization based on the Judeo-Christian framework.[15]

In the promotional literature, Yorktown's president, Richard J. Bishirjian, asks, "Do you trust mainstream universities today? Are you worried that members of your family are being attracted to left-wing ideas at the college they attend?" and assures prospective students and parents that the university is for real:

> I'm proud of our faculty which includes some of the top scholars in America. Really top notch scholars in their own right, many of

whom, like myself, were political appointees in the Reagan and first Bush Administrations, or who were GOP Congressional staff to US House and Senate members. Two of our Faculty, Dr. William B. Allen and Dr. Art Laffer, ran for the U.S. Senate nomination from California. All of us have found a home in the more traditional and conservative culture at Yorktown University.[16]

Strangely, this appeal seems not to appeal to the conservative elites who actually run the country; for some reason they prefer to send their children to the Ivy League, to Duke, to Berkeley, just as young Ben Shapiro, author of *Brainwashed* (an account of his undergraduate years at UCLA),[17] managed to resist the brainwashing programs of UCLA and then decided to attend Harvard Law School rather than Pepperdine, where he would have had the benefit of studying with Professor Kenneth Starr.

Even culturally conservative pundits—the kind who spend a good deal of ink decrying the state of American campuses—know better than to ship their offspring off to Bob Jones University or to urge them to "attend" YorktownUniversity.com. Witness *U.S. News and World Report*'s John Leo, who opened a January 2005 column with these words:

> In the fall of 2000, I promised my daughter the freshman that I wouldn't write about Wesleyan University (Middletown, Conn.) until she graduated. As a result, you readers learned nothing from me about the naked dorm, the transgender dorm, the queer prom, the pornography-for-credit course, the obscene sidewalk chalking, the campus club named crudely for a woman's private part, or the appearance on campus of a traveling anti-Semitic roadshow, loosely described as a pro-Palestinian conference.[18]

Well, Wesleyan sure does sound like a hopping place, with plenty of nudity, sexual experimentation, and even an anti-Semitic roadshow. A queer prom must be a terrible thing to witness. One can only admire Leo's restraint in not writing about these travesties for four full years so as not to interfere with his daughter's life. I don't doubt for a moment that the Wesleyan student body is every bit as liberal as the Leo family says it is:

> After the 2000 election, my daughter told me that 80 percent of the students had voted for Al Gore.
>   "Bush got only 20 percent of the vote?" I asked.
>   "No, Dad," she explained, "the 20 percent was for Nader."

I'm one of those Democrats who don't see any meaningful distinction between voting for Nader and voting for Bush. Still, I don't doubt for a moment anything in Leo's final paragraph:

> I should add that I think my daughter got a decent education at Wesleyan. You can do this if you are strong-minded, independent, and willing to pick your courses very carefully. But admission to the university should come with a warning label: If you are fainthearted, go somewhere else.

And I should add that I wish every American undergraduate were strong-minded, independent, and willing to pick his or her courses very carefully. But my guess is that even the fainthearted among the offspring of the conservative elite would rather follow the Bush family to Yale or follow John Leo's daughter to Wesleyan than take their chances with the really top-notch scholars at Yorktown University.com.

Leo's column is also remarkable for what it does not contain: a full-dress Horowitzian denunciation of Marxist faculty and their brainwashing techniques. In the course of his career, Leo has not been shy about denouncing Marxist faculty and their brainwashing techniques, so I am left to wonder at his reticence here. Perhaps it's because, to gauge by books such as Ben Shapiro's *Brainwashed* and films like Evan Coyne Maloney and Stuart Browning's *Brainwashing 101*, we left-liberal faculty seem to be doing the most incompetent, most ineffectual job of brainwashing the world has seen since the North Koreans first patented the technique in the early 1950s. Or perhaps it's because we're simply not trying hard enough: apparently, we've even let John Leo's daughter slip through our fingers. Certainly, the majority of the stories about political correctness on American campuses over the past fifteen years have had less to do with clashes between conservative students and liberal faculty members than with students (often, but not always, conservative students) caught up in Kafkaesque administrative proceedings and kangaroo courts, like Eden Jacobowitz at Penn, who was charged with calling a group of black female undergraduates "water buffalo," and Steve Hinkle at California Polytechnic State, who was subjected to a seven-hour "hearing" for putting up posters advertising a lecture by black conservative author Mason Weaver (his case was taken up both by the Foundation for Individual Rights in Education and the ACLU).[19] That hasn't stopped the right from complaining about liberal and leftist faculty, by any means. But of all the conservative complaints about American higher education, oddly enough, the intimidation, oppression, and/or indoctrination of conservative students *in the courses of liberal professors* has proven to be the most difficult thing to document. This is not to say that it doesn't happen; after all, we have a few charter members of the Monty Python left, and furthermore, there have been numerous reports, particularly since September 11, of liberal professors openly expressing hostility for George Bush and for American conservatives. Whether this amounts to open intimidation is another question.

The Students for Academic Freedom take their cue, however, from their leader, who is fond of construing "intimidation" and "indoctrination" very generously indeed. In his 2004 *Chronicle of*

Higher Education essay advocating "intellectual diversity," for instance, Horowitz revealed that the assignment of a single book can constitute a hostile environment for conservative thought:

> At the University of North Carolina at Chapel Hill, a required summer-reading program for entering freshmen stirred a controversy in the state legislature last fall. The required text was Barbara Ehrenreich's socialist tract on poverty in America, *Nickel and Dimed: On (Not) Getting By in America*.... That reflects an academic culture unhinged. When a university requires a single partisan text of all its students, it is a form of indoctrination, entirely inappropriate for an academic institution.[20]

Ehrenreich is indeed a socialist, and *Nickel and Dimed* is indeed a left-wing book. Many conservative students will survive the reading of it, however. Some may even learn how to argue with socialists. Others will, conceivably, be offended or outraged. At which point the University of North Carolina will have to adopt John Leo's proposed warning label for Wesleyan: If you are fainthearted, go somewhere else.

Arguments like those of Horowitz and the aggrieved students at the SAF's Academic Student Abuse Center lead professors like me to believe that there's a significant difference between students who legitimately don't want to be harangued on subjects that are tangential or irrelevant to the course material, and students who just don't want to encounter any liberal professors or liberal arguments on their way through college. But even the most fainthearted of this second group of students need not be quite so fearful. Liberal professors like me are professionals, and all but a very few of us deal with student disagreement professionally. As I noted at the outset of this book, most of the time when students disagree with me about something, I have no idea whether they do so out of religious convictions, admiration for George Bush and Ronald Reagan, adherence to the free market, or just because they think my reading of a book or a passage or a character is mistaken. Most of the time, I enjoy and try to encourage the comments of students who disagree with me in some way. That's because in the liberal arts corner of the campus, we believe in critical thinking even when it's applied to us. What we love more than anything else is critical intelligence, and we don't assume that all forms of critical intelligence will wind up on the political left; on the contrary, we know it's illiberal to think that. Any liberal professor will tell you the same thing; we'd much rather read a well-written, well-argued conservative essay than a careless, shoddy liberal-minded screed. It is, to use a term that's thoroughly inappropriate in this context, a no-brainer.

Now I'LL RETURN to my own classroom. In the following two chapters, I'll let you in on a couple of my courses: a basic entry-level American literature survey and the honors seminar in postmodernism. I can't (and won't) reproduce every aspect of those courses, but I'll try to give you some idea of what my classes look and sound like. I think you'll find that, in some respects, my classes don't look anything like the popular caricature of literature courses; I don't encourage students to read tendentiously for the "politics" of a literary work, I don't subordinate fiction and poetry to literary theory, and I don't ask anyone to master (or reproduce) the technical jargon of criticism—either of the old school (which spoke of hendiadys and anagnoresis) or of the new (which speaks of phallogocentrism and performativity). On the other hand, you'll find that in some respects, my classes are everything the cultural right fears they are, and more; we certainly do talk about race, class, gender, and sexuality in novels that address such things, and you might be surprised how many American novels address such things. And in my postmodernism seminar, I don't espouse all things postmodern, but I do make a case for pragmatist antifoundationalism, which its critics (wrongly) associate with moral relativism. But I never—explicitly or implicitly—ask my students to agree with anything I say, in or out of class; in fact, as you'll find in chapter 6, one of the reasons I make a case for pragmatist antifoundationalism is that I think it offers not only a compelling rejection of moral absolutism but also a supple way of grasping the problem of incommensurability, that is, the impasse that results when people disagree so completely and fundamentally that they can't even agree to disagree.

You are, of course, free to disagree with me about that too, when you get to chapter 6. But first, I'll introduce you to my lower-level "American Fiction Since 1865" survey. I'll start with a detailed reading of the first novel on the fall 2003 version of my syllabus, William Dean Howells's *The Rise of Silas Lapham*, and then I'll offer more general remarks on some of the material in the rest of the course—the way I taught it in 2003, and the way I teach it in general.

5. Race, Class, Gender

Nobody loves *The Rise of Silas Lapham*. And when I introduce the novel to my undergraduate survey class, I do not promise that they will come to love it. On the contrary, I promise them that if my past experience is any guide, most students will find it offputting and dull at first. Though William Dean Howells was once rightly called the dean of American letters, and at the time of *Silas Lapham*'s publication was one of the most important figures in American literature (Twain was just as famous, but not as well-connected in New England circles; Howells was editor of the *Atlantic Monthly* and wielded considerable influence as a gatekeeper and promoter), his reputation has fallen on hard times in the past few decades, and now he is appreciated—not loved—chiefly by scholars of American literature who specialize in literary realism and late-nineteenth-century American culture. But, as I tell my students, people who read *The Rise of Silas Lapham* carefully will wind up agreeing with me that it is a fascinating book.

Howells's prose is not musical; it's actually fairly . . . prosaic. And Howells is writing a novel of manners set in Boston in the mid-1870s, so most of the social manners he describes are going to be alien to us. It's a fair bet that no one in my classroom (myself included) has ever received a dinner-party invitation that compels us to wonder anxiously whether it is proper to wear gloves to the event, and no one in the room is going to understand Howells's many allusions to the architectural tastes of moneyed Bostonians in the Gilded Age. We do not know, for instance, whether it is fashionable or unfashionable to order black walnut for one's house; we read that Lapham's suggestions include "black-walnut finish, high-studding, and cornices" and that "the architect was able to conceal the shudder which they must have sent through him,"[1] but we don't know why the architect shudders, or whether we should trust his shuddering. Still, Howells is writing at a time of extraordinary social and cultural change in America, and he registers that change with an insider's keen eye. The question he poses himself—and us—is something like this: What, in a democracy, are the grounds for having an elite? And what kind of elite are we talking about? Before the Industrial Revolution, the political, economic, and cultural elites in the United States were pretty much all the same people. Only after the Civil War did we develop a society in which rural bumpkins like Silas Lapham could become millionaires overnight—and lose it all the next day. And even though rich men could buy political influence, then as now, many of them stayed out of politics themselves, leaving it to a newly emergent political class that has since turned into the professional politicians, staffers, advisors, pollsters, and commentators we're familiar with today. Meanwhile, of course, our contemporary cultural elite—a group which includes curators of major museums, directors of artistic nonprofits, and even college literature professors like me—has practically no economic or political power to speak of, whereas once upon a time the membership list of the cultural elite corresponded quite closely to the membership list of the economic elite. All this is at stake in *The Rise of Silas Lapham*, and for no extra cost you even get a marriage plot, too.

But if students have such a hard time with Howells, why don't I just teach *Adventures of Huckleberry Finn* instead? Actually, sometimes I do. The brilliance of Twain's book is not marred for me by Twain's liberal use of the n-bomb, even though I have to correct students' mistaken belief that the term was not especially pejorative in Missouri in the 1830s. (When it comes to reading the word aloud, I tell students at the outset of the term that although I will not say "nigger," "fuck," or any variants thereon in my own speech, I will indeed read them from the texts if they appear there, because this is college, and we shouldn't need to bowdlerize "bad words" in a college literature class.) And though there are two scenes in which Huck's exchanges with Jim come straight from the minstrel show, on balance I think there's no question that the novel is overwhelmingly sympathetic to Jim and to abolition—even if it did appear a generation too late to do any good in the struggle against slavery (and therefore shouldn't be compared to antebellum novels on this score). Nonetheless, I have found *Huckleberry Finn* frustrating for three other reasons.

One, many students cannot read it—not because of its rendering of Jim, but rather because they have read it before and already "know" what it is about. As a result, they're overwhelmingly inclined to dismiss the final third of the book, just as Ernest Hemingway famously did when he declared that Twain was "cheating" by bringing Tom back onto the scene and turning the narrative into a burlesque.[2] "It's only a kid's adventure story, after all," said about half the class in the late 1990s, the last time I asked why in the world Twain would write such a scorched-earth, black-humor conclusion that undermines both Huck's and Jim's humanity and makes Tom look like a fiend. "A kid's adventure story—featuring a slave hunt, a deadly family feud, a pair of sleazy con men, and scenes of astonishing cruelty and stupidity? Are you kidding?" I replied. "That's like trying to make a Disney musical out of *Schindler's List*." But those students couldn't be persuaded to take the novel seriously; it was just a picaresque lark down the Mississippi, full of spills and chills.

Two, the students who did take it seriously identified with it too completely—and they, too, wrote off the final chapters. More specifically, most of my white students could not detach themselves from what I have since come to call the Huckleberry Finn Fantasy—the seductive notion that if *we* were alive back then, even if we were poor backwoods kids whose only formal education included lessons about how abolitionism was immoral and "lowdown," we would somehow, all by our lonesomes, come to the conclusion that we should save Jim and go to Hell. (The same emotional appeal is at work in *Schindler's List*, of course; when we identify with Oskar Schindler or Huck Finn, we do so, in part, because we so desperately want to believe that we'd have wound up on the side of the angels "naturally," even if we'd had no strong feelings about slavery or genocide to begin with.)

And three, many students could not understand how I could be so skeptical about *Huckleberry Finn* and still consider it a great piece of work. My students have no such problem when it comes to works like Willa Cather's *My Ántonia* or Ralph Ellison's *Invisible Man*, the conclusions of which I find unconvincing or unappealing, so I've had to conclude that *Huckleberry Finn* is simply so iconic— the literary critic Jonathan Arac calls it "hypercanonical"[3]—that students' impressions of the novel, and of its cultural impact, are unchallengeable by ordinary mortals like myself.

I haven't given up on teaching *Huckleberry Finn* in undergraduate survey courses, but if I want to grab a class's attention and ask them to read the syllabus with fresh eyes, *The Rise of Silas Lapham* does the job. Even if no one winds up loving it.

THE MARRIAGE PLOT, as in the British novels from which Howells took his cue, is also the class plot: Will the Lapham daughter marry into the Corey family? Will the rural Vermont nouveau riche climb into the ranks of the Boston Brahmin? Young Tom Corey certainly seems smitten with one of the daughters, but Tom's parents, predictably enough, are aghast at the idea of having an "alliance" with the Laphams. What's at stake is not money but culture, and what French sociologist Pierre Bourdieu calls "cultural capital"; the Laphams have no idea where to vacation, or how to decorate a house, or what books to own, or how to have—or even attend—a formal dinner party. They live in the wrong part of town, having "bought very cheap of a terrified gentleman of good extraction who discovered too late that the South End was not the thing."[4] None of this would matter to Silas and Persis Lapham, simple country folk that they are, except that—as they are subtly made to perceive— their lack of sophistication will surely damage their children's chances of advancing in the world. Even though Silas is quite wealthy when the book opens—able to boast of Corey, "I could buy him and sell him, twice over"[5]—he is wealthy after the fashion of Jed Clampett of *The Beverly Hillbillies*, having discovered on his farmland the basis for a new mineral paint that beats anything on the market. "Lapham had not yet reached the picture-buying stage of the rich man's development," Howells writes, "but they decorated their house with the costliest and most abominable frescoes; they went upon journeys, and lavished upon cars and hotels; they gave with both hands to their church and to all the charities it brought them acquainted with; but they did not know how to spend on society."[6]

I ask my students: What does Howells mean by "society"? And what does it have to do with "culture"? The words "society" and "culture" can have either a limited or an expansive sense; think of what we mean when we say "America is an open society" or even "America is a classless society," and when we say, "In our culture, self-made men like Lapham are widely admired," or, "Some cultures are matriarchal." More often than not, "society" and "culture" are all-inclusive, all-encompassing terms, the one meaning "the whole bunch of us, organized in some political entity," and the other meaning "the myriad ways of life that make the whole bunch of us into a bunch that's distinct from that other bunch." In *Silas*

Lapham, we're reminded that these terms also have a specialized sense; here, "society" is used in the sense we associate with the society pages of a major newspaper, and "culture" is used in the sense we associate with people who are "cultured and refined." And, of course, the "cultured and refined," under these definitions, are the people who make up "society."

A student suggests that our—ahem—society doesn't work that way any longer; look at Donald Trump, he says. Trump makes the society pages, but he's hardly an aficionado of high culture; he has lousy, lavish taste, and a truly hideous haircut to boot.

Point taken, I reply, but it actually reinforces Howells's point as well. If you take the long view on society and culture, after all, Trump is a classic *parvenu*, a loud nouveau riche boor whose cultural taste has been formed by—and is best expressed in—casinos. Yet even in saying that, I sound like an aristocrat or a snob, don't I, because who cares what nouveau riche families put in their living rooms? The poor couldn't care less; it's the aristocrats, the economic and cultural elites, who have turf to defend. But who are these aristocrats in the novel? The Coreys, of course, and to understand them you have to understand that while we have no landed aristocracy in this country, no earls and dukes, we do have, in many of our oldest cities, a set of very old families from whose perspective the Kennedys, say—whom the rest of us think of as American royalty—are a bunch of brash kids just off the boat.

I ask my students how many of them are familiar with the Astors or the van Rensselaers. No hands. "I didn't think so," I say, "I don't know them personally, myself. How about the Adamses and the Roosevelts?" Everyone in the room raises a hand. "The first families of Virginia? The elite of old Atlanta?" No hands again.

You get the idea. I don't tell my students the Coreys are the last of a dying breed, because families like them are assuredly still around, and still throwing debutante balls. But when *Silas Lapham* opens, it's 1875, and the Coreys are about to be supplanted—or at least challenged for cultural dominance—by a new class of entrepreneurs, inventors, and outright robber barons who will become the Carnegies, the Mellons, the Morgans, and the Rockefellers of the late nineteenth century. And yet "culture" still matters, if you're going to ingratiate yourself with the right people; as Persis puts it, when Silas tells her that they have enough money to get their girls "into society," "there's got to be something besides money, I guess."[7] There is: to get into society, you need culture. Watch what happens when Tom Corey tries to give young Irene Lapham advice on how to stock the library the Laphams have planned for their expensive, fashionable new house on Boston's Back Bay:

> The young man looked at her, and then said, seriously, "You'll want Greene, of course, and Motley, and Parkman."
>
> "Yes. What kind of writers are they?"
>
> "They're historians, too."
>
> "Oh, yes; I remember now. That's what Gibbon was. Is it Gibbon or Gibbons?"
>
> The young man decided the point with apparently superfluous delicacy. "Gibbon, I think."
>
> "There used to be so many of them," said Irene, gayly. "I used to get them mixed up with each other, and I couldn't tell them from the poets. Should you want to have poetry?"
>
> "Yes; I suppose some edition of the English poets."
>
> "We don't any of us like poetry. Do you like it?"
>
> "I'm afraid I don't very much," Corey owned. "But, of course, there was a time when Tennyson was a great deal more to me than he is now."
>
> "We had something about him at school, too. I think I remember the name. I think we ought to have *all* the American poets."
>
> "Well, not all. Five or six of the best: you want Longfellow and Bryant and Whittier and Holmes and Emerson and Lowell."[8]

The scene should strike us as comic, not merely because Emerson is the only poet on Tom's list whose reputation has survived the past century and a quarter, but also because Irene clearly has no idea what Tom is talking about. But it doesn't so strike us, not in my classroom, because the overwhelming majority of my students are with Irene; they, too, have no idea how to stock a library in a fancy new house. Furthermore, what the hell does that crack mean, "There was a time when Tennyson was a great deal more to me than he is now," and why should Tom say it to someone who barely remembers Tennyson's name from school?

I tell my students this: our society no longer has much of a sense of "society" in which it is important to know the names of the major poets and historians. In fact, by the time we get to *The Great Gatsby*, we'll see (by way of the man with the owl-eyed spectacles) that the nouveaux riches aren't expected to have opened the books in their new mansions' libraries—and today, they're not expected to have libraries at all. (Gatsby's books, the owl-eyed man tells us, are "absolutely real—have pages and everything. . . . What thoroughness! What realism! Knew when to stop, too—didn't cut the pages.")[9] But I assure my students that many of them have had conversations like Tom's and Irene's, with friends, on dates, whenever they're trying to determine whether someone else has cultural tastes similar to theirs. Tom is displaying, among other things, the fact that he knows enough to know the "right" kind of thing to say about Tennyson in 1875; he's basically saying, "I like his early work, but his recent stuff is kind of weak," the same way my students would say, "I liked Radiohead up until they released *Kid A*, but since then they've been spinning their wheels," or, "Scorsese did great things up through *Goodfellas*, but I really haven't paid attention to him since." After all, if you're really interested in music and movies, if you think such things are important, you don't want to find yourself waking up next to someone whose idea of a musical genius is Rod Stewart and whose favorite movie is *Father of the*

Bride. (Depending on how finicky your taste in movies is, you may not want to wake up next to someone who thinks Scorsese is a genius, either.) And why are flirting and "hooking up" at issue in a conversation about taste? Because Irene, poor deluded Irene, thinks Tom is courting her—and that mistake turns out to be the twist at the heart of the marriage plot; Tom isn't interested in cute, blond, culturally illiterate Irene. He's in love, to everyone's surprise, with the other sister—dark-haired Penelope, whom Tom's mother calls a "little, black, odd creature."[10] Pen knows her major literary figures; she's read *Middlemarch* and *Daniel Deronda*, and her verbal wit is more than a match for Tom's, which is largely why he falls for her. When you superimpose the marriage plot and the class-conflict plot, the implication is clear: the clash between old money and new, in Gilded Age Boston, will be reconciled by appeal to a kind of cultural meritocracy in which the sharp, witty, well-read daughter wins the heart of the young cultural aristocrat.

Penelope is, so to speak, a curious vehicle for this reconciliation. Endowed by Howells with a talent for subtle irony and gentle mockery (Howells based her, in part, on his daughter Winny, who died a few years after this novel was published), Penelope has little tolerance for the Coreys' displays of class privilege. At one point, the haughty and overbearing Mrs. Corey unexpectedly calls on the Laphams, finding only Penelope and her mother at home; Mrs. Corey, in the course of making small talk, praises the Laphams' new house, saying, "You will enjoy the sunsets on the Back Bay so much." Penelope crisply bats away this pleasantry, retorting, "Well, not unless they're new ones. I don't believe I could promise to enjoy any sunsets that I was used to, a great deal."[11] Penelope's brand of wit—lying somewhere on the decorum continuum between Jane Austen and Dorothy Parker—stops short of giving direct offense, and accordingly is too elusive for most of my students. "Try this, then," I say. "Are there radically different sunsets where you live, Mrs. Corey? I had no idea. Does the Back Bay orbit a different sun than the rest of Boston?" Scattered laughter. "But that's far too insulting," I add. Penelope is remarking on the fact that the sun sets on Boston's fashionable and unfashionable neighborhoods alike, and, in so doing, she's flouting the protocol of class status that Mrs. Corey both displays and enforces here. But she's doing it obliquely, wittily, not with a middle-finger salute.

I know my students find Penelope's demeanor inscrutable, but I assure them that they know this character. They've seen her before, and I tell them I'm willing to bet they've seen her quite recently, perhaps in the last week or two. Just look at the profile: here's a smart, sardonic, dark-haired teenage girl with clueless parents and a popular, blond younger sister. She spends much of her time in the narrative providing a dry, ironic commentary on the rest of the proceedings, almost as if half her body is outside the frame altogether and she's saying directly to us, "Will you just look at the material I have to work with here?" Anyone who's familiar with the MTV cartoon series *Daria* will know the type: it's Daria herself, in every detail. Granted, it's a less caustic Daria, and 1875 is way too early for Doc Martens, but there's no question that the sister scenarios of *Silas Lapham* and *Daria* are drawing on the same dark–light, smart–ditzy motif that has driven so many romance narratives over the centuries. And I'm not simply drawing on a pop-culture reference in order to appear hip or Daria-snarky to my students; the pedagogical device works. Everyone in the room knows MTV's alienated, wisecracking, Garofalo-esque cartoon character—I can see (and hear!) the shock of recognition, combined with the ancillary shock of "Hey, my literature professor likes *Daria*!" Good, I think, they have a connection to the novel, and a reason—however mediated—to identify with one of the characters. Now we can get down to business.

Because the rest of the plot is all about business: Silas's "rise," it turns out, is predicated on his financial ruin. The second half of the novel is the narrative of Silas's precipitous decline, and though the

novel (and Silas himself) pins the blame on Silas's ethically question-
able dealings with a former partner, Milton K. Rogers (whom he
forced out of the business just before it took off), things are actually
much more complicated than that. I won't rehearse every detail of
the plot, but suffice it to say that Silas has invested badly (a shameful
thing, this, since both he and his wife have this quaint notion that
participating in the stock market amounts to "gambling");[12] he has
flooded the market with his paint, even as a new West Virginia firm
has emerged as a serious competitor; he accidentally burns his new
house to the ground just after he has forgotten to make an insurance
payment; and the massive economic collapse that will become the
crash of 1877 has begun. (In a subplot, it also turns out that Silas has
been supporting the dissolute wife of a Civil War comrade who'd
saved his life, and Persis, upon first discovering evidence of the pay-
ments, suspects Silas of having an affair.) The moral drama—Silas's
"rise"—has to do with whether, in his distress, Silas will sell some
mills out west in order to save himself even though he knows they
will be next to worthless once the Great Lacustrine and Polar Railroad makes its bid for them. Interestingly, according to the business
ethics of the day, Silas is under no obligation to mention the railroad's interest in the property if the prospective buyer does not ask,
but Silas holds himself to a considerably higher standard. Late in
the book, a shady group of investors (pretending to be British) is
brought to him by none other than Rogers, and even when Silas
warns these people about the mills, they still insist on buying. When
Silas refuses, on the grounds that he would eventually be party to
someone else's fraud, Rogers demands that he sell the mills *to him*,
in order to save *him* from financial ruin.

We are well above the ethical bar here, I tell the class. After all,
as Rogers points out, we don't know for a certainty that the railroad will come forward and lowball Lapham on the mills, and, as
Rogers insists, Lapham is committing no crime in selling the mills
to Rogers himself, since Rogers is fully aware of what he's buying.

In fact, Rogers insists that Lapham has a positive duty to sell: "I want you to give me this chance to get on my feet again. You've no right to deprive me of it; it's unchristian."[13] Now, faced with an appeal like that—and faced also with the likely prospect of bankruptcy—who among us would agree to sell the property to Rogers?

Not a hand goes up. "You're kidding me, right?" Time after time, I can't believe this response. Perhaps the students think I'm trying to sucker-punch them? "Believe me," I tell them, "I won't think less of you—and I won't report you to the Securities and Exchange Commission, either. You're all with Silas on this?" Yes, they're all with Silas on this, because it's the only way to believe in the plot; if Silas gives in, he's no longer worthy of our admiration as a businessman, and, more importantly, the logic of the marriage plot—in which Penelope's marriage to Tom is somehow related to Silas's fall, so that the Laphams get to marry into the Coreys on the implicit condition that they return to Vermont and never darken the Coreys' dinner parties again—falls apart as well.

I remind the students just how high the stakes are in the mid-1870s; we are dealing with pure, unregulated, turbocharged industrial capitalism. No income tax, no unemployment benefits, no welfare, no Social Security, no Federal Deposit Insurance Corporation. No Antitrust Act, either, and of course no Occupational Safety and Health Administration. It's another world altogether; Silas is living amidst the great and terrifying boom-and-bust cycles of the American economy after the Civil War, which gave us incredible economic expansion and three or four catastrophic depressions leading up to the global meltdown in 1929. The novel barely registers that wider world, just as it never mentions the notoriously contested election of 1876; there is but one brief allusion to national politics, when Lapham remarks, "I hate to see them stirring up those Southern fellows again."[14] (The novel does not explain what exactly is stirring up those Southern fellows, or why Lapham hates to see it.)[15] Likewise, the novel does no more than gesture at the turbulent social unrest of the time. That unrest almost crept into the novel through a side door; Howells's first draft had Bromfield Corey talking of "applying dynamite to those long rows of close-shuttered, handsome, brutally insensible" new houses in the Back Bay. "If I were a poor man, with a sick child pining in some garret or cellar at the North End," Corey says, "I should break into one of them, and camp out on the grand piano."[16] A commendable sentiment coming from an aristocrat, but then again, dynamite had only recently been invented (by Alfred Nobel in 1866), and its use was associated mainly with anarchists and nihilists and assassinations.[17] Howells was persuaded by his editor, Richard Watson Gilder, to cut the reference to dynamite, and he struck it for roughly the same reason an American novelist in 2006 would think twice about having a character speak angrily of hijacking commercial planes and flying them into skyscrapers; the term was simply too closely aligned with acts of terrorism. Still, even though Howells cut the novel's most incendiary (though indirect) reference to current events, the fact remains that the novel is set at a time when the American economy is about to go into a temporary freefall, workers are on the brink of starving or striking, and the safety net hasn't yet been invented. So when Silas thinks he might lose everything, we really are talking about *everything*.

For his part, Silas is no robber baron; he made his money honestly (not in speculation), with little harm to the environment (unlike the coal industry), and he has always treated his workers well (no labor riots and head-busting private security forces for him). As one of his employees notes: "when everybody is shutting down, or running half time, the works up at Lapham are going full chip, just the same as ever. Well, it's his pride. I don't say but what it's a good sort of pride, but he likes to make his brags that the fire's never been out in the works since they started, and that no man's work or wages has ever been cut down yet at Lapham, it don't matter *what* the times are."[18] In a famously corrupt era, Lapham has exceptionally clean hands; it would be hard to imagine a more sympathetic portrait of a Gilded Age businessman. He brags a bit too much, and he lacks certain social graces; most embarrassingly, he gets drunk at the Coreys' dinner party (in part because of his nervousness, in part because he so rarely drinks at all). But as an entrepreneur and as an employer, he's as good as it gets. To my students, his story reads like the Uplifting Tale of an Honest Man Who Did the Right Thing.

I can't do much to dent this reading, I've found. I've tried pointing out that Silas is quite conflicted about his own social ambitions; on one hand, "he knew who the Coreys were very well, and, in his simple, brutal way, he had long hated their name as a symbol of splendor which, unless he should live to see at least three generations of his descendants gilded with mineral paint, he could not hope to realize in his own,"[19] but on the other hand, he is gratified when Bromfield Corey calls on him: "he was not letting his wife see in his averted face the struggle that revealed itself there—the struggle of stalwart achievement not to feel flattered at the notice of sterile elegance."[20] It's a peculiar use of the term "struggle," particularly in a period when the most brutal struggles of the day turned on the question of whether laborers should have a day of rest. Howells gives us no means of entry into those struggles. (It's also a peculiar use of the term "sterile," since Bromfield is no less capable than Silas when it comes to producing progeny. But, of course, Bromfield is not economically productive, as Silas is.) And on the upper-crust front, my students find Bromfield Corey so unfathomably alien—with his studied careerlessness as an "amateur" painter, his patrician mannerisms, and mildly Wildean drolleries ("Ah, we shall never have a real aristocracy while this plebeian reluctance to live upon a parent or a wife continues the animating spirit of our youth")[21]—that they cannot begin to imagine why Lapham is intimidated by him, and when he expresses disdain for the way Lapham markets his wares ("I will tell you plainly that I don't like the notion of a man who has rivaled the hues of nature in her wildest haunts with the tints of his mineral paint"),[22] the class recoils.

I explain to them that Corey is objecting to Lapham's habit of advertising his paint by making billboards out of rocks and trees, and that, back then, advertising itself was considered a generally disreputable business no matter what medium it adopted. The very idea of a national ad campaign for a specific brand of product didn't occur to anyone until the 1890s (the era of "Uneeda Biscuit"); before that, ads were associated primarily with snake-oil salesmen and patent-medicine frauds. So from Corey's perspective, I tell my students, we should think of Lapham as the rough equivalent of the guy who got rich with the *Girls Gone Wild* videos. He's a multimillionaire in his twenties, that kid, but you wouldn't necessarily want your daughter to marry him, now, would you?

Still no dice. They're not sympathizing with Corey on this or on anything else. For similar reasons, I can't get most of the class to agree that there's something vaguely unnerving about the logic of the novel's conclusion, as Penelope marries Tom and the rest of the Laphams retreat to Vermont while the young couple heads offstage to open the incipient global market for Lapham's mineral paint in Mexico:

> The marriage came after so such sorrow and trouble, and the fact was received with so much misgiving for the past and future, that it brought Lapham none of the triumph in which he had once exulted at the thought of an alliance with the Coreys. Adversity had so far been his friend that it had taken from him all hope of the social success for which people crawl and truckle, and restored him, through failure and doubt and heartache, the manhood which his prosperity had so nearly stolen from him.[23]

Ahh, come again? Adversity had done wha-aaa-aa-t? Did we read that right? First, you can get what you've wanted only if you no longer care about it, very well. That solves the social-ambition problem: the nouveaux riches can marry into the establishment, only so long as they lose their money and disappear. But what's this about Lapham's manhood? Is Howells seriously suggesting that money makes you a girlie-man? It's one thing to insist that the Laphams are happier being poor—as we hear of Persis, "she was glad the prosperity was going; it had never been happiness."[24] It's quite another to imply that wealth strips you of your *cojones* and seduces you into a Bromfeldian life of "sterile elegance." Back when he was thinking of building that house on the Back Bay, Silas had said to Persis, "A man can be a man on Beacon street as well as anywhere, I guess";[25] but guess what? He guessed wrong! A man *can't* be a man on Beacon Street. Isn't that strange? No, it seems, by and large, the students are all right with this too. The whole discussion of cultural capital has made some of them uneasy, knowing as they do that they're probably not going to climb their way into any rarified elite, be it political, economic, or cultural, and they're willing to see the question of "culture" as a trivial pursuit, a matter of knowing the right things to say about the right kinds of art and literature. "Besides," says one student, "the Laphams really are happier back in Vermont—they never did fit into Boston society, and they knew it."

But that's precisely the problem with this ending, I reply. We admire the self-made man—and by "we" I mean not only the people in my classroom but the whole country—and Silas is not only an entrepreneur but a rigorously honest man. In the historical drama the novel unfolds, we're rooting for him to displace the effete Coreys and all their like. But then we're supposed to cheer his financial ruin as well, because it restores his manhood through failure and doubt and heartache, and because it sends him back to the farm where he's more comfortable? Talk about mixed messages: it's a great nation and an open society where a guy like Silas can strike it rich, but really, social ambition is a bad thing and we shouldn't try to reach too far beyond our station. I ask the class point-blank: is that what I'm hearing?

Yes, that's what I'm hearing. The students are basically echoing *Silas Lapham*'s ambivalence about society and culture (or, if you like, its contradictions), endorsing both the novel's portrait of social mobility and its image of simple country people with their simple country culture. Very well, so they find Howells's account of Silas more compelling than mine. That's understandable: Silas is Howells's creation, not mine. Moreover, Howells was rather ambivalent about his own social climb from the remote provinces of Ohio to the inner circle of New England literati, so it is hardly surprising that *Silas Lapham* is ambivalent about social climbing.

But before my class moves on, I'm going to take one last stab at this ending. As Kermit Vanderbilt notes in his introduction to the Penguin edition, the Tom–Penelope marriage may involve some class-crossing, but it is also "a happy alliance of insider and outsider" that manages to "preserve the continuity of unmistakable Anglo-Saxon enterprise and culture"[26] The terrain of the novel is quite deliberately limited in this respect: I direct students to the brief Penguin appendix, where they find two passages in the *Century* serial version of the novel in which Howells alludes to casual anti-Semitic prejudice in Boston society. In one of those passages, Silas explains to Persis that Jews drive down property values:

> You see, they *have* got in—and pretty thick, too—it's no use denying it. And when they get in, they send down the price of property. Of course, there aint any sense in it; *I* think it's all dumn foolishness. It's cruel, and folks ought to be ashamed. But there it is. You tell folks that the Saviour himself was one, and the twelve apostles, and all the prophets—I don't know but what Adam was—guess he *was*—and it don't make a bit of difference. They send down the price of real estate. Prices begin to shade when the first one gets in.[27]

Here, Silas is both admirable and right: it's just dumn foolishness that when one points out that Jews are not all that "different," the argument don't make a bit of difference. But apparently they were different enough to matter, so Howells deleted them from the final manuscript, just as he deleted the reference to dynamite.

"Well, so he took out that stuff," says a student, "probably because he didn't want to give needless offense or the wrong impression." "No doubt," I reply. "Howells was no anti-Semite. But look where that leaves the novel—with no Jews; one black servant, nearly invisible; a bare reference to Italians; and not an Irishman to be seen anywhere. In Boston in 1875, for crying out loud." The students are puzzled. What's my point, they ask. Just this: that in rendering this picture of class conflict and its reconciliation via the Lapham–Corey marriage, Howells came up with the safest possible version of that conflict, and in so doing he had to decide to keep a lot of his actual Boston surroundings out of his novel. That's not a flaw, it's not a bad thing; every artist works with principles of selection. But as readers, we should think about what's *not* in the narrative and why, just as you think about what *is* in the narrative and why. Adding race and ethnicity to the mix would have complicated Howells's plot considerably—just think if Tom had fallen in love with a clever working-class Irish lass, or a nice Jewish girl—and so Howells consciously chose not to go that route. So we wind up, in the end, with a social challenge to the Coreys' dominance that's about as mild a social challenge as you could find in Boston in the mid-1870s, and even then, the challenge is finally rebuffed as Silas is restored to, of all things, his "manhood." The "success" of the marriage plot is predicated on Silas's "failure," except that his failure is actually his triumph, and except that the marriage brings "none of the triumph" that Silas had expected. That's why I think this is so fascinating a book. And that's why I hope my students will be fascinated, as well, even if they don't come to love what they've read.

* * *

NEXT WE READ James Weldon Johnson's *The Autobiography of an Ex-Colored Man*. It's a great novel for kicking off a class discussion of race and literature, since the novel is based partly on the premise that black folk don't write novels—and it's also based on the premise that the book itself is not a novel, written by a black man who doesn't appear to be a black man.

Before I get to Johnson's novel-masquerading-as-an-autobiography, though, I'll explain what I mean by "race and literature." For most of African-American literary history, African-American writers were praised by white critics only if they had managed somehow to "transcend" merely "racial" subject matter and speak to "universal" themes. This is a pernicious set of terms—as if black folk don't also speak of birth, death, joy, suffering, war, and peace?—and it was ubiquitous in American literary criticism right through the 1960s. The idea was that once Negroes stop going on about Negro themes and Negro concerns, then, and only then, will they be admitted to the ranks of the "universal," where the great writers live. Many of the greatest writers in the African-American tradition have grappled with this formulation of blackness and universality, as did W. E. B. DuBois when he closed his essay "Of the Training of Black Men," with a ringing endorsement of the value of Western Civ:

> I sit with Shakespeare and he winces not. Across the color line I move arm in arm with Balzac and Dumas, where smiling men and welcoming women glide in gilded halls. From out of the caves of evening that swing between the strong-limbed earth and the tracery of the stars, I summon Aristotle and Aurelius and what soul I will, and they come all graciously with no scorn or condescension. So, wed with Truth, I dwell above the Veil.[28]

DuBois follows this vision of raceless, color-blind culture, however, with a pointed question: "Is this the life you grudge us, O knightly America? Is this the life you long to change into the dull red hideousness of Georgia?" For DuBois, the point of insisting on Shakespeare's wincelessness was twofold: one, to assert the transcultural, transhistorical value of writers from Aristotle to Balzac and Dumas, and two, to contrast the world of ideas with the world of Jim Crow, where black intellectuals like himself were indeed met with scorn and condescension, and where aspiring black scholars would be met with winces—and worse—whenever they attempted to sit next to their white peers. If you get the first point and miss the second, seeing in this passage a simple celebration of "universal" themes and values rather than a righteous demand that black students finally be granted access to the intellectual treasures of the West, you wind up replaying the very assumption that DuBois is trying to challenge, namely, that there's something indelibly ununiversal about being black.

The idea of the "universal" is something of a straw figure here; it really means "not overtly racially marked," which in turn means "racially marked in such a way as to align with the majority or default position, which doesn't see itself as racially marked." And by the time we've reached this point in the argument, we're already in a place where, in certain classrooms, things can get weird. I don't want my white students to go around thinking, "What a horrible thing it is that I have been racially marked all this time without knowing it. I have been abusing my White Privilege as a member of the majority!" I want to avoid this reaction not because I want my white students to avoid feeling "uncomfortable" about the pervasive assumption, in white-majority cultures, than nonwhiteness is somehow a barrier to the expression of "universal" themes (for I do want them to challenge that assumption), but because I do *not* want my white students to make a show of expiation, of liberal guilt or (even worse) faux-liberal guilt. I recall a kind but misguided soul at a small liberal arts college who came to class one day—a class taught by an acquaintance of mine—having painted his pale torso "person of color" only to be told by a student of tint, "But honey, yours washes off." The "unmarked" nature of white privilege in the United States is not a function of white evilness and depravity or white supremacy; it is a simple corollary to majority status, as many white people have learned when they've found themselves in social situations where they are visibly in the minority, and where they have to take their whiteness into consideration in some way.

The dynamic was named by DuBois in that famous passage on "double consciousness" that opens "Of Our Spiritual Strivings" (and *The Souls of Black Folk*):

> After the Egyptian and Indian, the Greek and Roman, the Teuton and Mongolian, the Negro is a sort of seventh son, born with a veil, and gifted with second-sight in this American world,—a world which yields him no true self-consciousness, but only lets him see himself through the revelation of the other world. It is a peculiar sensation, this double-consciousness, this sense of always looking at one's self through the eyes of others, of measuring one's soul by the tape of a world that looks on in amused contempt and pity.[29]

Most people (and most of my students who've heard of DuBois) associate "double consciousness" with this passage's next sentence: "One ever feels his twoness,—an American, a Negro; two souls, two thoughts, two unreconciled strivings; two warring ideals in one dark body, whose dogged strength alone keeps it from being torn asunder." This second sense of "doubleness," it turns out, can be assimilated to any state of hyphenated-Americanness, if one feels his or her just-off-the-boatness sufficiently keenly (at once Italian and American, at once Korean and American, at once Polish and American, etc.). But the more elusive, more existential problem of always seeing oneself through the eyes of another—*that* is the state of being among the not-normal subgroup in a sea of normals: of being of African or Asian descent in a European culture, of being disabled in an able-bodied culture, of being the only woman in the meeting, of being the only Jew in the club, of being always unsure of whether you are being perceived as an individual or as an instance of one of the myriad subdivisions of intraspecies difference. Of always wondering, are they looking at me, talking to me, holding the door for me, rolling their eyes at me this way because I'm X? Or would they behave the same way if I were not X? And when I speak of birth, death, joy, suffering, war, and peace, will I be heard as just another human speaking to humans, or will I be heard as a provincial, as an instance of "identity politics"?

Now that we understand that much, I tell my class, let's understand the transcultural nature of African-American literature; almost all of it deals with one or another aspect of African-American life and speech and culture, but that hardly renders it incomprehensible to non-black readers. It's a literature; it can be read, it can be taught. Can it be taught by white guys like me? Of course it can. It can be taught by anyone who studies it deeply and seriously, anyone who does his or her homework. The question of whether a white guy can teach African-American literature is not a serious epistemological or cultural question; indeed, many African-American writers of generations past would have been quite pleased to know how seriously their work is now—finally—taken in college literature courses, by both black and white faculty. The question is, rather, merely—and I say this with some sense of irony—a political question. As I put it to my first group of African-American literature students in 1990, if you're skeptical about taking this course with a white professor, give me a couple of weeks and see if I do or don't know this material sufficiently well. At the time, I wasn't worried about that. The only thing I worried about was whether I might have been taking someone else's job—whether the English depart-

ment of the University of Illinois at Urbana–Champaign could have
hired an African-American scholar to teach that course. But then
again, we shouldn't assume that all African-American PhDs in English literature will necessarily want to specialize in African-
American literature, either. The social pressures on them to do so are
enormous, and of course for many African-American scholars it
makes all kinds of sense to work in African-American literature. But
it's not like it's in anyone's interest—including the interest of minority undergraduates—for the rest of the entire English department to
be understood as the preserve of the non-black faculty. Black graduate students who want to specialize in Victorian literature or
medieval studies should damn well be encouraged to do so.

I am not a specialist in African-American literature; I know
more about it than some Americanists, less than some others, but I
have always believed that it is part of my job as a reader and critic of
American literature to be conversant with the history of African-
American literature. Occasionally—three times in fifteen years, to
be exact—I have offered undergraduate courses exclusively in
African-American literature, most recently in the spring of 2004. In
more general undergraduate surveys in American literature, I see
no need to tie the syllabus to any demographic disposition of the
United States, past or present; on the contrary, the idea of doing so
seems to me patently absurd, particularly if one factors in literacy
rates over the course of US history. The number of works by
African-American writers on a syllabus in 2006 should not have to
correspond to (a) the proportion of African-Americans in the population in 2006, (b) the proportion of African-Americans in the population in 1885, (c) the proportion of literate African-Americans in
the population in 1850, or (d) any other number whatsoever. I therefore have no reason to apologize for assigning works by James Weldon Johnson, Zora Neale Hurston, and James Baldwin all in one
semester, as if this constitutes an illegitimate "overrepresentation" of
African-American writers relative to their numbers in the republic

of letters between 1912 (the publication date of Johnson's *The Auto-biography of an Ex-Colored Man*) and 1953 (the date of Baldwin's debut, *Go Tell It on the Mountain*). I'm happy to say that in twenty years of reading students' evaluations, I have come across only two or three complaints that my syllabus was too, um, "multicultural." The overwhelming majority of my students simply want a chance to read works with which they're not already familiar—and although Toni Morrison is a staple among contemporary writers and Hurston has enjoyed one of the most spectacular posthumous comebacks in American literature since Herman Melville was redis-covered and reinterpreted in 1924, it's usually safe to say that most undergraduates are not familiar with most of the major figures in African-American literature.

Of course, the terms of teaching the "transcultural" depend on which cultures one needs to trans. When I teach Hurston in a gen-eral survey class, as I did in the fall of 2003 to a class of thirty-two that did not contain any African-American students, I usually have to do an exposition on "signifying" and other salient aspects of African-American vernacular English. *Their Eyes Were Watching God* is a raucous, cutting, vigorously politically incorrect book (from its allusion to an apparently consensual sexual liaison between a slave and a master to its variously scathing renderings of episodes of envy, dissension, and resentment in the black community), and unless you're familiar with the kind of rhetorical indirection with which someone might challenge an obnoxious partygoer by saying, "Tell me, what post office did *you* ever pee in? Ah craves tuh know,"[30] you're going to miss a great deal of what makes the novel so delightful. So, in November 2003, when I ask the class, "How many of you are familiar with 'signifying,' 'the dozens,' and expres-sions like 'talking out your neck'?" One hand goes up: that of the precocious freshman who happens to be taking the African-American literature survey taught by one of my colleagues. By con-trast, in January 2004, when I ask the same question in my

African-American literature class, every black student—sixteen out of a class of thirty-four—raises a hand (as do two of the remaining eighteen white students). It was as if I'd asked the class, "How many people are familiar with features of the black oral tradition," and the black students replied, in signifying fashion, "Yes, professor, we're black."

It's not that I have nothing to tell these students; I can fill them in on the terms of the Herskovits–Frazier debate in African-American studies,[31] and I can let them know about Henry Louis Gates Jr.'s brilliant work on signifyin(g) and Western theories of signification in his 1988 book, *The Signifying Monkey*.[32] My black students usually don't come into class already knowing about those aspects of the tradition. Gates offers an account of trickster figures and their crafty rhetorical practices that ranges from the Yoruba figure Esu-Elegbara and Anansi the Spider all the way to Ishmael Reed's *Mumbo Jumbo* (whose PaPa LaBas is a version of the Benin god Legba, a manifestation of Esu). The idea that West African trickster figures are still with us today, from Br'er Rabbit to Bugs Bunny (if you want to get someone's attention fast, just tell them Bugs was black) is at the heart of the Herskovits–Frazier debate, and it concerns the question of whether African cultural forms survive in contemporary American culture, as Melville Herskovits argued in *The Myth of the Negro Past*, or whether, as E. Franklin Frazier insisted, "nothing remains" of the "habits and customs as well as the hopes and fears that characterized the life of their forebears in Africa." But teaching black students about Esu or Henry Louis Gates is usually quite a different matter from teaching non-black students about African-American cultural figures like Stagger Lee and High John the Conqueror; my students' cultural literacies, and my pedagogical approaches, differ from class to class.

Students' responses to the works, not surprisingly, depend in part on their familiarity with the figures of African-American culture, past and present; it was a black woman, some years ago, who insisted to me during a discussion of *Their Eyes Were Watching God* that there was no way Tea Cake was telling the truth about what he did with Janie's secret two-hundred-dollar stash when he disappeared for a day during their honeymoon. (He claims to have thrown a big chicken-and-macaroni party, and "stood in the door and paid all the ugly women two dollars *not* to come in."[33] "You musta thought yo' wife was powerful ugly," replies Janie. "Dem ugly women dat you paid two dollars not to come in, could git tuh de door. You never even 'lowed me tuh git dat close.")[34] "I *know* this man," my student insisted, "and he is *lying*." Although I replied that I thought this was unlikely (since the tale Tea Cake tells upon returning to Janie is quite damning enough), I had to admit that Hurston gives us no way of corroborating his story, so that we, like Janie, have to take him on faith if we will. Likewise, it was one of my black male students who suggested that Janie, in marrying the much younger Tea Cake after her twenty-year marriage to Joe Starks, scandalizes the town because "she was married to the mayor, she was like the town's first lady, and here she is getting it on with Tupac."

When it comes to some of the more excruciating and unpleasant details of the African-American tradition, I do have some general ground rules for students. General civility in addressing one another, of course; students should not critique each other ad hominem, and everyone should begin from the premise that his or her peers speak out of a desire to advance the conversation (as opposed to a desire to provoke or goad one's real or imaginary antagonists). And I will tolerate no faux-liberal grandstanding. No one gets any points, in the twenty-first century, for denouncing the obscenity of slavery. When we discuss *The Autobiography of an Ex-Colored Man*, whose plot turns on a lynching, no one gets any extra credit for speaking out against lynching. And if there is no be no faux-liberal grandstanding, so too there is to be no contrarian or faux-contrarian denial; no one is allowed to pretend that slavery was beneficial to the slaves, and no one is allowed to blink away the fact that the United States witnessed roughly sixty lynchings a year from 1875 through 1925, as lynching became a standard means of enforcing perceived breaches of the color line, and not exclusively those "breaches" that challenged the taboo of interracial sex (as Ida B. Wells reported in 1892, 728 lynchings of black Americans had occurred in the previous eight years alone).[35] The subject of lynching is simply too serious to be blinked away.

I presume that no one in my classrooms has ever seen or would ever condone a lynching, and I know that many of my students come from families that didn't live in the United States when Johnson's book was published. So, I tell my students, the only thing you can possibly do "wrong" about such atrocities, at this late date, is to deny them or to pass over the various justifications for them advanced by white supremacists of a century ago. Should there be any doubt about the vileness of those justifications, I could direct "dissenting" students (who might think, for whatever reason, that I am exaggerating about the pervasiveness of lynching and the popularity of its justifications) to the white supremacist books of the time, perhaps Thomas Dixon's *The Klansman* or *The Leopard's Spots*, or Charles Carroll's *The Negro A Beast*, a bestseller of 1900. I am confident that this material will shock even the most complacent reader today, regardless of his or her political stripes. But, so far in my teaching career, I haven't had to do that; so far, it's been a fairly simple matter of explaining to students that lynching was, at one time, so ubiquitous that a writer like James Weldon Johnson would hinge a novel's plot on it—and would devote a good deal of his political life, as general secretary of the NAACP, to trying (and failing) to get an anti-lynching bill passed by the United States Congress.

For although most of *The Autobiography of an Ex-Colored Man* is actually about music—and my classes on Johnson's novel are dominated, once they get going, by discussions of the narrator's musical career, the history of black musicians' "crossover" success with white audiences, and the history of white musicians' appropriations, adaptations, and emulations of African-American musical forms—there is no question that Johnson wrote the book, in large part, to try to stem the tide of lynchings sweeping his nation. He did so not by trying to point out, in fictional form, that lynching was simply wrong; perhaps that would have been too directly polemical, but then the book is, at points, directly polemical, featuring a number of discussions of "the Negro question" and an extensive disquisition on the class distinctions among African-Americans, which remains compelling one hundred years later. Rather, I think Johnson avoided the "lynching is wrong" line because, by 1912, it clearly wasn't working; too many white Americans believed that lynching was terrible but ultimately necessary, and far too many white Americans believed that lynching was a positively good thing that they should commemorate with celebratory photographs and postcards.[36] There was no way that Johnson could challenge those beliefs directly and win. Instead, crafty writer that he was, Johnson set about creating a plot in which lynching is not merely wrong but also counterproductive, insofar as it stokes the very fears about racial "passing" that made white supremacists lose sleep at night. The book says as much in its preface: "these pages also reveal the unsuspected fact that prejudice against the Negro is exerting a pressure which, in New York and other large cities where the opportunity is open, is actually and constantly forcing an unascertainable number of fair-complexioned colored people over into the white race."[37] That's what Johnson wants supremacists and other apologists for lynching to take away from the book: An unascertainable number, oh, my God. And they may even be among us right now!

For when the narrator witnesses a lynching in the South, he is moved not to dedicate his life to African-Americans' civil rights—that is, to become James Weldon Johnson himself—but to disaffiliate himself from black folks altogether: "A great wave of humiliation and shame swept over me. Shame that I belonged to a race that could be so dealt with; and shame for my country, that it, the great example of democracy to the world, should be the only civilized, if not the only state on earth, where a human being would be burned alive."[38] This shame eventually leads the narrator to give up his dream of becoming a black composer, transcribing the "sorrow songs" and gospel melodies of the rural black South into the stuff of symphony and opera, and to spend the rest of his life passing as a white man:

> I argued that to forsake one's race to better one's condition was no less worthy an action than to forsake one's country for the same purpose. I finally made up my mind that I would neither disclaim the black race nor claim the white race; but that I would change my name, raise a mustache, and let the world take me for what it would; that it was not necessary for me to go about with a label of inferiority pasted across my forehead. All the while I understood that it was not discouragement or fear or search for a larger field of action and opportunity that was driving me out of the Negro race. I knew that it was shame, unbearable shame. Shame at being identified with a people that could with impunity be treated worse than animals. For certainly the law would restrain and punish the malicious burning alive of animals.[39]

It is a searing passage, as is the narrator's description of the lynching itself, which I will not reproduce here (it's too long and too gruesome, and, besides, you should go and buy the book). Sometimes I remind my students that humans have burned other humans alive for centuries. The Inquisition specialized in it, and the smell emanating from the innocent "witches" and "heretics" of Europe did not differ significantly from the smell of the charred bodies of innocent African-Americans who were tortured and maimed before being immolated. But once my students have taken in—if they can take in—the sheer brutality and horror of the scene, I have two questions for them. One, what does it mean that this narrator is fictional, and that this "autobiography" about a black man passing as white is in fact a novel passing as an autobiography? (It was published anonymously, and Johnson, who could not have passed for white and would not have wanted to, did not reveal that he was the author of the book until 1927.) And two, what is going on in that first sentence, "to forsake one's race to better one's condition was no less worthy an action than to forsake one's country for the same purpose"?

To the first question I've gotten every kind of response. Some students are outraged, outraged that Johnson is "lying" to us, and that he kept up the "lie" for fifteen years. For them, amazingly (and, for me, distressingly), the whole book falls apart when it's revealed to be the novel that it is. Other students—more sophisticated or practiced readers—are fascinated that Johnson managed to compose a fictional scenario that critiques both lynching and passing (the narrator closes the book on a note of deep regret: "I am an ordinarily successful white man who has made a little money. They are men who are making history and a race. . . . I cannot repress the thought that, after all, I have chosen the lesser part, that I have sold my birthright for a mess of pottage")[40] while partially justifying the practice of passing as a defensive response to lynching. Almost all my students over the years, black, white, and other, have been critical of the narrator's decision to pass, which would probably please Johnson; but often they've rested their arguments on a kind of racialist appeal to what the narrator "really" is. Whenever I hear that argument, I ask, in devil's-advocate mode, whether my students are saying that the narrator is somehow indelibly "black." I suggest in return that if he's successfully passing as white, then he's not much darker than most of the white students in the class; and besides, isn't the idea of "indelible" blackness part of the logic of Jim Crow—the "one-drop" rule in which anyone of mixed parentage is deemed a Negro?

Maybe, students tend to say, but Americans didn't have the

"mixed race" category back then, and besides, the narrator himself accepts his designation as "Negro" until he sees that lynching. This is a good point, I think—and it takes us to that line about forsaking one's country to better oneself. I'd originally read it more or less benignly, as an analogy between passing and emigrating: I'm just leaving my native land to better myself. But over the years, many students have insisted on reading the sentence more cynically, as establishing an analogy not between passing and emigration but between passing and treason. I think that reading is entirely plausible. It depends, as I told one class, on what one thinks of the very idea of "forsaking" one's country, which does seem to be a stronger, more charged term than merely "leaving" one's country. So perhaps the narrator suggests that he is betraying "his" people, and if so, then my students are right to be suspicious of a man who forsakes "his race" for his own personal gain. It also depends on how you read the phrase "no less worthy." If the sentence were "forsaking one's race to better one's condition is just as laudable as forsaking one's country" there would be no ambiguity; but because we're not sure that forsaking one's country is a "worthy" action, we can't be certain about what "no less worthy" might mean. Following that train of thought, I asked the class to go back and look at the narrator's earlier decision to claim "his" race, because that decision is not entirely noble. When he decides to leave his patron in Europe and become an African-American composer, to "voice all the joys and sorrows, the hopes and ambitions, of the American Negro, in classic musical form,"[41] he asks himself, "was it more a desire to help those I considered my people, or more a desire to distinguish myself, which was leading me back to the United States? That is a question I have never definitely answered."[42] Moreover, he admits explicitly that he chooses to embark on a career as a black composer because he knows he'll be a scarce commodity: "I should have greater chances of attracting attention as a colored composer than as a white one."[43]

I dwelt on this question for about half an hour during one class period in the fall of 2003, not only because it's a good question in and of itself but also because it opens onto the larger question of whether Johnson invites us to read his narrator ironically, and, if so, what to make of that irony. I don't think Johnson leads us to a simple condemnation of his narrator's careerism; but I do know that Johnson—a composer himself, in partnership with his brother J. Rosamond Johnson (they wrote, among other things, "Lift Every Voice And Sing," also known as the "Negro national anthem")—believed passionately that black musicians and artists weren't getting their due. But just then, in early October 2003, a funny thing happened. Two days after I brought up the question of the narrator's self-interest in declaring himself to be a "colored composer," and my students had responded by asking why he wants to convert African-American music to "classical form" in the first place (another good question), Rush Limbaugh resigned from ESPN in response to the controversy over his remarks about Philadelphia Eagles quarterback Donovan McNabb the previous Sunday. The Eagles had gotten off to a shaky start that season, and Limbaugh had said, on the *NFL Countdown* pregame show, "I think what we've had here is a little social concern in the NFL. The media has been very desirous that a black quarterback do well. There is a little hope invested in McNabb, and he got a lot of credit for the performance of this team that he didn't deserve. The defense carried this team." At the time, the rest of the ESPN crew—all of whom were former NFL stars, black and white—took issue with Limbaugh, but not with regard to the "little social concern" statement; they argued simply that McNabb was not overrated, and that was the end of that . . . until Tuesday, when McNabb told the Philadelphia *Daily News*, "It's sad that you've got to go to skin color. I thought we were through with that whole deal." And then the storm broke, and by late Wednesday night Limbaugh had resigned.[44] So, Thursday afternoon, I opened the class with him.

"You may have heard that Rush Limbaugh resigned from ESPN," I said as the attendance sheet made the rounds. Sure enough, the entire class was aware of this; it was the topic *du jour* in the campus newspaper and in the hallways and food courts. I quoted the statement he'd issued the previous night, which read, in part, "My comments this past Sunday were directed at the media and were not racially motivated." I asked my students to take Limbaugh at his word, on the grounds that he very likely thought he was not saying anything racist, and quite sincerely believed that the NFL and the media were tacitly rooting for a black quarterback. This second belief, I suggested, has something to do with the economics of black scarcity, on which Johnson's narrator relies when he decides he'd be better off as a black composer.

The class snapped to attention—some of it curious, some of it skeptical. I got the sense that even the Rush fans in the room were giving me the benefit of the doubt, since, from what I'd gathered in the local Pennsylvania media during the previous two days, central Pennsylvania's Rush fans seemed to be torn between the desire to defend their hero from the forces of political correctness and the desire to smite anyone who badmouths their beloved Iggles.

I told my students I wasn't going to get into the question of whether Limbaugh should have resigned; they could save that for their journalism ethics classes. Instead, I suggested that Limbaugh's remark was badly dated. I agreed with McNabb: I thought we were through with that whole deal. But, I said, that's not because I think we're completely post-racist; it's just because there are about ten black starting quarterbacks in the NFL.

"Nine," said one young man.[45]

"Thanks," I replied.

Those nine or ten quarterbacks, in 2003, ran the gamut of the talent spectrum from star players like McNabb, Daunte Culpepper, Michael Vick, and Steve McNair, who really do carry their teams and are basically a new kind of player, the mobile 240-pound quarterback who can run for 100 yards a game, to mediocre guys like Aaron Brooks and Jeff Blake, to marginal players like Quincy Carter and . . . uh, who's the quarterback for the Tampa Bay Buccaneers . . .?

"Shaun King," a dozen students, not all of them male, called out.

"Right, Shaun King," I answered. "No disrespect, but he's no McNabb or McNair."

My point was this: the idea that the NFL would pick just *one* of these guys, and have "a little social concern" to hype him and promote him because of his color, was really rather bizarre in 2003. But, fifteen years earlier, I noted, in Super Bowl XXII, the Washington Redskins, with unheralded Doug Williams at the helm, beat the heavily favored Broncos after a stupefying thirty-five-point second quarter in which Williams made the Broncos' secondary look like the local high school JV, throwing for a record-setting four touchdowns. Was there, in 1988, some excitement about that performance specifically because Williams was black? Damn straight there was—Williams was the first black quarterback in the Super Bowl, *still* the last black quarterback to win a Super Bowl, and he wound up as the MVP of the game, no less. I had black friends—and white friends—who were indeed thrilled that "a brother" had done all that. To make things even sweeter, Williams had toiled in obscurity with the Tampa Bay Buccaneers for some years, and some people were glad for him just because he'd done time with a team where you could expect to lose twelve games and get sacked hard fifty times every year. So yes, back in 1988 there really was "a little social concern," a desire that "a black quarterback do well."

Now to put that social concern in social context. Before that Super Bowl, if you go back to the mid-1970s—as I do—you find only one black starting quarterback, James Harris of the Rams (who had become pro football's first black quarterback in 1969 with the Buffalo Bills). There was also Joe Gilliam, a Steelers backup who saw little action behind Terry Bradshaw; only much later, in 1984, did Warren Moon arrive on the scene, and even he, for all his talent, spent six years in the wilds of Canadian football before being signed in the NFL. Back then, you really could hear whispers that black players didn't have the intelligence or the leadership skills to be quarterbacks, and sometimes the remarks were louder than whispers. But I haven't heard that kind of thing in years, not from anyone who knows anything about the game. Nor have I heard any whispers—let alone comments on ESPN, with the exception of Limbaugh's—that certain black quarterbacks are overrated because of their race. That's not because the league put out new guidelines one day for how to discuss race in the NFL; it's simply because there are now a significant number of black quarterbacks, some of whom are among the league's elite and some of whom aren't, and they've made the case for their skills on the field. But back when you had only one or two black quarterbacks, their very blackness was matter for commentary, good and bad. They stood out, just as Tiger Woods stands out for being the first player of color—or Cablinasian, as he puts it—ever to dominate the PGA tour. That's what the ex-colored man is counting on; when his patron says, "I can imagine no more dissatisfied human being than an educated, cultured, and refined colored man in the United States,"[46] he thinks, fair enough, but exactly how many African-American classical composers are there? He thinks he has a legitimate shot at becoming what they call, in the tradition, a "Negro first."

The class then embarked on a discussion of whether the ex-colored man is deluded about his prospects, and we looked at the novel's depictions of black performers who are being overlooked and underestimated, like the minstrel who frequents the club at which the ex-colored man plays ragtime: "Here was a man who made people laugh at the size of his mouth, while he carried in his heart a burning ambition to be a tragedian; and so after all he did play a part in a tragedy."[47] I pointed out, as does William Andrews in his introduction to the Penguin edition, that sometimes black scarcity does not work in such a way as to overvalue black individuals; one of the reasons Johnson wasn't more explicit about the fictional status of his book was that "in 1912, the publication of African-American novels by Northern commercial publishers was still a new and risky venture."[48] Johnson knew that an anti-lynching treatise by a black writer wouldn't get much play, and an anti-lynching novel by a black writer wouldn't even have a chance to play; but an anonymous "autobiography" by a man of ambiguous racial status, in which racial "passing" is revealed to be partly a response to the ubiquity of lynching—now that's a saleable commodity! The economics of black scarcity simply would not work for Johnson as a writer in the way the ex-colored man believes they will work for him as a black composer. It was a far better rhetorical and political strategy for Johnson, then, to "forsake" the race by writing anonymously about a man who has forsaken "his" race.

After the class, one student approached me and said he loved the segue from the NFL to the novel, but that Limbaugh's comments *were* racist, and I should have said so. Privately, I agreed with the first part. But I insisted that Limbaugh himself doesn't think of things that way; he seems sincerely to think that the media and the NFL are full of liberals overrating McNabb in the service of their liberal social agendas. But, my student asked, isn't that in itself a kind of racist thing to think? I said that it's surely a bizarre thing to think, but that I had another point to make about Johnson's narrator, and didn't want to provoke a whole side discussion about Rush Limbaugh; I just wanted to show that the form of the statement, "You just think that way about X because he's black," sounds more and more absurd the more black folk there are in the conversation—or the room, or the league.

I mention this episode for two reasons. One, to give an example of how, on occasion, I use a topical event in order to set up a discussion. Two, to show that even when I'm demonstrating that Rush

Limbaugh doesn't know what he's talking about with regard to Donovan McNabb, my classes contain plenty of students who are more outspokenly "liberal" and/or left-leaning than myself. I know as much from their papers and their exams; I know it from their approving citations of Michael Moore; and I know it from the questions—which also came up in that 2003 class—of whether Willa Cather is trying to "queer the prairie" in *My Ántonia*, and whether *The Great Gatsby* can be read as a critique of capitalism and bourgeois individualism. Sometimes, when I read conservatives' accounts of campus life and classroom "intimidation," I wonder what's happening with the liberal students on American campuses. Don't *they* ever feel uncomfortable? Don't they ever make their professors uncomfortable? I've begun to suspect that for some critics on the right, it's a mystery why liberals exist at all; they sometimes speak as if no one, left to his or her own devices, would wind up as a liberal but for professorial indoctrination and brainwashing. And it certainly doesn't occur to them that some of their demonized liberal faculty members have our share of undergraduates who find us not liberal enough for their tastes.

Late in the semester, long after we'd finished discussing Johnson's novel, I learned that one of my students belonged to the College Republicans; Kevin, a wiry kid who hadn't said a word all term, sent me an e-mail in which he apologized for being late to class because he'd had to attend the noontime rally for Conservative Coming Out Day. I laughed out loud when I received the e-mail, because—as I gently noted in my reply to Kevin—he hadn't *been* late to class. The point was, of course, that he was "coming out" to me. No problem, I replied; you weren't late, and I hope you had an enjoyable rally. (This turned out to be the Coming Out Day that backfired a few days later when the president of Penn State's College Republicans was discovered to have those disturbing Halloween-party photos on his website. I did not mention the story to Kevin when it broke, because I thought it was entirely up to him to decide whether he wanted to discuss it with me; otherwise, it was none of my business as Kevin's professor.) But the e-mail made me go back and look at my response to Kevin's first paper, partly to see if I had made any comments that might have struck him as biased or unfair. What I found instead was even more illuminating: Kevin had written an essay in which he'd argued that Johnson presents "black" culture as being somehow superior to "white" culture, and that even the narrator's decision to "pass" should be regarded as a triumph for "black" culture. At the time, when I graded the paper, I told Kevin that I didn't think this reading could be supported by the novel itself. In my comments, I wrote, in part:

> I see a major problem with your argument: when it comes to the narrator's life-changing decision to pass as white, you seem to say that (a) he hangs on to black culture all the same, and (b) even his marriage should be seen as a kind of triumph for black culture. Argument (b), I think, is simply implausible, since the narrator has to deny being black in order for his marriage to be socially accepted; argument (a) is more problematic, and you should have made it more carefully. Perhaps like so: yes, the narrator values black popular cultural forms like ragtime, spirituals, and the cakewalk even after he decides to pass for white; indeed, he values them more highly than some black people do, and never comes to believe that white culture is simply better than black culture. At the same time, though, he certainly *does* turn his back on black culture: it's as if, once he sees that lynching, he says, "yeah, yeah, ragtime and spirituals, very nice, yeah, very nice, but I'm outta here, see you later, like maybe never." All the worthy black cultural achievements in the world don't manage to prevent him from concluding that he'd be better off living as a white guy if he can.

In retrospect, I realized that Kevin had almost surely written the kind of paper with which he thought I would agree politically; apparently he thought I would approve of a paper whose argument is that black culture is better than white culture and somehow triumphant in the end. If Kevin learned nothing else that semester, I hope he learned he was mistaken about this much: I don't like papers that indulge in such facile cheerleading. I like papers whose arguments are plausible, grounded firmly in the details of the literary works in front of us. I thought I had said so quite clearly in my paper handout, but perhaps I should "come out" to my students more emphatically in the future, lest any of them waste their time and mine trying to concoct strained arguments they imagine to be compatible with what they imagine my politics to be.

DOES WILLA CATHER "queer the prairie" in *My Ántonia*? When the question was asked, in that 2003 class, some of my students were sure that there was no chance that Cather was trying to do any such thing; an even larger group wondered just what it would mean to queer a prairie in the first place. In one sense, that larger group included me; although I believed I knew what that student was asking, I wanted him to be more specific about whether he was talking about Cather's depiction of gender roles, Cather's personal life, or Cather's aesthetic decisions about how to represent her Nebraska childhood. So I'll back up and explain how that question arose in the course of our classroom discussion.

"Willa Cather leaves me feeling intensely nostalgic," one student wrote in her weekly response in my fall 1989 American literature survey, "but I have no idea what for." It's hard to come up with a more succinct summation of the emotional effect of *My Ántonia*. Having taught the novel half a dozen times, I've learned that there really are only two kinds of people in the world: those who fall under Cather's spell, emerging from *My Ántonia* suffused with the warm red glow of the summer sun setting on the vast, verdant prairie, and those who find the novel horrifying or annoying, with its insistence on glorifying the remarkably fecund and nearly toothless Ántonia and elevating her to the ranks of the timeless. "She lent herself to immemorial human attitudes which we recognize by instinct as universal and true," Cather writes. "She was a rich mine of life, like the founders of early races."[49] I find that first sentence especially grating, skeptical as I am that there are any such things as immemorial human attitudes which we recognize by instinct as universal and true. How come other prominent female characters, like Lena Lingard and Tiny Soderball, don't get to be immemorial and universal? They head west, strike it rich (Lena by dressmaking, Tiny in Klondike real estate), and live as single women in San Francisco. What's wrong with that? It's a "pioneer" version of the road Cather herself took, after all; she didn't stay at home in Nebraska and have eleven children and a fertile orchard like Ántonia Shimerda. She lit out for the big city where she worked in a male-dominated industry and lived as a single woman of ambiguous sexuality with her longtime companion, Edith Lewis. Ah, but perhaps modern women like Lena, Tiny, and Willa are necessarily something other than timeless insofar as they are modern. If that's the case, then some poor shlub has to stay home in the wheat fields, have lots of kids, and serve ever after as a Timeless Symbol to those who, like Cather and her narrator, Jim Burden, go to college and flee the prairie. And yet the novel is profoundly autobiographical nonetheless, mixing Cather's fondness for her childhood friend, Annie Pavelka (the model for Ántonia), with her regret over the marriage of a woman with whom she had forged another intimate emotional friendship, Isabelle McClung (a marriage that took place just before Cather began writing *My Ántonia*).

You can already tell, I suppose, that I tend to be one of Cather's skeptical readers. Take the overwhelmingly nostalgic conclusion of the novel:

> I had the sense of coming home to myself, and of having found out what a little circle man's experience is. For Ántonia and for me, this

had been the road of Destiny; had taken us to those early accidents of fortune which predetermined for us all that we can ever be. Now I understood that the same road was to bring us together again. Whatever we had missed, we possessed together the precious, the incommunicable past.[50]

I think this conclusion depends on a kind of narrative legerdemain, as the novel attempts (so to speak) to make us forget all the strange, horrific things—both in the wilds of nature and in the intrigues of the town—the novel itself has depicted in the first two-thirds of the narrative. But each time I've taught My Ántonia I've gotten a different reaction from students. Those who are altogether too enchanted by the novel, I try to disenchant; those who are too disenchanted, I try to re-enchant. Neither of these is hard to do; the long first section of the novel, recounting Jim's first year in Nebraska after the death of his parents, is wonderfully evocative of the uncanniness of the American plains.

I wanted to walk straight on through the red grass and over the edge of the world, which could not be very far away. The light air about me told me that the world ended here: only the ground and sun and sky were left, and if one went a little farther there would be only sun and sky, and one would float off into them, like the tawny hawks which sailed over our heads making slow shadows on the grass.[51]

I kept as still as I could. Nothing happened. I did not expect anything to happen. I was something that lay under the sun and felt it, like the pumpkins, and I did not want to be anything more. I was entirely happy. Perhaps we feel like that when we die and become a part of something entire, whether it is sun and air, or goodness and knowledge. At any rate, that is happiness; to be dissolved into something complete and great. When it comes to one, it comes as naturally as sleep.[52]

I love passages like this, even Cather's eerie association of happiness with oceanic-at-oneness and death, and I appreciated them all the more when I first moved to Illinois, having never seen the great American Midwest after living for twenty-eight years in New York and Virginia. Yet Cather's evocations of the plains are always mediated by something else—partly by the new inhabitants, who turn out to be an assortment of troubled folk from the Old Country who are fleeing terrible histories in Europe and Russia or tragically wasting away in sod houses (like Ántonia's father, who commits a grisly suicide in the middle of his first bitter Nebraskan winter), and partly by the ghosts of the former inhabitants, about whom Cather writes as if they belonged to another era, as in the reference to a snake so old that "he must have been there when white men first came, left on from buffalo and Indian times."[53] No kidding, left on from buffalo and Indian times? Exactly how many eons would that be? Cather was born in Virginia in 1873 and moved to Nebraska when she was nine; Jim's story begins, appropriately enough, in the early 1880s. And yet there are no Indians in the novel, and the only signs of them are rendered as if they are evidence of an ancient civilization. This doesn't mean that Cather is an after-the-fact accessory to genocide, I assure my class. But it is worth noting, because it's every bit as striking as Howells's refusal to mention the Irish in a novel about Boston. The massacre at Wounded Knee—just over the northern border in South Dakota, as Red Cloud (the town on which Cather based Black Hawk) lies on the southern border—is still in the future, in 1890. There are plenty of Sioux and Pawnee in the area; "left on from buffalo and Indian times" around Black Hawk could very well mean "here since last Friday." But Native Americans would complicate the picture considerably, so we're going to pretend, for now, that they're prehistoric.

And what is the picture? In one respect, it's one of the most enthusiastic representations of immigration and multiculturalism in the American canon. Out on the empty, featureless land ("not a country at all, but the material out of which countries are made"),[54] a motley assortment of Swedes, Czechs, Germans, Austrians, Russians, Norwegians, and others forge a new nation (stop asking about those Indians!) despite their linguistic, national, and religious differences, all of which give them plenty of reasons for mutual distrust. The Shimerdas are a bit of a problem; they're Catholic (which means, in this context, "weird and superstitious"), the mother is a shrew, they live in extreme poverty, having been taken advantage of by a fellow Czech, and of course the father's suicide is terrible—not only because he blew his brains out in the barn, but because he leaves his neighbors with the question of where to bury him. The Norwegian graveyard will not have him, and Jim's grandmother is outraged: "If these foreigners are so clannish, Mr. Bushy, we'll have to have an American graveyard that will be more liberal-minded."[55] Yet Mrs. Shimerda and her oldest son insist that he be buried on the very corner of their own land, which would mean that eventually his resting place would consist of a crossroads. Now Jim's grandfather is outraged: "I don't know whose wish should decide the matter, if not hers. But if she thinks she will live to see the people of this country ride over that old man's head, she is mistaken."[56]

The details of cultural difference and the limits of cultural tolerance are everywhere, even on the open prairie; when Mrs. Shimerda demands that her youngest child touch her father's corpse at the funeral, Jim's grandmother intervenes: "'No, Mrs. Shimerda,'" she said firmly, 'I won't stand by and see that child frightened into spasms. She is too little to understand what you want of her. Let her alone.'"[57] My students fail to agree about whether Mrs. Burden is justified in this, so we look back at other examples of the Shimerdas' otherness—the dried mushrooms that the older Burdens somewhat ignorantly reject as "dried meat from some queer beast,"[58] or Mr. Shimerda's bizarrely devout gesture of worship to the Burdens' Christmas tree, to which Mr. Burden responds tactfully ("Grandfather merely put his finger-tips to his brow and bowed his venerable head, thus Protestantizing the atmosphere")[59] before saying, in an ecumenical spirit, "the prayers of all good people are good."[60] Here, too, the relations between "culture" and "society" are at issue, but this time, not in the conflict between old and new money in the rarefied, finely reticulated world of Boston's Back Bay, but in the extremely primitive, seemingly pre-social conditions of the wild plains. It is not clear, in the early 1880s, what kind of cultural differences will or won't prevent these immigrants from forming a society. The dried mushrooms don't pose too much of a problem; the differences in burial practices do.

When Jim moves to town, he becomes a fierce advocate for the immigrant girls of Nebraska. Noting that "there was a curious social situation in Black Hawk,"[61] he explains that the new arrivals are not constrained by the ideology of feminine domesticity, and therefore wind up driving the engines of prosperity and success in a stunningly short time:

> The daughters of Black Hawk merchants had a confident, unenquiring belief that they were "refined," and that the country girls, who "worked out," were not. The American farmers in our country were quite as hard-pressed as their neighbours from other countries. All alike had come to Nebraska with little capital and no knowledge of the soil they must subdue. All had borrowed money on their land. But no matter in what straits the Pennsylvanian or Virginian found himself, he would not let his daughters go out into service. Unless his girls could teach a country school, they sat at home in poverty.
>
> The Bohemian and Scandinavian girls could not get positions as teachers, because they had had no opportunity to learn the language. Determined to help in the struggle to clear the homestead from debt, they had no alternative but to go into service. . . . The girls I knew

were always helping to pay for ploughs and reapers, brood-sows, or steers to fatten.

One result of this family solidarity was that the foreign farmers in our country were the first to become prosperous. . . .

I always knew I should live long enough to see my country girls come into their own, and I have. To-day the best that a harassed Black Hawk merchant can hope for is to sell provisions and farm machinery and automobiles to the rich farms where that first crop of stalwart Bohemian and Scandinavian girls are now the mistresses.[62]

Not only do the immigrant girls help the families take over the region; they're also better dance partners than the American girls, about whom Jim sneers, "when one danced with them, their bodies never moved inside their clothes; their muscles seemed to ask but one thing—not to be disturbed."[63] Ántonia, by contrast, is a vivacious and exciting dancer: "she had so much spring and variety, and was always putting in new steps and slides."[64] Jim gets in trouble a few times for crossing the social borders and hanging out with the "disreputable" foreign girls, but this only adds to their allure, and to Jim's distinctive mode of self-congratulation: "I looked with contempt at the dark, silent little houses about me as I walked home, and thought of the stupid young men who were asleep in some of them. I knew where the real women were, though I was only a boy; and I would not be afraid of them, either!"[65] In the multiculturalism debates of 1918—which were even more vicious and nativist than most of what we've witnessed in the past twenty years—there's no question where *My Ántonia* stands: firmly on the side of the spirited, cosmopolitan, industrious foreigners. And as they assimilate—a process marked, in part, by Ántonia's pronunciation of the very word "country," which is first rendered phonetically as "kawn-tree" and then assimilated to the novel's standard English as Ántonia's speech improves—they become the flesh, blood, and muscle of the body politic.

But somewhere between Jim's departure from Black Hawk and his return twenty years later (when he is a lawyer working for one of the great railroads), something goes quite wrong with the novel's titular character. Ántonia does not assimilate; she is knocked up by a scoundrel in Denver, returns home in disgrace, gives birth, and eventually marries a fellow from the old kawn-tree and has ten more children with him. She has a fine farm with her pleasant and undemanding Czech husband, and tells Jim, "I've forgot my English so. I don't often talk it any more."[66]

The first time I taught the novel, I asked my students why Jim doesn't marry Ántonia in the first place; he winds up in a sterile, loveless marriage to a woman who, as we're told in the introduction, "finds it worth while to play the patroness to a group of young poets and painters of advanced ideas and mediocre ability. She has her own fortune and lives her own life."[67] He's a lawyer in New York, but his "quiet tastes irritate her," so she hangs out with some B-team modernists while he pines for the prairie girls and "loves with a personal passion the great country through which his railway runs and branches."[68] He even thinks, when he recalls dancing with Ántonia, "if, instead of going to the end of the railroad, old Mr. Shimerda had stayed in New York and picked up a living with his fiddle, how different Ántonia's life might have been!"[69] So why didn't Jim sweep up Ántonia and take her to New York where they could dance the night away together?

Asking this question, I've learned, is like pulling at a loose thread in the novel. We sometimes start with Jim's profession of love to Ántonia, just before he leaves Nebraska for twenty years: "I'd have liked to have you for a sweetheart, or a wife, or my mother or my sister—anything that a woman can be to a man. The idea of you is a part of my mind; you influence my likes and dislikes, all my tastes, hundreds of times when I don't realize it."[70] Some of my students flinch at this passage, just as I do. A sweetheart *or* a wife *or* a mother *or* a sister? No wonder he can't marry her! Or we can start with Jim's one ill-fated attempt to kiss Ántonia, which she decisively rebuffs, saying, "You know you ain't right to kiss me like that. I'll tell your grandmother on you!"[71] What follows this is extremely strange. Jim objects to being infantilized ("You'll always treat me like a kid, I suppose"), and Ántonia replies that he's "a kid I'm awful fond of"; she tells Jim how proud she is of him, and he thinks, "if she was proud of me, I was so proud of her that I carried my head high. . . . Her warm, sweet face, her kind arms, and the true heart in her; she was, oh, she was still my Ántonia!"[72] He's proud of her for repelling his kiss, and she's still his? It is here that he thinks dismissively of the "stupid young men" of the town and praises his own taste in foreign girls, and then the chapter ends like so:

> Toward morning I used to have pleasant dreams: sometimes Tony and I were out in the country, sliding down straw-stacks as we used to do; climbing up the yellow mountains over and over, and slipping down the smooth sides into soft piles of chaff.
>
> One dream I dreamed a great many times, and it was always the same. I was in a harvest-field full of shocks, and I was lying against one of them. Lena Lingard came across the stubble barefoot, in a short skirt, with a curved reaping-hook in her hand, and she was flushed like the dawn, with a kind of luminous rosiness all about her. She sat down beside me, turned to me with a soft sigh and said, "Now they are all gone, and I can kiss you as much as I like."
>
> I used to wish I could have this flattering dream about Ántonia, but I never did.[73]

When I ask my students what they think might be going on in this passage, most of them play it safe, noting the difference between the innocent hay-play with Tony (Ántonia) and the serious making-out with Lena, and concluding that it just doesn't work with Ántonia, and that's why they never marry. Look at that kiss, after all—it's too much like slipping the tongue to your older sister. But one semester, a student ventured, "Um, what's with Lena's reaping-hook? It's like she's killed them all or something," and the remark lit up the class. "No kidding," I replied. "Suddenly we move from *Little House on the Prairie* to *Nightmare on Elm Street*, and what's up with that?" It was a cheap laugh line, and it got some cheap laughs. But the serious point is that Lena Lingard's sexuality is dangerous. It messes men up and makes them go mad, like poor Ole Benson, who, people say, was driven out of his mind by the sight of her voluptuous figure out in the fields. And there is definitely the suggestion here that "they are all gone" because Lena the Reaper has seen to it somehow.

Not long thereafter, things get still stranger. The Black Hawk section of the novel ends not with Cather's famous image of the iconic plough silhouetted against the setting sun (that's in the section's penultimate chapter), but with a sexual assault—intended for Ántonia but instead perpetrated on Jim, who unwittingly serves as her decoy. Ántonia is working in a house owned by a notorious old molester named Wick Cutter, and that night he comes home to rape Ántonia, finds Jim in her bed, and beats him savagely. This is how Jim reacts to the episode, having saved Ántonia from a brutal rape:

I heard Ántonia sobbing outside my door, but I asked grandmother to send her away. I felt that I never wanted to see her again. I hated her almost as much as I hated Cutter. She had let me in for all this disgustingness. Grandmother kept saying how thankful we ought to be that I had been there instead of Ántonia. But I lay with my disfigured face to the wall and felt no particular gratitude. My one concern was that grandmother should keep everyone away from me. If the story once got abroad, I would never hear the last of it. I could well imagine what the old men down at the drugstore would do with such a theme.[74]

Could this get any weirder? Now it's somehow Ántonia's fault for letting Jim in for all this disgustingness, and suddenly our Jim, who was once so disdainful of petty Black Hawk gossip and petty Black Hawk people, is fretting away about what the old men at the drugstore might say. Most of my students agree: Jim should be damn proud for saving Ántonia. And if his manhood is at issue, he can take some pride in giving old Wick Cutter (a name which needs no elaboration) almost as good as he got. But Jim thinks no such thing, and—curiouser and curiouser—even the novel itself seems to "punish" Ántonia for her sexuality. "I asked grandmother to send her away"—but it is Cather who sends her away, for a long, long time. She does not appear for years after this scene, and when she returns to the novel, she returns as a fallen woman, pregnant and abandoned by the man who'd promised to marry her.

Meanwhile, the book is taken over by none other than Lena Lingard, for whom the third section is named. Jim briefly dates her in Lincoln, while he is attending the University of Nebraska, and Lena even extends him a most Mae West–like open invitation, "Come and see me sometimes when you're lonesome,"[75] but they do not roll in the hay. Instead, in her final scene with Jim, Lena delivers what will stand as the novel's most stinging rebuke to its own closing glorification of Ántonia, as she rips into the conventions of marriage and childbearing: "She told me she couldn't remember a time when she was so little that she wasn't lugging a heavy baby about, helping to wash for babies, trying to keep their little chapped hands and faces clean. She remembered home as a place where there were always too many children, a cross man and work piling up around a sick woman."[76] As for men, Lena says, "I don't want a husband. Men are all right for friends, but as soon as you marry them they turn into cranky old fathers, even the wild ones. They begin to tell you what's sensible and what's foolish, and want you to stick at home all the time. I prefer to be foolish when I feel like it, and be accountable to nobody."[77] Striking as this is, Lena isn't quite doing herself justice here. She is accountable to her mother time and again, vowing that "I'm going to get my mother out of that old sod house where she's lived so many years. The men will never do it,"[78] and reminding her younger siblings that their mother might like to receive handkerchiefs with her initial, B for Berthe, instead of M for Mother: "I'd get the B, Chrissy. It will please her for you to think about her name. Nobody ever calls her by it now."[79]

Indeed, although Lena is talked about—by absolutely everyone in the novel—as if she is a brazen hussy, "scantily dressed in tattered clothing"[80] while out in the fields and a threat to the morality of any civilized society when she moves to town, she enters the novel saying, "I've seen a good deal of married life, and I don't care for it,"[81] and leaves the same way, having established herself as a successful, independent dressmaker and having bought her mother the house she'd promised. Gradually, we learn that her tattered clothing was an index not of her immodesty but of her extreme poverty, and that far from driving Ole Benson insane out in the fields, as was rumored, she was the victim of his stalking—as well as of his wife's potentially homicidal madness. Still, despite all this, even the Widow Steavens, who seems to serve as Black Hawk's moral arbiter in such matters, refuses to alter her opinion of the girl: "My Ántonia, that had so much good in her, had come home disgraced. And that Lena Lingard, that was always a bad one, say what you will, had turned out so well, and was coming home every summer in her silks and her satins, and doing so much for her mother. I give credit where credit is due, but you know well enough, Jim Burden, there is a great difference in the principles of those two girls. And here it was the good one that had come to grief!"[82]

It's really quite astonishing when you take a good look at it. Time and again, Lena Lingard delivers the most pointed critiques of the patriarchal social conventions of her time, and she flouts them all. She turns into a self-made businesswoman and remains sexually untethered, and yet—or, more likely, as a result—the townspeople don't give her the time of day. I have a very hard time believing that Cather wrote this character into the novel by accident. She is almost certainly Ántonia's foil and counterpart, and Cather is almost certainly offering us a biting critique of the hypocrisy and provinciality of people who insist that Lena was always a bad one, say what you will.

It was at this point, in my 2003 class, that one of my students asked if Cather was trying to "queer the prairie." When I asked him to be more specific, he said he believed that Cather was deliberately depicting social relationships that challenge or trouble the traditions of heterosexual marriage, and deliberately creating sexually ambiguous characters. Very possibly, I replied, but remember, as to the first point, the novel's not called *My Lena*. Although Cather's novel contains a serious critique of wife-and-mother domesticity, the novel ends in a resounding affirmation of wife-and-mother domesticity. I think that's the truly singular thing about the novel— the nostalgic, sentimental conclusion combined with all the events in the narrative that work precisely against that conclusion. As for whether Cather actually attempted to create "queer" characters in order to queer the prairie, there seems to me no decisive reason to conclude that Jim Burden himself is "really" gay, or that (even more reductively) Cather was writing from a "lesbian" position by adopting the narrative voice of a man (she'd already had some experience at this, having ghostwritten magazine-publishing magnate S. S. McClure's autobiography). Some critics have suggested that Jim's sexuality is elusive, as if he's playing at being a little man when he kills a rattlesnake on the prairie and then playing at being a gay-man-in-training when he weeps and gushes over the opera *Camille* in Lincoln. Some have suggested that Ántonia's sexuality is almost as elusive, as she shifts back and forth between the vivacious Ántonia and the tomboy Tony.[83] But there's no question that Jim is queer, because the novel itself says so: "Anna knew the whisper was going about that I was a sly one. People said there must be something queer about a boy who showed no interest in girls of his own age, but who could be lively enough when he was with Tony or Lena or the three Marys."[84]

"Now, wait a second," students say, "Cather didn't mean 'queer' in *that* sense." That's right; the passage suggests that "queer" is a rough synonym of "sly," and Jim's queerness has less to do with homosexuality than with a kind of ethnic border-crossing. He has no interest in girls of his own age . . . unless they're the immigrant girls, and his liveliness around *them* makes him queer. Sexuality and ethnicity are all tied together here, and though Jim isn't marked as gay, he is marked as "a sly one." There's just something not quite right about the boy, or so the people of Black Hawk tell themselves. For my part, I think Jim is, appropriately, about as elusive as was the writer who created him. He may look in some respects like a gay man who has plenty of girlfriends, a passionate love of opera, and a loveless, sham marriage; but he also has erotic dreams about Lena and reaping-hooks, and an unfathomable blame-the-intended-victim reaction to Ántonia's foiled rape. It simply doesn't add up, and *that's* what is really queer about it all. If Jim were unambiguously presented as gay, in the literary conventions of the time, we could "place" him. But we can't. And that makes his character even queerer—and more interesting—than it would be if we could say with interpretive certainty that Cather deliberately gave us a gay protagonist to go along with Lena Lingard's critiques of coupledom and child-rearing.[85]

Time and again, I find that my undergraduates will entertain just about any reading of a literary work—as long as there is some reasonably plausible evidence that the author intended it that way. With Howells I get relatively few questions on this score; with Johnson, the debate centers on how the author wanted us to view the narrator; with Cather, I often throw up my hands. I tell students that Cather was an exceptionally nostalgic writer who got more nostalgic as she got older, and that, even when she was writing in 1918, there seems to be no question that much of Jim's nostalgia for old Nebraska is also hers. She famously remarked, later in life, that the world "broke" for her in 1922, and the Virgilian epigraph to the novel, *"optima dies . . . prima fugit"*—the best days are the first to flee—seems to be echoed both in her work and in her life. But at the same time, maybe Cather is not merely expressing, but working with or working out, that sense of nostalgia in *My Ántonia*, so that she also provides us with a critique of it.

Lest my students get too bent out of shape about Cather's intentions, I remind them that there's no sense in which Cather owns the literary-criticism copyright to every possible interpretation of her work. There are intended meanings and unintended meanings in any complex human utterance, and literary works are certainly no exception. If a student wants to write an essay that proposes a reading of this novel that she doesn't think Cather herself might have intended, that's fine with me—as long as she's aware that that's what she's doing, and as long as she has the necessary textual evidence in front of her. Still, my students want to know: how can we tell the difference between an intentionalist reading and some other kind of reading, and what makes that other kind of reading OK or not OK? I tell them to think of it this way: take the difference between the claim, "Cather wrote a novel about the prairie that is also a novel about gender roles," and the claim, "Cather meant to write a novel about the prairie that is also a novel about gender roles." The second statement clearly obliges one to provide evidence of Cather's explicit intentions; the first merely requires one to show that Cather's novel addresses questions of gender and sexuality, regardless of whether she wanted it to or not. Furthermore, we can take up those questions in ways Cather herself might not have liked—again, as long as we're aware that this may be what we're doing. This reading might sound like it involves a lower interpretive standard, insofar as it is not beholden to an author's statements about his or her work. But such a reading still needs to win the assent of both its real and hypothetical readers; the real ones should come away from such a paper thinking, "Hmm, I never really paid attention to those passages, but yeah, sure enough, Lena offers a counterweight to the closing glorification of Ántonia." And that's why I tell my students that when they start to plan their essays, they don't have to write only those things they think Cather would agree with—or, for that matter, only those things they think I might agree with. Such considerations should be irrelevant to them. All I ask is that their interpretations be plausible, and my criteria are lawyerly and austere. One, I read their essays to see how well they handle textual evidence, that is, how well they support whatever claims they make by reference to the material in front of them; and two, I want to know how well they anticipate and head off plausible counterarguments. That's it. Meet those two criteria in my classroom, and the field of interpretation is open.

Now THAT WE'VE historicized postbellum Boston, revisited lynching, and queered the prairie, what manner of harm can we inflict on F. Scott Fitzgerald? Surely a course like mine can come up with some way of transforming Gatsby's doomed love for Daisy into a critique of capitalism and bourgeois individualism?

Actually, a course like mine can't quite manage that feat. Fitzgerald's novel offers a complex and skeptical revision of the notion of the self-made man; it manages to deromanticize and then to reromanticize Gatsby, and it questions the distinction between legitimate and illegitimate ways of accumulating wealth. But I have to admit that it probably wasn't intended as a full-blown critique of capitalism and bourgeois individualism. To say this is simply to remark that *The Great Gatsby* was not written by Tony Kushner.[86] Still, because I have found time and again that the major challenge in teaching *The Great Gatsby* is to prevent undergraduates from writing generic essays about Jay Gatsby and the American Dream, the day that some clever twenty-year-old decides to read Fitzgerald "against the grain" is a good day. So I take seriously all such questions about capitalism and bourgeois individualism. Indeed, for most students, the novel is unreadable for the same reason *Adventures of Huckleberry Finn* is unreadable; they have read it in high school, and they have faithfully memorized the green light, the fresh green breast of the new world, and (yes) the American Dream. Teaching the novel to those students is a far more difficult challenge than teaching it to students who wish it had been written by Tony Kushner.

The Great Gatsby is more familiar to my students than the other novels I've discussed in this chapter, and more familiar to most general readers as well; for that reason, I won't bother summarizing the book. I will, however, insist that Nick Carraway is, in some ways, almost as elusive as Jim Burden; asking students to explain Nick's attitude toward Gatsby is tantamount to asking them to reread more than half of the book. Gatsby, Nick says, "represented everything for which I have an unaffected scorn" and yet had an "extraordinary gift for hope, a romantic readiness such as I have never found in any other person and which it is not likely I shall ever find again."[87] Much later, he tells Gatsby, "They're a rotten crowd. . . . You're worth the whole damn bunch put together."[88] Slight praise, this, since Tom and Daisy are a truly rotten crowd, yet Nick follows it with a disclaimer: "I've always been glad I said that. It was the only compliment I ever gave him, because I disapproved of him from beginning to end."[89] This disclaimer isn't quite true, either; when Gatsby admits to Tom that he attended Oxford for only five months as part of "an opportunity they gave to some of the officers after the Armistice," Nick says, "I wanted to get up and slap him on the back. I had one of those renewals of complete faith in him that I'd experienced before."[90] Unaffected scorn, tempered by admiration; disapproval from beginning to end, punctuated by renewals of complete faith. Odd, isn't it?

It's odd, too, that Nick ends the third chapter with the sly line, "Every one suspects himself of at least one of the cardinal virtues, and this is mine: I am one of the few honest people that I have ever known."[91] But he says this just after letting us know that all the time he's been dating Jordan, "I knew that first I had to get myself definitely out of that tangle back home. I'd been writing letters once a week and signing them: 'Love, Nick'."[92] We don't know anything about this other love interest; we know only that Tom and Daisy have asked him whether he had been engaged to be married: "Of course I knew what they were referring to," Nick writes, "but I wasn't even vaguely engaged. The fact that gossip had published the banns was one of the reasons I had come East. You can't stop going with an old friend on account of rumors, and on the other hand I had no intention of being rumored into marriage."[93] Nick's treatment of this other woman may or may not be dishonest; it is certain, however, that in his relation to us, he occasionally forgoes honesty in favor of discretion.

This is a minor example (Nick's love interest in the Midwest is not critical to the novel), but it suffices to make a larger point: Nick's ambivalence about Gatsby structures the entire narrative. As he begins, in chapter 6, to reveal (and unravel) Gatsby's real history as Jimmy Gatz, he tells us, "I've put it down here with the idea of exploding those first wild rumors about his antecedents, which weren't even faintly true."[94] Fair enough: Nick's account of James Gatz of North Dakota is unquestionably more reliable than the rumors that Gatsby was a German spy, or that he killed a man. And it's far more reliable than Gatsby's initial account of himself:

> "I'll tell you God's truth." His right hand suddenly ordered divine retribution to stand by. "I am the son of some wealthy people in the Middle West—all dead now. I was brought up in America but educated at Oxford, because all my ancestors have been educated there for many years. It is a family tradition. . . .

"After that I lived like a young rajah in all the capitals of Europe—Paris, Venice, Rome—collecting jewels, chiefly rubies, hunting big game, painting a little, things for myself only, and trying to forget something very sad that had happened to me long ago."[95]

Nick responds not merely to the implausibility of all this, but also (and particularly) to its secondhand quality, as if Gatsby were the author of lousy genre fiction: "With an effort I managed to restrain my incredulous laughter. The very phrases were worn so threadbare that they evoked no image except that of a turbaned 'character' leaking sawdust at every pore as he pursued a tiger through the Bois de Boulogne."[96] As I tell my students, we instinctively trust Nick at such moments; he is a deft deflater of pretension, and has been since the moment when, in the opening pages of the novel, he deflated his own family's pretensions. "The Carraways are something of a clan," he writes, "and we have a tradition that we're descended from the Dukes of Buccleuch, but the actual founder of my line was my grandfather's brother, who came here in fifty-one, sent a substitute to the Civil War, and started the wholesale hardware business that my father carries on to-day."[97] Obviously, the narrator who disclaims the lineage of the Dukes of Buccleuch in favor of the story of two generations of hardware dealers will have little patience with Gatsby's ridiculous capsule autobiography, and will, conversely, want to get up and slap Gatsby on the back when he finally admits to the truth about his brief time at Oxford.

We trust Nick to see through Gatsby, and through his house, that "imitation of some Hôtel de Ville in Normandy, with a tower on one side, spanking new under a thin beard of raw ivy."[98] The raw ivy is the key, as is Nick's ability to spot it—an ability which turns out, before too long, to be of a piece with his ability to spot less obvious forms of counterfeit. After Daisy professes to world-weariness and despair at her life with Tom, Nick responds:

The instant her voice broke off, ceasing to compel my attention, my belief, I felt the basic insincerity of what she had said. It made me uneasy, as though the whole evening had been a trick of some sort to exact a contributory emotion from me. I waited, and sure enough, in a moment she looked at me with an absolute smirk on her lovely face, as if she had asserted her membership in a rather distinguished secret society to which she and Tom belonged.[99]

Nick is right on both counts: the purpose of the evening, and the meaning of that smirk. But, I ask my students, if Nick is so perceptive about such tiny gestures and inflections, how is it that he is so enchanted by Daisy's voice, and how is it that Gatsby, of all people, punctures the illusion more deftly than he? Nick tells us, with a full flourish of Fitzgerald's remarkable lyricism:

it was the kind of voice that the ear follows up and down, as if each speech is an arrangement of notes that will never be played again. Her face was sad and lovely with bright things in it, bright eyes and a bright passionate mouth, but there was an excitement in her voice that men who had cared for her found difficult to forget: a singing compulsion, a whispered "Listen," a promise that she had done gay, exciting things just a while since and that that there were gay, exciting things hovering in the next hour.[100]

Compare this to Gatsby's seemingly brutal and reductive line, "her voice is full of money." To which Nick abruptly assents: "That was it. I'd never understood before."[101]

Gatsby gets it, and Nick doesn't, partly because Gatsby is far more vividly aware of just how much those gay, exciting things cost, and partly because he is (as a result) less deceived, in this respect, about his love for Daisy. His account of their first kiss might well have been full of "appalling sentimentality," as Nick suggests,[102] but, at the same time, Gatsby freely acknowledges the more, shall we say, mercenary aspects of his infatuation. "It excited him, too," Nick writes, "that many men had already loved Daisy— it increased her value in his eyes."[103] Daisy is a hot property, in this sense, and her hotness depends in part on her distance from the "hot struggles of the poor"; "Gatsby was overwhelmingly aware"— see, it's right there in the text—"of the youth and mystery that wealth imprisons and preserves, of the freshness of many clothes, and of Daisy, gleaming like silver, safe and proud above the hot struggles of the poor."[104] Gatsby is terribly romantic and sentimental about Daisy, never quite realizing that the woman of his dreams is only the woman of his *dreams*, and that the real Daisy is not merely as shallow and as self-dramatizing as Nick perceives but so morally corrupt that she will allow Gatsby to take the blame for Myrtle's death. But by the same token, Nick turns out to be rather romantic about Gatsby, and never more so than when he recounts Gatsby's death.

It took me two readings of the novel to realize just how much of the paragraph about Gatsby's death is the work of Nick's imagination, so I try not to let students leave the class without trying to come to terms with it. Gatsby, you'll recall, is waiting for word from Daisy rather than taking Nick's advice and fleeing "to Atlantic City for a week, or up to Montreal"; "He wouldn't consider it," says Nick. "He couldn't possibly leave Daisy until he knew what she was going to do":[105]

No telephone message arrived, but the butler went without his sleep and waited for it until four o'clock—until long after there was any one to give it to if it came. I have an idea that Gatsby himself didn't believe it would come, and perhaps he no longer cared. If that was true he must have felt that he had lost the old warm world, paid a high price for living too long with a single dream. He must have looked up at an unfamiliar sky through frightening leaves and shivered as he found what a grotesque thing a rose is and how raw the sunlight was upon the scarcely created grass. A new world, material without being real, where poor ghosts, breathing dreams like air, drifted fortuitously about . . . like that ashen, fantastic figure gliding toward him through the amorphous trees.[106]

What a flight of fancy this is, coming from someone whose self-appointed task it had been to set the record straight about Gatsby. But just before Wilson (for it is he) creeps up to kill Gatsby and himself (for this is no doubt what is about to happen), can we stop to remark at the stunning quality of this passage, its stark vision of the unfamiliar sky, the frightening leaves, the grotesque rose, and the raw sunlight upon the scarcely created grass? It is a "new world," all right, the demonic counterpart to the "fresh green breast of the new world" evoked on the novel's final page; it is uncanny in the sense of the German word *unheimlich*, a word which philosopher Martin Heidegger insisted on rendering as "not-at-home." That's how Gatsby feels here, not-at-home among the frightening leaves and the scarcely created grass—or so we think, until we realize that everything after the first sentence of this passage is Nick's doing: "I have an idea," "perhaps," and then a supposition within a supposition, "if that was true." Actually, we don't know that Gatsby died for a dream. For all we know, one of his mob connections might have arrived—we know that Gatsby's phone line "was being kept open for long distance from Detroit"—and killed both Wilson and Gatsby before fleeing the scene. Not likely, I know. But it would give another color entirely to Gatsby's death, and another meaning to Nick's description of the "foul dust" that "floated in the wake of his dreams."[107]

The argument here is a simple one: just as Gatsby creates a "Daisy" in the course of re-creating himself as Gatsby, so too does Nick create a "Gatsby" in the course of "temporarily clos[ing] out my interest in the abortive sorrows and short-winded elations of men."[108] One is left to wonder whether the object is really worth it;

on that justly famous final page, after all, Nick likens Gatsby's "wonder when he first picked out the green light at the end of Daisy's dock"[109] to the wonder of Dutch sailors at the sight of the new world. The analogy runs the risk of rendering Gatsby ludicrous again, as does the phrase in the penultimate paragraph, "Gatsby believed in the green light";[110] maybe, on second thought, Gatsby is just a vainglorious dweller in the valley of ashes, a Mr. Nobody from Nowhere with a pink suit and an ostentatious house with brand-new ivy, in love with a vacuous beauty whose voice is full of money. But it invites us, also, to ask whether Nick's re-presentation of Gatsby partakes of what is either Gatsby's extraordinary gift for hope or Gatsby's plumb foolishness. Nick wants to believe that Gatsby was disillusioned at the very end—that he knew Daisy would not call, and (perhaps) no longer cared. But (perhaps) this is only Nick's illusion. Such, at least, is one of the traditional readings of the novel: humans can't handle too much reality, as T. S. Eliot once told us, and we have to delude ourselves about something in order to beat on, boats against the current.

But then I add to this observation, some version of which many students have encountered in high school, the following question: does it matter that Gatsby is a bootlegger? Assuming that one of Meyer Wolfsheim's associates did not, in fact, murder Gatsby at the end, and that he dies because Daisy did not admit that she had been driving the car that struck Myrtle, do we care that Gatsby makes his money illegitimately? If so, why?

I ask my students this question for two reasons: first, because it gives some historical specificity to airy talk about the American Dream, and second, because it is (or should be) part of the larger question of "value" in the novel, in which Daisy is a desirable commodity and Gatsby is worth the whole damn lot put together. Gatsby was swindled out of his first inheritance of $25,000, left to him by Dan Cody; he turns to bootlegging only because it represents the surest way of amassing enough wealth to peer across the bay at Daisy's house, and make a play to take her away from Tom. As far as I'm concerned, Gatsby's road to riches isn't much more corrupt than any real estate magnate's or robber baron's; though he's involved in organized crime, it's not like he's dealing hard drugs. He's simply selling alcohol over the counter in "drug" stores—though I admit that when Tom says, "you've got something on now that Walter's afraid to tell me about,"[111] a more sinister note is sounded, and in the final chapter we learn that Gatsby may also have been involved in passing stolen or counterfeit bonds. But I bring up the question of Gatsby's legitimacy not because I'm a moral relativist (as I insist to the class), but because if you look at, say, The Godfather, The Sopranos, or most other organized-crime narratives, they quite explicitly question the distinction between legitimate and illegitimate business. And it's the 1920s—it's Prohibition we're talking about, for goodness' sake. I ask the class: how many of you think it's more or less OK for Gatsby to sell alcohol during Prohibition? No hands. All right, then, how many students support Prohibition? Still no hands. This doesn't make any sense. I decide not to ask how many of them have engaged in underage drinking.

In 2003 I was especially skeptical of my students' disapproval of Gatsby. This was the same class that had insisted, a few months earlier, that they would not have sold the mills to Rogers if they were in Silas Lapham's position. So I mentioned the names of Enron, of Tyco, of WorldCom, and of our little local scandal, Adelphia. You've got corporate crime up and down the street these days, I noted, and yet no one wants to cut poor Gatsby a little bit of slack? Come on, people, I urged, the crash of 1929 wasn't caused by bootleggers. It was brought on by corporate creeps and crooks and Ponzi schemers, the Jazz Age counterparts to Kenneth Lay and Dennis Kozlowski and Bernard Ebbers. Jay Gatsby is not a threat to the financial—or the moral—health of the nation. I'm not suggesting that Tom Buchanan's family made their money by defrauding pensioners and stockholders, of course; we don't know where Tom's money comes from. We know that Nick is a bond trader, and that, as he puts it, "Everybody I knew was in the bond business, so I supposed it could support one more single man."[112] But we do know how Gatsby made his money, and Fitzgerald is clearly inviting us to think about the possible sources of wealth—and above and beyond that, cultural legitimacy—available to a savvy but penniless striver like Jimmy Gatz who has none of the vast inherited wealth of a Buchanan and none of the (recently accumulated) cultural capital of a Carraway.

Did Fitzgerald intend to write a critique of capitalism and bourgeois individualism? I doubt it. None of his remarks on *Gatsby* suggest such a thing. But then again, is it possible to read *Gatsby* as a novel that asks what our culture values and how? Is it possible to press the question a bit further, and ask about how value itself is rendered in the novel? Though it's far too reductive (actually, it's downright silly) to imagine Daisy as a junk bond, look again at the language of Nick's lyrical account of Gatsby's murder; perhaps he had, after all, "paid a high price for living too long with a single dream." This is the language of unwise investment strategies. Gatsby's world, like the world of (legitimate) bonds in which Nick works, is somehow "material without being real." And perhaps the story of Gatsby's wealth is something more than just the story of Gatsby's wealth; perhaps it is also an account of the times, an updated Howellsian tale of the clash between new money and old. "A lot of these newly rich people are just big bootleggers, you know," says Tom, and though Nick replies, defensively, "not Gatsby," we know Tom is right.[113] Perhaps *The Great Gatsby* is not only about love and the green light across the bay, but also about culture, society, and systems of value that traverse both "legitimate" and "illegitimate" economies. But to suggest such a thing, I think, is only to suggest that *The Great Gatsby* is a great novel, a novel whose intellectual complexity and beauty become only more vivid when you can get a class of undergraduates to reread the fresh green breast of the new world with fresh eyes.

And sometimes, when you want to get undergraduates to reread a book—knowing, as you should, that many of them do not yet see the point of rereading something they read only a few years ago—you need to historicize it for them. You need to take a "timeless classic" and show them that it's not timeless, but that it can, with some effort, be seen as belonging to both its time and ours. Yes, there are themes that run through literary works from vastly different times and places. On some level, both *Hamlet* and *Invisible Man* are "about" betrayal; on some level, both Edmund Spenser's *The Faerie Queene* and Robert Frost's "The Need of Being Versed in Country Things" or "After Apple-Picking" are "about" the question of whether literary form can salvage order from chaos and entropy. But to work at that extraordinary level of generality in the college classroom seems to me irresponsible. Literary criticism, college version, should at least ask students to ask how literary works speak to, from, about, and out of their cultural moment—not so as to advance this or that historicist agenda, but so as to lead students to see just how complex and remarkable works like *The Canterbury Tales* or *Madame Bovary* or *The Great Gatsby* truly are, and that their complexity has as much to do with their vigorous participation in the literature and culture of late-fourteenth-century England or mid-nineteenth-century France or pre-Depression New York as with their uncanny ability to speak to us across hundreds of years and thousands of miles.

I have never quite understood why, in the academic culture wars of the past generation, intellectual conservatives have been so opposed to this position. Why is there so little "conservative" historicism in the humanities? Why, exactly, should the division of intellectual labor have fallen out this way, in which the intellectual left says, "Let's try to understand how feudalism, mercantile capitalism, industrial capitalism, post-industrial capitalism, etc., inflected the production and reception of works of art," and the intellectual right says, "No! works of art are timeless, timeless, timeless"? And then the intellectual left says, "But aren't you curious as to why some works of art survive and remain powerful for centuries, whereas others gradually drop out of sight, and still others are acknowledged only long after their creators are dead?" And the right replies, "There's nothing to be curious about! Some artists are great and some aren't, that's all." In this, as in other schools of cultural criticism, the intellectual right hasn't brought anything to the table in decades. No doubt that's one reason why liberals and leftists have dominated literary criticism and theory, and it's certainly contributed to a state of affairs in which historically informed readings of literary works are associated exclusively with the left, either in the person of Stephen Greenblatt, inventor of the so-called new historicism, or in the person of Marxist critic Fredric Jameson, whose well-known motto is the bite-size dictum, "Always historicize!" Perhaps the student who asked me about capitalism and individualism in *The Great Gatsby* was picking up on this, and assuming that any professor with an interest in historical context would necessarily be a critic of capitalism and individualism. If that was the case, and if this assumption is widely shared, then I have some words for you:

> To perceive a work not only in its isolation, as an object of aesthetic contemplation, but also as implicated in the life of a people at a certain time, as expressing that life, and as being in part shaped by it, does not, in most people's experience, diminish the power or charm of the work but, on the contrary, enhances it.[114]

Those words were written not by a contemporary Marxist critic but by Lionel Trilling, liberal humanist man of letters and cultural critic. Paradoxical as it may sound, I think they have stood the test of time quite well over the years.

6. Postmodernism

THE "POSTMODERNISM AND AMERICAN FICTION" class is the most rigorous undergraduate course I've taught. It covers a wide range of material, some of which is forbiddingly difficult to read, and because it's an honors seminar, which some people (mistakenly) consider to be an easy teaching assignment, I find that I do three or four times more preparation-and-response work for this course than I do for the standard American literature survey. Although I've taught versions of this course six times (twice as a graduate seminar), I've never taught the same lineup of readings twice, partly because I like to keep myself on my toes and partly because I'm never convinced that everything really worked the last time around. I always ask students for feedback on this in their written evaluations of the course, and I always find that something—some theorist, some novelist—just didn't go over for some reason. So I go back and reshuffle the deck. I've opened the course with three straight novels (*Pale Fire*, *The Crying of Lot 49*, *The Left Hand of Darkness*), with Thomas Kuhn's *The Structure of Scientific Revolutions*, and (most recently) with Ridley Scott's 1982 film *Blade Runner*. I usually assign a range of contemporary novelists, from well-known figures like Thomas Pynchon, Kathy Acker, Richard Powers, and Toni Morrison to relatively unsung writers like Richard Grossman (author of *The Alphabet Man* and *The Book of Lazarus*) and Randall Kenan (*A Visitation of Spirits*). I also assign a packet or two of contemporary critical theorists, some of whom shaped the contours of the postmodernism debate (Fredric Jameson, Jean Baudrillard, Jean-François Lyotard), and some of whom filed critical minority reports (Nancy Fraser, Stuart Hall, Andreas Huyssen).

Once the course gets rolling, my students and I talk about what it means to be an antifoundationalist—that is, one of those secular people who believe that it's best to operate as if our moral and epistemological principles derive not from divine will or so-called "natural" law but from ordinary social practices. Starting first with Kuhn's history of science (and threading our way through the many misreadings of Kuhn among humanists),[1] we turn to Richard Rorty's antifoundationalist philosophy, a pleasant kind of enterprise in which people converse about the good and the true without thinking about whether their claims can be grounded in something that is not merely another claim. We argue about whether antifoundationalism is any different from moral relativism. We linger over postmodernism's critiques of Jürgen Habermas's theory of communicative action, debating whether any critique of reason can be cogent or persuasive unless it, too, implicitly relies on some norms for communication. Then we debate what counts as legitimate debate, and what happens when debaters disagree so fundamentally and violently that they can't even find the words in which to disagree. For the most part, students find it to be confusing, stimulating, and fun, and they tend to leave with the impression that they've engaged some of the most important intellectual issues of our day.

But I'm getting ahead of myself. What is postmodernism in the first place, and why should anyone be subjected to courses in it? Some of my students—and most people outside of academe—understand "postmodernism" either as a shorthand epitaph for the bygone trendy, jargon-ridden bullshit of the 1980s and 1990s or as a synonym for trendy, jargon-ridden bullshit in general. So perhaps a few preliminary explanations are in order.

The simplest answer (though it turns out to be trickier than it sounds) is that postmodernism is the stuff that comes after modernism, and that's how the term was used by art critics in the 1960s and by architecture critics and theorists in the 1970s. Or you could say, as literary critics Andreas Huyssen and Charles Newman have done, that postmodernism follows from the institutionalization of modernism, well after the modernist revolution was over and the artworks themselves had been officially designated as classic.[2] After all, there's a pretty clear dividing line between the titanic, anguished paintings of abstract expressionists like Willem de Kooning and Jackson Pollock, on the one hand, and the apparently superficial, cool, commercial art of Roy Lichtenstein or Andy Warhol. That's a standard reference point for modern–postmodern discussions: the lone, tormented, avant-garde artist and his (almost always his) struggles to discover the very essence of painting, over against the wry, ironic hipster whose "artworks" seem to be indistinguishable from comic-book clichés, Hollywood posters, or soup cans. Likewise, in architecture, the modern–postmodern divide is clear, and has widely-agreed-on reference points: Le Corbusier's rational, steel-and-glass cities are modern, whereas Las Vegas's anything-goes combination of roadside stands and rhinestone-studded excess is postmodern.[3] It just so happens that the two New York buildings most often cited as examples of modernism and postmodernism are only a few blocks from each other: Gordon Bunshaft's Lever House on 52nd Street and Park Avenue, completed in 1952, one of the first International Style buildings in Manhattan, and Philip Johnson's AT&T building on 54th Street and Madison Avenue, completed in 1984 and immediately derided as the world's first Chippendale skyscraper. Today, both buildings are enveloped in historical ironies; in 1992, Lever House became the first steel-and-glass building in New York to be designated an official landmark (over the screams of a few dogged traditionalists), and now it seems to evoke an earlier, more innocent era of Manhattan office buildings in that it uses only a fraction of its available airspace. And in 1992, AT&T moved out of the AT&T building, reportedly, in part, because the corporation did not want to be associated with a massive, granite-and-limestone headquarters that looked like a neoclassical piece of furniture. The building itself remains, however, and has spawned two decades' worth of imitations—even though none of them has precisely duplicated that Chippendale top.

In architecture and art, then, it's possible to sketch out a rough draft of modernism and postmodernism in a single class. Literature, by contrast, isn't so simple. Experimental postmodern literature resembles experimental modern literature more than it resembles anything else, and although there are some noticeable differences between the two—postmodern experimentalists tend to be somewhat more enamored of hallucinatory or conspiratorial alternative histories than their modernist counterparts—these differences are relatively slight, on balance. The problem is that every attempt to define postmodern fiction in stylistic terms—as a form of writing that defeats readers' expectations of coherence, as experimental narrative that plays with generic conventions, as fiction that dwells on ambiguity and uncertainty—winds up being a definition of modernist fiction as well. Worse still, such definitions can also cover novels like Laurence Sterne's eighteenth-century masterwork, *Tristram Shandy*, or Miguel de Cervantes's *Don Quixote*. If it's authorial self-reflexivity you want, try the second half of *Don Quixote,* in which every character has read the first half of the book and humors the old knight-errant accordingly. (There's even a surreal scene in which Don Quixote catches another character reading Avallenada's counterfeit version of Book Two and denounces its lack of realism.) You want fictional narrative flaunting its own fictionality? Been there, done that, seen that, not only in André Gide's modernist classic, *The Counterfeiters,* but also in key moments of Chaucer's *The Canterbury Tales* and Spenser's *The Faerie Queene.* Experiments with traditional genres? *Ulysses.* Infinite circularity?

The Thousand and One Nights. Sure, there are postmodern novelists whose sense of the contingency of all narrative goes a bit beyond that of their modernist predecessors, but, by and large, there's nothing uniquely postmodern about most of the experiments conducted in contemporary experimental fiction.

The standard rejoinder to that statement runs like so: yes, there were experimental works in other eras and other centuries, but they were exceptions, not representative of the vast majority of works produced at the time. *Tristram Shandy* aside, most eighteenth-century fiction remains interested in more or less realistic renderings of individual consciousness and social settings. True enough. But then again, so-called postmodern works of fiction are *still* singular exceptions to the contemporary rule. As the novelist and critic William Gass once put it, the dominant form of fiction in the twentieth century was the nineteenth-century novel, if by "dominant" you mean the kind of literature most people actually read. There's nothing postmodern about most of today's popular writers, like Maeve Binchy or John Grisham. More tellingly, there's nothing especially postmodern about most critically acclaimed writers of "quality fiction," either. Richard Ford, E. Annie Proulx, Michael Chabon, Philip Roth, Madison Smartt Bell, Ann Beattie, Oscar Hijuelos—those are some of the most prominent writers of our time, and you can't plausibly call them postmodernists. For the most part, they seem to be capable, mimesis-minded chroniclers of contemporary life.

So, in the past, my attempts to explain to students the difference between modern and postmodern literature have involved some nervous coughing and jingling of keys in the coat pocket, as I've acknowledged that modernist fiction is fragmentary, experimental, and self-reflexive, but that postmodern fiction is, um, well, more so. I've recently discovered, however, that there are any number of postmodern writers and critics out there who defend the distinction fiercely. Some of them have written me scorching e-mails that

begin, "YOU FOOL!!! Don't you KNOW that I and I ALONE
have broken with the Western mimetic tradition since Plato!!!! In
my recent cryptofiction I have proven this beyond the last Cartesian
shadow of metaphysical doubt!" Some of them have raised interesting questions about whether science fiction is postmodern, and how
we should try to account for recent experiments with hypertext.
And some of them have suggested that there's an informal International Magic Realism Association, ranging from Salman Rushdie to
Zadie Smith to Gabriel García Márquez to Toni Morrison, that
constitutes a kind of global postmodern and/or postcolonial fiction
consortium. I'm willing to entertain most of these suggestions, even
the ones written in random caps-lock mode. But the fact remains
that there's a five-decade history of definitions of literary postmodernism, and that the first attempts to create such definitions in the
1960s and 1970s amounted largely to self-promotional brochures on
the part of a couple of experimentalists (such as Raymond Feder-
man and Ron Sukenick) trying desperately to distinguish themselves from previous generations of experimentalists. To say that
those theories are chiefly of historical interest today is, I think,
merely to give them their due—and to make the ancillary point
(always useful for students) that we should expect theories of postmodernism to change with each decade, since what we're really
dealing with, in such theories, are our contemporary attempts to
grasp the contemporary.

The question of whether science fiction is postmodern, curiously
enough, is structurally similar to the question of whether feminism
is postmodern. As I point out in the "feminism" section of the class,
feminists and postmodernists didn't seem to have much use for
each other through most of the 1980s, even though some feminist
artists—Jenny Holzer, Sherry Levine, Cindy Sherman, Barbara
Kruger—were doing work that could plausibly be considered
among the best postmodern stuff out there. Yet feminism wasn't
invented in 1968; its contemporary roots go back to the nineteenth

century, and the same thing can be said of science fiction, which, for all of its cyberpunk and posthuman manifestations today, can trace itself to Jules Verne and H. G. Wells. Some of the phenomena that we call postmodern might actually predate modernism; meanwhile, the vast majority of the cultural work going on today isn't postmodernist. Is postmodernism an era, then, or a style, or something else? A candy mint, or a breath mint?

There's another way to think about this—in terms of what I call the means of cultural transmission.[4] Here's what I mean: there is no one cultural center, no Academy that authorizes certain forms of art and delegitimates others, and therefore there are no distinct cultural margins, either; as a result, seemingly avant-garde artists like Sherman can wind up being profiled in the pages of USA Today (as she was in 1993).[5] At the same time, what the prewar German Marxist critic Walter Benjamin called the problem of "the work of art in the age of mechanical reproduction" has quite dramatically given way to the problem of the work of art in the age of electronic transmission, and anyone with a laptop and an Internet connection can take a virtual tour of the Louvre. In this sense, postmodernism, as a means of cultural transmission, has the capacity to absorb anything from neo-medieval architecture to conceptual art involving rotting meat, or the capacity to revisit and revise anything, as if it were what art critic Hal Foster aptly called "a computer virus in the history mainframe."[6] Something like that computer virus seems to be at work in the literary subgenre of "historiographic metafiction," in which writers like Thomas Pynchon, Ishmael Reed, Robert Coover, E. L. Doctorow, Don DeLillo, and company mix the features of the traditional historical novel with aspects of surreal or carnivalesque nonfiction *and* with implicit and explicit meditations on the relation between writing fictional narratives and historical narratives. In fact, the reason I now open the course with *Blade Runner* (the director's cut, of course, without that horrible narrative voiceover) is to try to make this initial point about postmodernism's omnivorousness. Think of those huge ceiling fans humming over the initial interrogation scene in *Blade Runner,* the blue cigarette smoke curling around the characters as the detective tries to determine whether Leon is human: we're in a future where androids are so technologically advanced as to be nearly indistinguishable from humans, and we still have the fans-and-smoke props from the noir films of the forties and fifties? That's postmodern pastiche for you. "And yet," I add on the opening day of the course, "even as the visual style of *Blade Runner* evokes the past, it has become enormously influential as a way of representing the future as a dystopian extrapolation of the present. Let me put this more dramatically: we couldn't have the future without *Blade Runner*." This always furrows a few brows in the room, particularly among students who are familiar with science fiction, so I add a few sentences of explanation. In *Blade Runner*, the near future isn't cool and streamlined and filled with bright white corridors as in films like *2001: A Space Odyssey* or *THX 1138*, and it's not a wasted landscape filled with twisted metal, either, as in *Terminator* or *The Matrix*. It's actually a lot like Times Square crossed with São Paulo. It's got artificial intelligence together with smoke-filled rooms with ceiling fans, just as we live in a polyglot world that has instant messaging together with Chippendale skyscrapers.

The class reads *Do Androids Dream of Electric Sheep?* (on which *Blade Runner* is based) the next week, noting the film's many differences from the book. The book is fascinating and incoherent (it is a Philip K. Dick novel, after all), and leads in completely different directions from the film, into topics such as religion, the nature of empathy, the post-nuclear depopulation of the planet, and the effects of cognitive disability. But what the film loses in these respects, it gains in visual power: that enormous Coca-Cola ad looming over the drizzling cityscape of Los Angeles, Detective Deckard magnifying an android's photographs with a visual-enhancement technology so acute as to be indistinguishable from hallucination—these haunting images, and their very obvious interest in the imagery *of* images, will stay with us for the rest of the semester.

Students who have some acquaintance with media studies and communications tend not to think of "postmodernism" in terms of experimental or pulp literature or Chippendale skyscrapers; they seem instead to associate postmodernism with the *Matrix* hypothesis—the proposition that what we naively think of as the real world is but a computer simulation. I don't mean to say that these students believe we're all living in the Matrix, and that in actuality we're encased in a pod of pink goo while artificial-intelligence machines use our body heat for electricity; I mean only that they think of postmodernism in this way, as if postmodernism proposes that the real world is a simulation (even if postmodernism is silent or agnostic about the pink goo). From what I can gather, they get this idea—as the Wachowski brothers got the idea—from their understanding of French theorist Jean Baudrillard, who is cited twice (once by name, once for his line, "Welcome to the desert of the real") in *The Matrix* and whose writings of the 1980s and 1990s do, indeed, mount seemingly absurd arguments that the real world has been effaced by "simulacra" and that, as one of his recent books puts it, *The Gulf War Did Not Take Place*.[7]

Most of the pop-culture Baudrillardisms I've heard in the world at large are remarkably banal: "Look, a video camera taking pictures of a video camera—it's so postmodern!" Or, "Reality shows are more real than reality—that's postmodernism for you!" But then again, some of those banalities come straight from Baudrillard himself, even if they don't sound like banalities when he utters them, and even if he himself thinks he's talking about banality. A couple of passages from Baudrillard's most well-known work, "The Precession of Simulacra," have made their way into the general culture, like his famous pronouncement that "Disneyland is there to conceal the fact that it is the 'real' country, all of 'real' America, which *is* Disneyland" (though people tend not to quote the dubious parenthesis that fol-

lows this, "just as prisons are there to conceal the fact that it is the
social in its entirety, in its banal omnipresence, which is carceral";
yeah, I think, tell that to people on the inside).[8] More pervasive,
though, is the sense that the mass media *are* our reality: they don't
simply "construct" reality, they are the reality itself. The tail wags the
dog, everything becomes mass entertainment, and politics is determined by how the photo op will look on the TV news. This
communications-theory insight, however, isn't really Baudrillardian;
it's more commonly associated with fairly traditional media critics on
the left, many of whom became convinced in the Reagan years that
only a media-drugged society could tolerate a president as odious as
Reagan. "Postmodern," for them, became almost synonymous with
"unreal," and the fact that Reagan confused World War II with
World War II movies was taken as a sign of the times—that is, the
times when signs were finally cut free from their signifying function
and floated loose in the air in waves and streams, the times when
signs signified anything or nothing. Not until the mid-1990s did I
start to see similar complaints on the right, as in Lynne Cheney's
denunciation of the "postmodern presidency" of the Clinton era,[9]
whereupon I realized that I was hearing the same howls of outrage
and betrayal I'd heard ten years earlier: Only a media-drugged society could tolerate a president as odious as Clinton! Surely we have
lost all sense of the real!

But, for what it's worth, Baudrillard emphatically does not say
that media images have distorted reality. Early in "The Precession
of Simulacra" he lays out what he calls "the successive phases of the
image" (an unfortunate phrase which leads readers—including this
one—to wonder whether he's suggesting a chronological or developmental "succession"):

- it is the reflection of a basic reality
- it masks and perverts a basic reality
- it masks the *absence* of a basic reality

- it bears no relation to any reality whatever: it is its own pure simulacrum.[10]

Most people who talk loosely about "simulacra" and "simulation," I've found, really mean "the image masks and perverts a basic reality." That's what *The Matrix* shows us, certainly, which is why the film, far from being Baudrillardian, actually depicts a dystopian-SF version of good old-fashioned Marxist consciousness-raising: the matrix, like ideology, is all around you, even in the air you breathe— but the figure of Morpheus (ably played by Laurence Fishburne) is here to lead you out, to show you the *real* reality behind the mass illusion. Now, as I've just noted, occasionally some agitated soul on the left or on the right will declare that there is no reality anymore: how can there be, if we've gone from May '68 to Reagan–Thatcher–Kohl in just over a decade? Or how can there be, if Bill Clinton can lie under oath and get away with it? But very, very few people, in my experience, are willing to ride the Baudrillard bus to the last stop, the fourth phase of the image, where we seem to be living among the "images that yet / fresh images beget" from Yeats's uncanny poem "Byzantium." Can we even imagine such a thing?

I usually line up "The Precession of Simulacra" with DeLillo's 1985 novel *White Noise*, for the obvious reason that DeLillo's novel is fascinated with representations that occlude their ostensible object, from the "most photographed barn in the world" (to which people flock with cameras because it is the most photographed barn in the world, a Mona Lisa of the prairie that no one sees because they are "taking pictures of taking pictures")[11] to the scene in which Jack Gladney has the following conversation with a SIMUVAC official who's overseeing the evacuation of the town in the wake of the "airborne toxic event":

> "But this evacuation isn't simulated. It's real."
> "We know that. But we thought we could use it as a model."

"A form of practice? Are you saying you saw a chance to use the real event in order to rehearse the simulation?"

"We took it right into the streets."[12]

But there's a way to approach Baudrillard from the other side of literary history, as well: not to note his influence on postmodern literature but to note how much he and Jean-François Lyotard (whom I'll get to in a moment) owe to Samuel Beckett. Baudrillard was a disciple of Guy Debord, the leader of the Situationist International (the political–artistic movement widely credited with inspiring the student uprising in Paris in May 1968) and the author of *The Society of the Spectacle*, and his debt to Debord is obvious to people who know their French intellectual history. But his debt to Beckett seems palpable, as well; it's striking (at least, I find it striking) how often Baudrillard predicates his argument on the claim that it is no longer possible to do X because X no longer exists and we no longer can speak of doing X. The next time you come across a copy of "The Precession of Simulacra" (especially if it's your first time!), just look at how often the phrase "no longer" appears in the text. The first couple of times I taught it, in the early 1990s, some of my savvier students thought they heard a weird kind of lament in there, a kind of basso continuo of despair, as if Baudrillard were really mourning the passing of the King and the Center and the Real, the gold standard and the face-to-face encounter and all that has been effaced by the postmodern, post-something simulacrum. Students wondered whether there wasn't an anguished cry behind what appears to be Baudrillard's nihilist glee, the cry of a leftist driven mad by the belief that if we've gone from the utopian dream of Paris in May '68 to the conservative ascendancy of Reagan–Thatcher–Kohl in only thirteen years, then nothing makes sense any longer and nothing ever will.[13]

I think those readings are plausible—no, more than that, I think those readings were terrific, the best kind of acute "amateur" responses to a flamboyantly arrogant piece of work that dares you to meet it on its own barely comprehensible terms. As I remind my students, you have to remember that after a certain point in his career Beckett wrote primarily in French (and translated himself back into English), and his influence can be felt on thinkers from Sartre to Derrida to Baudrillard. In that spirit, I suggest, we can read Baudrillard and Lyotard as Hamm and Clov in *Endgame,* spinning out exchanges about how there is no more nature, there is no more meaning, just the dialogue to keep us here, but it will keep us here no longer, it will end, it must end, if one could only speak of ending . . .

In every class I've had a few students who can't proceed with this kind of material until they know one thing: are we supposed to believe this? To those students, and to all my students, I say what my wife, Janet, once said to one of her students who was puzzled beyond words by one of the loopier modernist manifestos she'd assigned to her class: "I'm not asking you to believe any of it. All I ask is that you learn how to read it." To which I add, once more with feeling: Remember, this is literary study. Remember what drew you to this strange, amorphous field in the first place. Think of us as the Department of Studying People Who Created Extraordinary Things You Don't Necessarily Have to Believe.

STILL, AFTER WE'VE HAD our fun with Baudrillard and reality shows and *The Matrix,* I have to say that I now teach "The Precession of Simulacra" largely out of historical interest. Maybe that's just one of those odd postmodern post-ironic ironies. But I think it makes sense; that wing of postmodern media and cultural theory simply isn't holding up very well. In another decade or so, I just might ditch it altogether (maybe by then we'll finally be post-postmodern), because there are more pressing matters urging themselves on our attention. Matters such as the Lyotard–

Habermas debate, for example, which is looking more and more important with each passing year, and which, I think, poses such intractable questions for critical theory and political practice that our era may well be defined by them.

This sounds like a large and dramatic claim—possibly too large and dramatic to be taken at face value. So I'll elaborate this one at some length, with the proviso that what follows is the kind of explanation I offer to my undergraduates. It is not meant as an original philosophical contribution to the debate over the legacy of the Enlightenment; it is meant simply as an introduction to that debate, and it will deal in general paraphrases and broad strokes. I will also say in advance, to readers who might be skeptical as to whether even advanced American undergraduates "get" this kind of material, that the vast majority of my honors students have understood the debate very well, even if they do sometimes tell me, as one student did in a written evaluation of my 2001 class, "Take it easy on us sometimes—we're undergraduates, you know."

Habermas is an eloquent defender of the universalist promises of the Enlightenment.[14] He considers the Enlightenment a "modern" phenomenon, that is, as something that helped to free humanity from unquestioning adherence to the institutions of church and state by proposing reason as the standard for political and moral deliberation. But he sees modernity as an unfinished project, insofar as Enlightenment universalism has not yet been made been available to all persons and is therefore universal only in aspiration. On that score, Habermas is unquestionably right; many contemporary societies do, in fact, subordinate rational deliberation to the dictates of church and state, and (as you may have heard in the news lately) some of those societies deny full human status to roughly half their populations, practicing a form of religious patriarchy that, in the West, was marginalized—though not completely defeated—by the end of Europe's long and brutal religious wars. Furthermore, Habermas sees verbal communication as one of the key social practices that can help to advance the cause of universal rights, because in verbal communication the parties thereto are oriented toward understanding. They may disagree, sure, but they want to make their disagreement intelligible to the other party or parties. Habermas therefore favors social practices that increase our chances for "reciprocal recognition," and he considers the "ideal speech situation" to be one in which all persons speak as moral equals, regardless of race, gender, sexual practice, and so on. In the ideal speech situation, no one is coerced, all are oriented toward understanding, and all use the potential for mutual recognition—a potential which is integral to language itself—in the service of human emancipation.

If you think this sounds too much like a friendly seminar discussion, you've got a point. But most of my undergraduates—who just happen to be participating in a friendly seminar discussion—don't see what's wrong with this. How can you be against mutual understanding?

So we turn to Lyotard. Lyotard's *The Postmodern Condition* shares many features with Baudrillard's work; it's occasionally inscrutable and often provocative, and it sometimes sounds more apocalyptic than it needs to, as when Lyotard proclaims that "postmodern science" is "changing the meaning of the word *knowledge*."[15] Nevertheless, Lyotard's work (especially two of his follow-up books, *The Differend: Phrases in Dispute* and *The Inhuman*) has been extremely influential—and, more to the point, undismissable in at least one way: there really are "incommensurabilities" between different human belief systems that cannot be negotiated away or finessed by appeal to impartial third parties. Yet the weakest part of Lyotard's general argument is his anti-Habermasian suggestion that the Enlightenment runs directly from the great German philosophers of the eighteenth and nineteenth centuries to the atrocities of the Holocaust. For while there's a sense in which the faculty of instrumental reason, left to its own devices without any moral mooring,

can sit down one day and try to figure out the most rational and effi-
cient method for exterminating Jews, Lyotard underestimates the
profound influence of German *anti*-Enlightenment thought on the
Holocaust—the appeal not to universal reason but to emotional,
irrational celebrations of "blood and soil." The intellectual origins of
the Holocaust are quite complex, and Lyotard does not do them
justice.

However, Lyotard's skepticism about the Enlightenment is not
entirely wrongheaded. In practice, the Enlightenment was not in
itself a universalist enterprise; at one moment, Hume and Kant are
talking about universal human reason, and in the next moment
they're mouthing off about how Africans don't happen to have it.
The contradiction looked bad then, and it looks worse now. The
domestic version of this dynamic, of course, gives us Thomas Jefferson scribbling "all men are created equal" onto a piece of parch-
ment and dreaming of universal emancipation while being
surrounded by a house and plantation full of slaves. It's no surprise,
then, to find skeptics—some of whom were among those originally
excluded from the Enlightenment on the grounds that they were
incapable of reason, and some of whom speak today in the names
of those so excluded—suggesting that this much-touted universalism is really just a front for Western imperialism and domination,
that it hides its partiality by sneakily pretending to be critical of all
partialities, and that it offers a blueprint not for universal emancipation but for the ruthless eradication of difference. These claims
may sound misguided or hyperbolic at first to many Western ears,
and certainly to the Western ears attached to my students' heads,
but at the same time they're not all that strange, either; we all know
how vexing it is to be locked in a debate with someone who says, "I
represent the claims of universal truth, and the only reason you disagree with me is that you are intellectually deficient." It's even
more vexing, certainly, when that someone happens to be running
an imperialist outpost somewhere in the southern hemisphere, and

follows that sentence with, "Now bring me more rubber/oil/dia-monds/ivory or I'll chop your hands off."

Habermas replies that this is exactly why the project of moder-nity is unfinished; its original formulation was flawed, and only gradually have we come to see that the rule of reason dictates that one can't pronounce X to be universally true and then go about oppressing or killing everyone who doesn't think so. For Habermas, then, the problem with the Enlightenment is that it needs more enlightenment. But at least it set the wheels in motion; if all received truths are now open to skeptical scrutiny from everyone on the planet, then surely Enlightenment philosophers' ignorant remarks about Africans are available for universal scrutiny, as are the brutali-ties of European imperialism. The ideal speech situation is not a reality, and has never been a reality; it is merely a useful regulative ideal—something by which to weigh our current world and find it wanting. Again, in the United States, the relevant argument would run something like this: yes, there is a deep and fatal contradiction between the universalist promise of the Declaration of Indepen-dence and the Constitution's institutionalization of slavery. We know the contradiction is fatal to the Union, because it led to the Civil War; but the best course of action here is to use the former to criticize the latter, rather than junking the universalist promise alto-gether on the grounds that it is fundamentally fraudulent.

So far my paraphrase makes the universalists sound pretty good, I think—as if Habermas is saying, "Fair enough, we got it wrong before, but the potential for good is still there if only we follow through on a truly universal universalism." And yet here's where Habermas makes his most telling misstep, and allows Lyotard his most cogent retort. Habermas imagines the "ideal speech situation" as something oriented not merely toward under-standing, as I said above, but toward *consensus*. This, I believe, is a terrible mistake, theoretically and practically. It basically says, "We will all sit down and deliberate as equals—and then, when we're done deliberating, we will agree." Of course, I know that there has to be a weak consensus in the room, so to speak, if there's going to be any discussion whatsoever; all participants have to agree to deliberate, at the very least. But in suggesting that consensus is the goal of the discussion, Habermas has left himself wide open to the charge that he does see universalism as the eradication of difference—that universalism will have done its job only when there is no one left to dissent from it. And that, Lyotard insists, puts us right back on the road to Terror. For what if we come across a discourse that is truly, thoroughly, incommensurable with our own? What, for example, if we come across a group of people who refuse to believe that disputes should be guided by reason and deliberation, and who insist instead that disputes should be conducted by means of sacrifices to Ba'al?

At this point in the exposition, some of my students are practically bouncing up and down in their chairs. How did we get from "peace, love, and understanding" to "terror"? Even before 9/11, the word was a charged term—and Lyotard, writing long before 9/11, did not hesitate to throw it around freely. Consensus is terror, reciprocal recognition is terror, mutual understanding is terror. Most of my students think this is just next door to insane; killing hostages and flying planes into buildings, they say, is terror. Asking people to sit down and work out their differences is not terror. On the contrary: if people sat down and tried to work out their differences there would be less terror.

I tell those students that I happen to agree with them, for the most part. But let's imagine someone who disagrees with all of us, and who thinks our agreement is really just a cover for our excluding him or her from the conversation—or from the protection of the state, or from the promises of universal human rights. To a person such as this, our agreement to agree looks a little like Paul McCartney's version of compromise in "We Can Work It Out": Try to see it my way, do I have to keep on talking till I can't go on, why do you see it your way, don't you see that your way of thinking will ruin everything? We can work it out, if only you'll admit that your point of view threatens the very foundations of our society. More seriously, I tell my students that the question of how to agree to engage in discussion, without agreeing that discussion will lead to consensus, is much trickier than it looks. Imagine, for instance, that someone comes to you and says, "I'll agree to deliberate a matter that is very important to us both, and I'll try to understand you if you try to understand me, but I'm not going to agree in advance that the purpose of our deliberation is to get us to agree." What exactly is the nature of that kind of agreement? Doesn't it involve only a very general agreement to participate in debate—leaving everything else up for grabs, such as the procedural rules of dispute, the means by which parties can appeal alleged infractions of the rules, and so forth—even before we get to the question of whether the agreement to participate entails an eventual agreement to agree? I tell my students that I'm sympathetic to Habermas in general, else I wouldn't be speaking in such a way as to invite their understanding and their questions. I wouldn't bother being a teacher at all. But the guy really does have his thumb on the scales when he speaks of consensus, and we have to find some way of fixing that before we proceed.

For comic relief—but also to demonstrate what another kind of seminar community would look like—I tell my undergraduate students the story of the first graduate seminar in which I explored the Lyotard–Habermas debate. My graduate students were almost unanimously convinced that Lyotard was right, that consensus was terror, that all the world's incommensurabilities must be respected in the cause of preserving difference. Even to attempt to negotiate those incommensurabilities and make them intelligible to each other, my students insisted, is to do irreparable harm to what Lyotard calls the heterogeneity of language games. "See," they said, "Lyotard says so right here: 'Is legitimacy to be found in consensus obtained through discussion, as Jürgen Habermas thinks? Such consensus always does violence to the heterogeneity of language games.'"[16] "OK," I'd replied, "then why don't we do some violence to the heterogeneity of language games?" Because that would be imperialism, they said. "How about just a little bit of violence— like, a teeny-weeny bit?" I asked. No, they answered. No harm! Not even a little bit! "Well," I remarked at the time, "I admire the consensus you've all achieved on this. I merely wonder where it came from." As if this scenario weren't strange enough on its face, I discovered a few days later that my students' anti-consensus con- sensus wasn't quite complete, when a shy young woman came in to talk to me during my office hours and told me how out of place she felt in the seminar—partly because she didn't agree with all her peers about Lyotard, and partly because, as she put it, she could tell from other discussions that she was the only Republican among her peers. So all my students agreed that agreement is terror, even as they were unaware of the one person who disagreed with them, who was too shy to speak up in class.

Now, it's not impossible to have a community of Lyotardians; it's just that even a group devoted to heterogeneity and dissensus requires something like a second-order consensus that dissensus might be a good thing.[17] After my lone Republican student left my office that day, I began to think harder about why one wing of the academic left would take Lyotard's position as axiomatic. I slowly realized (that is, at some point between 1995 and 1999) that my graduate seminar had testified to one of the academic left's weirder features—namely, its reluctance to consider that a defense of the heterogeneity of language games isn't necessarily a courageous blow against imperialism. Rather, it's morally neutral. It may sound like it's on the side of the angels, of course, but that's only because when *we* use it, we're thinking of preserving the language games of the exploited and the oppressed, as if it were a moral question akin to that of preserving species diversity in the natural environment;

we're absolutely *not* thinking of linking arms and marching down the street to fight for the principle that no harm be done to the unique and irreplaceable language games of Wal-Mart, the Family Research Council, or the World Bank. Or, for that matter, the Church of Jesus Christ of Latter-Day Saints.

Similarly, much of the academic left in the 1980s and 1990s endorsed another key aspect of Lyotard's argument in *The Post-modern Condition*, namely, the idea that the "grand narratives" of modernity (whether the Whiggish narrative of gradual progress and emancipation or the Marxist narrative of class conflict and dialectical materialism) had lost their charm—that such *"grands récits"* were, in fact, part of the terror of the modern (for they too suppress difference) and have rightly given way to *"petits récits,"* some of which are inevitably incommensurate with each other. Lyotard found allies in feminist standpoint epistemology, which championed "local" and "situated" knowledges against the domineering "view from nowhere" from which follows precisely the kind of false universalism that sees dissidence and difference as illegitimate. Yet this knee-jerk academic-left defense of "local knowledges," I fear, is every bit as strange and as blinkered as the knee-jerk academic-left defense of the heterogeneity of language games. I have never run across a fellow academic leftist who regarded Mormons or Islamists as practitioners of "local knowledges"; on the contrary, when we speak of "local knowledges"[18] we tend to imbue "local" with all the warm and fuzzy feelings we progressive lefties have for our local independent bookstores, our local independent food co-operatives, and our local independent media. "Local," in this sense, is good; it is opposed to "corporate" and "transnational" and "Wal-Mart." "Local" preserves difference and always offers alternative healing methods and organic produce from neighborhood farms; "universal" is homogenizing and oppressive and puts a McDonald's and a Starbucks on every street corner. I remark on this not to denigrate local bookstores (I'm as fond of them as anyone) or to claim that Lyotard had food co-ops on his mind when he was writing *The Postmodern Condition*. I'm only pointing out that just as the academic left tends not to think about whether religious fundamentalists might also be covered by an appeal to the heterogeneity of language games, so too do we tend to neglect the possibility that our defense of local knowledges might also cover the local small-town newspaper editor who supported David Duke for president in 1988. Perhaps, as I tell my students, it is possible to point out that "local" is often a synonym for parochial without thereby committing yourself to global imperialism or a career in Wal-Mart's public relations bureau. For "parochial" is quite literally another name for the local; it denotes the perspective of the person who has never left his or her parish.

In my 1999 class, I gave my students two examples that, I thought, should challenge any form of liberal sentimentality about the local: Brigham Young University and the Taliban. By 1999, the Taliban had been in power for three years, and had made quite a name for themselves as stoners of women, torturers of athletes, executioners of clean-shaven men, and destroyers of ancient sculptures and artifacts. For my BYU example, I drew on Martha Nussbaum's 1997 book, *Cultivating Humanity: A Classical Defense of Reform in Liberal Education,* in which Nussbaum insists that universities should cultivate cosmopolitanism and the ideal of "world citizenship."[19] Nussbaum's argument relies on the Enlightenment faith in reason, and she is accordingly skeptical of every kind of received wisdom and inherited tradition, but when she gets to BYU after surveying dozens of universities from Bentley College to Harvard, from Notre Dame to St. Lawrence University, from the University of California at Berkeley to the University of Nevada at Reno, Nussbaum finds that at BYU reason doesn't have the free hand that "reasonable" people have come to expect from Western universities. Rather, as one faculty member told her, "reason must operate within limits set by revelation." In 1996, accordingly, one of BYU's

English professors was fired because of an alleged absence of "gospel insights" and "spiritual inspiration" in her teaching. Let's think of this impasse as a potential incommensurability: the voice of untrammeled inquiry says, "The American Association of University Professors' principles of academic freedom must trump your parochial religious dictates"; the voice of unquestioning faith replies, "Your secular principles must yield to the revelations of divine truth." As for me, I'm on the side of untrammeled inquiry, but I freely acknowledge that, from some religious perspectives, this specific liberal conviction could well be construed as a liberal "bias." And, indeed, in that 1999 seminar my pair of examples of parochial localism had a profound effect on one of my brightest students—a tall, reserved woman who spoke to me after class (and many times thereafter) because she was a Mormon.

The first time we spoke, I started to apologize for any suggestion that the Latter-Day Saints were as extreme as the Taliban, and she said, no, that's not what she'd come to talk about; she wanted to say that the non-negotiable difference I'd described between reason and faith was a tension that she lived with every day, that her family had only reluctantly agreed to allow her to attend the University of Illinois, and that when she was done with all this postmodern gender-bending deconstructionist queer *Matrix*-watching college stuff, she was expected to come back home, get hitched, and have some babies. "I see," I said, taken aback. "And what do you want to do?" She said she wanted to go to graduate school, but wasn't sure she'd get the chance. In the meantime, she said, she wanted me to know that when I talked about the tensions between two incompatible belief systems, I was basically describing the emotional landscape of her life.

She became one of my most engaged and energetic students for the rest of the term, we kept up a lively e-mail correspondence through May, and, thanks to her and a handful of her fellow students, I began to focus more and more of the 1999 course on the question of incommensurability and difference, and less and less on simulacra. At the time, some students wanted to know what was distinctly postmodern about all this: certainly, they asked, different beliefs and worldviews had come into conflict before 1945 or 1973? Yes, I replied, but what's different this time around is that we've got people arguing that those conflicts must be preserved rather than resolved. They're calling into question the Enlightenment project of universal reason and universal rights, they're arguing that the establishment of moral norms is a form of imperialism or terrorism, and they're even arguing that our beliefs aren't grounded in anything other than our quotidian cultural practices—not in God, not in nature, not in the eternal verities of the human spirit. This is something new, and it's confusing. But, I added, before we go any further with all this, I want to frame the Lyotard–Habermas debate as a metadebate about the purpose of debate itself, and I want to start off by impressing upon you the uncomfortable fact that, at this meta-level, we can say neither that the debate is resolvable nor that it is unresolvable. It is impossible not to take a position on this one, and worse, it is impossible not to take a position that betrays the nature of the debate.

In 1999 and in 2001, this "framing" device met with a roomful of puzzled and/or exasperated looks, as well it should have. For, as I told both classes of students, it is a conundrum. It's infinitely recursive. I even wrote the form of the conundrum on the blackboard, and it went something like this: if you say that the dispute between Lyotard and Habermas can in fact be resolved by recourse to principles on which both parties can ultimately agree, you are, in effect, awarding the palm to Habermas and the pro-consensus, pro-communicative action party. If, on the contrary, you give up and say that this one is simply a fundamental impasse and can't be resolved, you have in effect resolved it by awarding the palm to Lyotard and the pro-incommensurability, pro-heterogeneity party. And you can't say "neither of the above," because that too defaults to Lyotard. "Now," I said to my students as time ran out, "think about that all weekend, and I'll see you next week."

IN THIS COURSE I have to remind myself constantly that while I'm devoting about half of my available brain capacity to the syllabus and to our discussions, my students are taking four or five other courses and maybe working at jobs ten to twenty hours on the side. And, as they say, I have to remember that they're undergraduates. As one young woman remarked to the class on our listserv, during that fall of 2001, it's like we spend all week challenging gender hierarchies and deconstructing every form of received thought, and then on the weekends we're dancing in the clubs with nut-flexers and singing about big pimpin'. "It's just funny," she said. "It is funny," I replied, "and those are the conditions of cultural analysis these days. Don't worry too much about it; even intellectuals can take a break over the weekend."

So, then, imagine that during the paragraph break above, you've spent a weekend in college-town dance clubs. You've spent two days nut-flexin' and big pimpin' and next-mornin' recuperatin', or maybe you've spent two days working at the record store or playing volleyball or babysitting or reading fiction, psychology, physics, or *People*. And now you're back in postmodernism class, being asked by your professor to recall the terms of the Lyotard–Habermas debate and to remember why it is that we can say neither that the debate is resolvable nor that it is unresolvable. Worse still, your professor has promised you that there's a way to approach this question as an antifoundationalist without necessarily being anti-universalist.

So, then, what better way to get back into the swing of things than to begin with *Pulp Fiction*? No, it isn't on the syllabus. But it will help me make an interesting point—or at least I hope it will.

It helps that every college student in the nation has seen *Pulp Fiction*. Together with *The Matrix*, it forms part of the common

culture we Americans aren't supposed to have. (I am being face-
tious about this. But I am always struck by the fact that when I ask
a class how many of them have seen these films, I am met with that
classroom cliché, the Sea of Hands.) And it doesn't take much, on
my part, to show that a good chunk of the movie is explicitly about
the conflict between systems of value, even if the movie likes to
address this question in low-comic form. Ron Rosenbaum's *New
York Times Magazine* essay of 1995 on (among other things) the the-
ology of *Pulp Fiction* pointed this out in some detail,[20] noting that
the conversation between Vincent (John Travolta) and Jules
(Samuel L. Jackson) begins with a light discussion of cultural differences: of hashish use and police searches in Amsterdam; of a
morally neutral conflict between classificatory systems, whereby the
French call a quarter-pounder a "royale with cheese" because of the
metric system; and the merits of mayonnaise on French fries and
beer in movie theaters. The discussion then gradually works its
way into a heated dispute over whether it is appropriate to throw
someone out a window, down four stories, and through a greenhouse roof, rendering him disabled ("he's kinda developed a speech
impediment"), if that someone has secretly given your wife a foot
rub. That dispute, in turn, then spawns a secondary disagreement
over whether a foot rub is analogous to oral sex—a proposition
Vincent defends and Jules dismisses out of hand as ridiculous.

By this point my students are bemused and curious. Sure, they
remember that argument between Jules and Vincent (mild chuck-
ling here and there), but what does it have to do with postmodernism and the problem of incommensurability? Here's what, I say:
sometimes the Lyotardians and the proponents of discursive heterogeneity tend to walk away from conflict and declare it unresolvable before they've really worked with it. They say, "Look, white
women and black women have different understandings of the TV
series *Dallas*—this must be evidence of cultural incommensurability,"[21] or, "Speaker A's language says the bird is singing whereas

speaker B's language says the bird is crying—these must be fundamentally incompatible belief systems." And when I suggest that
some postmodernists are too quick to declare a conflict unresolvable, I don't mean to reinstate the demand that the ideal speech situation should be oriented toward consensus; I'm not even thinking
about getting disparate parties to agree—about birds, *Dallas*, foot
rubs, Lyotard, or anything else. Instead, when I'm faced with the
conflict between two parties with well-developed belief systems, I
want to know one crucial thing above all: what internal protocols
do they have that would enable them to change their minds about
something? Do they have, for instance, an evidentiary standard,
and if so, what do they admit as evidence? And what forms of
authority are endowed with the capacity to decide such matters? Is
there a Supreme Court, a council of elders, a parliament, a workers' collective, a Leviathan? Are there competing moral imperatives within one or the other belief system that would be likely to
induce a person to reconsider his or her position on grounds that
are intelligible within the belief system itself? Nussbaum, among
many others, is fond of making the point (and it is a sound point)
that cultures are not monolithic, that they contain rich variegated
traditions, internal contradictions, and innumerable minority
reports. Any sufficiently well-developed culture will have, in other
words, ample resources for self-examination, historical revisionism,
searching moral debate, and other means of producing epistemic
change. It should, therefore, be possible to ask any belief system
something like the following: even though I cannot change your
mind about X, can you tell me what conditions would have to be
met in order for you to *consider* changing your mind about X?

This meta-question does not produce (or expect) consensus, but
it does attempt to make the grounds of dissensus intelligible. In this
way it manages to uphold the values of reciprocal communication
without seeking to guarantee that the goal of reciprocal communication will be a form of reciprocal understanding that leads to

agreement. If it were applied to Galileo's first observations of Jupiter's moons, which posed such a profound challenge to the early-seventeenth-century Catholic Church, it would ask, "What would you think, Father, if I were to show you that there are entities in orbit around Jupiter? Would that matter to you?" and invites you to make any number of possible replies:

(a) no, it would not matter, because Aristotle did not mention any such entities and therefore they cannot exist;

(b) no, it would not matter, because the Holy Father teaches us that Jupiter is in fact orbiting *our* planet;

(c) no, it would not matter, because your "telescopic" device is a fraud;

(d) no, it would not matter, because you did not slaughter a chicken before you began to speak to me (this is not a part of the Catholic catechism, but I hope you get the point);

(e) yes, it would matter, and I am convinced now that my conception of the heavens needs to be revised;

(f) yes, it would matter, and I will imprison you until you recant;

(g) yes, it would matter, but I am not sure exactly how it would matter because I do not yet know what to think about this.

This is more or less what happens between Vincent and Jules in *Pulp Fiction*; once they reach their standoff, when Jules refuses to entertain the proposition that a foot rub constitutes a form of intimacy with one's wife on a par with engaging in oral sex with her, Vincent essays two lines of argument that seek to make his position intelligible to Jules in Jules's own terms. First, he suggests that while foot rubs are not equivalent to oral sex, they are not trivial forms of intimacy; while they may not be "the same thing," Vincent says, they're in "the same ballpark." "It ain't no *ballpark* either," replies an outraged Jules. "Now look, maybe your method of massage differs from mine, but touchin' his lady's feet, and stickin' your tongue in her holiest of holies, ain't the same ballpark, ain't the same league, ain't even the same fuckin' sport. Foot massages don't mean shit." Undaunted, Vincent asks whether Jules has ever given a foot massage, to which Jules replies that he is "the fuckin' foot master"; then Vincent asks if Jules would give a foot massage to a man. You can imagine Jules's brisk, two-word retort; interestingly, the script reads, "Jules looks at him a long moment—he's been set up." Indeed he has: Vincent has led him to admit that foot massages do mean shit, that Jules prides himself on his technique, and that Jules thinks of them—quite fiercely—as a mode of heterosexual-only physical contact. Jules rallies, however, and the exchange culminates like so:

> JULES: Look just because I wouldn't give no man a foot massage, don't make it right for Marsellus to throw Antwan off a building into a glass-motherfuckin-house, fuckin' up the way the nigger talks. That ain't right, man. Motherfucker do that shit to me, he better paralyze my ass, 'cause I'd kill'a motherfucker, you know what I'm saying?
>
> VINCENT: I'm not sayin' he was right, but you're sayin' a foot massage don't mean nothin', and I'm sayin' it does. I've given a million ladies a million foot massages and they all meant somethin'. Now, we act like they don't, but they do. That's what's so fuckin' cool about 'em. There's a sensual thing's goin' on that nobody's talkin' about, but you know it and she knows it, fuckin' Marsellus knew it, and Antwan shoulda known fuckin' better. That's his fuckin' wife, man. He ain't gonna have a sense of humor about that shit. You know what I'm saying?
>
> JULES: That's an interesting point.[22]

That's an interesting point. It *is* an interesting point, especially since Vincent has conceded the major point at issue, namely, that Marcellus may not have been justified in throwing Antwan down four flights through a greenhouse roof. I acknowledge that Jules's is not the most eloquent of demurrals/deferrals; surely it's not in the same ballpark, the same league, even the same fuckin' sport as Oliver Cromwell's immortal "I beseech you, in the bowels of Christ, think it possible you may be mistaken." Yet in one way it is superior to Cromwell's plea, for it leaves open the possibility that Jules himself may be mistaken; he is not convinced by Vincent's argument, but he has understood it *as* an argument, and he appears to have taken it under advisement. The fact that the film renders the argument moot—first when Mia Wallace (Uma Thurman) ridicules the foot massage story, second when Vincent dies in a hail of bullets—is beside the point; what's important is that Jules tacitly agrees to consider Vincent's "interesting point" without seeking to rebut it.

Now, I could tell my students that Jules is exercising what Keats famously and obscurely called "negative capability," that is, "when man is capable of being in uncertainties, Mysteries, doubts, without any irritable reaching after fact & reason."[23] Or I could cite the term James Joyce invented for "doubt" in *Finnegans Wake,* "in twosome twiminds."[24] But it's more pedagogically useful, I think, to make the point by way of an actual (if fictional) argument (where the stakes are ludicrously small); besides, even though Quentin Tarantino has been grating on the cultural nerves for over a decade and I can stand him only in small doses (and yet I have even lower tolerance for many of the moralistic condemnations of the film, from both right and left), some parts of *Pulp Fiction* are still a fun read. This is one of them. When two people disagree about proposition X, they may not immediately agree to disagree, but they may find the discursive grounds on which to make themselves intelligible to each other, and they may, in the process, discover the grounds on which to make intelligible any further appeal to what the other person considers a plausible reason for reconsidering his (or her) position.

I told my students that I didn't want them to take this simply as a reading of *Pulp Fiction* but, rather, as a template for how to disagree with each other—and with me—for the rest of the semester. Very well, a few students replied, but how far does this principle go? Does it cover statements that we might find bizarre or counter-intuitive or noxious? What if someone comes along and says, "I think women should not be educated," or, "Africans are mentally deficient," or, "Gays and lesbians should be quarantined for the good of society"? Are we supposed to stop for a moment and think, "Interesting point"? Just what kind of contentless, cultural-relativist namby-pamby liberalism is this, anyway?

My students didn't say exactly that, word for word, but in both the 1999 and 2001 seminars, large pluralities of students made that general move; yes, we've agreed with you that reciprocal recognition is a useful regulative ideal, and we've agreed with you that we shouldn't preordain the goal of reciprocal recognition by decreeing that the purpose of conversation is consensus; furthermore, we've agreed with you that there might indeed be some forms of disagreement out there that are non-negotiable and that constitute true incommensurabilities, and that good Habermasians should be alive to these rather than seeing them as mere aberrancies or temporary obstacles. By gum (though they do not say "by gum," either), we've even agreed with you that it might be a useful meta-maneuver, when faced with a possible incommensurability, to ask the other party what resources his language game affords him for changing his mind, and what kinds of evidence or authority might be sufficient unto the task. But now you're leading us right back into moral relativism, by asking us to entertain outlandish and offensive propositions that do not even meet our minimal criteria for a well-formed proposition!

Yes, that's right, I say. I am asking you to entertain such things. But I am not asking you to believe them or espouse them, any more than I was asking you to believe or espouse Baudrillard. And the fact that they do not meet your minimal criteria for well-formed propositions is precisely the point: that's why we have an incommensurability here. The Taliban has just shown up and told you that both adulterers and rape victims must be stoned; the Khmer

Rouge has just appeared and informed you that you and your classmates have been suspected of being intellectuals and will be killed.
Or you're dealing with someone who defends widow-burning or
the torture of terror suspects. These are not capricious people; they
do this out of a profound sense of conviction. And your commitment to reciprocal recognition has obliged you to make the attempt
to understand them.

And then what? my students ask. Then they can kill us?

No, I reply. Then you can kill *them* . . . if critiquing them,
denouncing them, and vilifying them hasn't worked and they're
still at your throat with a knife. Nothing prevents you from stop-
ping someone from taking your life or from inflicting harm on
someone you deem innocent. So far, we've used the model of "conversation" and "argument" because we're talking about clashes
between language games and belief systems, and we've agreed to
try to negotiate those clashes before leaping to the conclusion that
they cannot be negotiated at all. But once it becomes clear that the
differences are in fact non-negotiable, then you have a range of
options: you can ignore the other party, live and let live; you can
keep trying to convert the other party to the cause of Christ or
Allah or Lenin or Hitler or liberal democracy; you can rail at the
other party from a safe distance; you can continue to point out that
the party espouses positions that betray his or her culture's best traditions of discussion and dissent; or, if you are in mortal danger,
you can kill the other party, unless your own belief system utterly
forbids you to kill under any circumstances.

In my 2001 class, I elaborated on these options by way of a short
essay that had recently been published by Andrew Sullivan in the
New Republic. The essay begins:

One of the most vivid experiences of my time as a graduate student at
Harvard was a seminar I took with the preeminent liberal political
theorist John Rawls. The discussion centred on Rawls's later work, in

which he divorced his liberalism from the claim of absolute truth. His argument was only cogent, he averred, if read and understood by people who already shared some basic premises—the need for consent, the reliance on reason, a tone of civility, a relatively open mind. With characteristic tactlessness, I asked him what his response would be if Hitler joined the debate and disagreed with him. Rawls answered that there could be no discourse with Hitler. We would have to agree that he was simply crazy, a madman at a Cambridge dinner party, a figure outside the conversation. To Hitler, Rawls had nothing to say, except please go away. But what if Hitler refuses to go away?[25]

Sullivan admitted, in his very next paragraph, that "the argument ad Hitlerum" is "such a high-school debating tactic that it should be employed only with extreme caution," and he issued the usual caveats about how the "geopolitical differences between anti-Semitism in Nazi Germany and anti-Semitism in the Arab world are vast." But the Nazi–Islamist analogy wasn't what jumped out at me about Sullivan's piece; rather, it was the suggestion that a Rawlsian response to Hitler involved removing him from a dinner party, or perhaps asking him to take his cappuccino to some other table in the Starbucks. Indeed, Sullivan closes the essay by painting Rawls as a jejune cultural relativist:

> It is not a revelation that large segments of the Arab world—at all levels of society—are not just anti-Israel, but fanatically anti-Semitic. . . . Why did I discount this anti-Semitism on the grounds that these are alien cultures and we cannot fully understand them, or because these pathologies are allied with more legitimate (if to my mind unpersuasive) critiques of Israeli policy? I guess I was thinking like John Rawls.

This, I told my class, is a severe underreading of what it means for Rawls to say that there can be "no discourse" with Hitler. Don't let the language of "discourse" and "argument" fool you: when we decide that someone is "a figure outside the conversation," we might, in fact, be providing grounds for imprisoning or killing him, on the grounds that he advocates—or is actually conducting—genocide. There is nothing flabby about this. Liberals, even liberals friendly to some of the theses of postmodernism, can kill you. But they are duty-bound to exhaust every other rational remedy first, and then to determine that the incommensurability facing them is not merely non-negotiable but deadly. This is not just another prescription for more liberal seminar chatter; the deliberation that the other party is a deadly enemy and an imminent threat may take millennia or milliseconds. But you are not compelled to go on talking—either in the mode of Habermas or the mode of Jules and Vincent—with someone bent on your extermination.

There was much relief in the classroom, along with some puzzlement as to whether this form of liberalism isn't really liberal at all. Indeed, my pacifist students found this conclusion all too aggressive for their tastes. But I didn't want the class to go off the rails into a discussion of pacifism and "just war" theory—or, for that matter, into a discussion of the vices of the Taliban and/or Nazi Germany. Instead, I reminded my students that thus far in the *Pulp Fiction* discussion of what it would take to change someone's mind, we're not fully postmodern yet. We're still arguing about arguing. One side says "equal rights for all"; the other says, "glory be unto the Creator"; and Lyotard says, "Preserve the differences." But what if yet another side comes along and says, "There are no grounds for my argument—in fact, the world would be far better off if we abandoned the notion of mind-independent concepts altogether (not mind-independent entities, mind you, just mind-independent concepts). Instead, let's admit that we're just making up our moral principles as we go along—not capriciously, either, but with what we believe are the very best of intentions. And let's try to make them up in such a way as to benefit as many of us as is conceivable."

Now the final stages of the discussion begin in earnest; now we begin to grapple not merely with belief A and belief B but with competing justifications for beliefs A and B. And this is the point at which I have to do something I almost never do in the lower-division undergraduate surveys or introduction-to-writing-about-literature classes: I have to show my own cards, and I have to do it in a way that comports with what I've just argued about argument.

I begin this phase of the class with Richard Rorty's introduction to *Consequences of Pragmatism: Essays, 1972–80*. Rorty, as I suggested at the outset of this chapter, is a thoroughgoing secularist who urges us to acknowledge the human origins of all human belief systems, and he thinks it dangerous to imagine that our beliefs come from someplace "outside" us, whether from God or Nature; moreover, he sees philosophy, paradoxically enough, simultaneously as an enterprise that can help deliver us from the last lingering remnants of theocracy and Platonism and as an enterprise that does not, in the end, have much influence over the affairs of the world. He also thinks that philosophers are particularly susceptible to professional self-aggrandizement; they are wont to conceive of themselves as the judges of everyone else's truth claims, just as poets in moments of cultural crisis are wont to declare themselves the unacknowledged legislators of the world.

Crucially, Rorty never backs himself into the corner of arguing that his antifoundationalist account of truth is itself true; he argues merely that it is useful, that it "pays its way," that it will serve us as a good tool for getting things done and for taking responsibility for our own moral propositions. He does not claim that Platonism and its ilk are inaccurate representations of the Way Things Really Are, either, precisely because he wants to jettison altogether such talk of the Way Things Really Are; thus, when he suggests that we substitute a "coherence theory of truth" (in which our beliefs "hang together" in such and such a way and are secured by intersubjective agreement among deliberating parties) for the "correspondence theory of truth" (in which we claim that our beliefs are secured by their correspondence to the way things really are in the world), he is not so foolish as to suggest that the coherence theory of truth better corresponds to the state of the world. Rather, he merely tells us that the correspondence theory of truth has nothing "interesting" left to say about the world, and that it no longer seems worth pursuing. This dismissal of most of the world's philosophical traditions is of course profoundly enraging to most of Rorty's critics. But anything else would involve Rorty in straightforward self-contradiction. Thus, when he offers you his groundless, foundationless, postmodern pragmatism, he doesn't say, "Here, this will fix you because it is right and true"; rather, he says, "Here, you might find this an interesting way to think about how we think—I tend to like it, and perhaps you will too." It is not for nothing that British philosopher Simon Blackburn has dubbed Rorty "the professor of complacence."[26] And, despite the fact that Rorty has been the single most important intellectual influence on my life, I have my problems with him too (some of which I've hinted at in this paragraph, and some of which I'll get to a bit later on). Still, I think he's onto something, and I ask my students—and you—to bear with me as I explain why I think so.

The critical passage in Rorty's introduction to *Consequences of Pragmatism* comes when he admits that it is "morally humiliating" to be an antifoundationalist, because antifoundationalists do not have the ability to say to their opponents, "You are simply wrong in a morally objective sense":

> Suppose that Socrates was wrong, that we have *not* once seen the Truth, and so will not, intuitively, recognize it when we see it again. This means that when the secret police come, when the torturers violate the innocent, there is nothing to be said to them of the form "There is something within you that you are betraying. Though you embody the practices of a totalitarian society which will endure for-

ever, there is something beyond those practices which condemns you." This thought is hard to live with, as is Sartre's remark: "Tomorrow, after my death, certain people may decide to establish fascism, and the others may be cowardly or miserable enough to let them get away with it. At that moment, fascism will be the truth of man, and so much the worse for us. In reality, things will be as much as man has decided they are."[27]

As I tell my students, I have never been able to decide whether this passage is humble or defiant: On one reading, it could be saying, "Admittedly, we antifoundationalists have no useful reply to offer when the fascists arrive to declare that they are the truth of man; if indeed they have established a totalitarian society that will endure forever, they have effectively created the truth of man in their image, and anything we say to the contrary—'No, the human carries the spark of the divine,' or 'No, we have a deep moral intuition that all are created equal'—is just so much self-consolation." On the other hand, it could be saying something more like, "We antifoundationalists, unlike the rest of you blatherers who natter on about the eternal rights of man, live without illusions. We know that rights are flimsy social things that can be made and unmade with each passing epoch, and we know that it would be the height of folly to think that we can give up the diurnal fight, safe in the knowledge that some higher or deeper forces are ultimately on our side."

My students are almost uniformly horrified by this passage: You mean there's nothing more to our moral intuitions and our deepest beliefs—it's just us, making stuff up? It's one thing to think of Baudrillard—or Beckett, or Yeats—as making stuff up. But this looks like simple nihilism, and it sounds dangerous and wrong. I tell them: Think of it this way. American bioethicist Leon Kass argues that we have deep moral intuitions built into our human apparatus, and that we have a natural revulsion against certain beliefs and practices.[28] It sounds reasonable enough—until you think of the good people (and I do mean "good people" in an unironic sense) who for centuries had a profound moral revulsion against what they called miscegenation. Think of their insistence that their revulsion was grounded in the laws of God and nature. Or think of the profound conviction with which our imaginary interlocutor insisted that both adulterers and rape victims must be stoned to death. He has a deep moral intuition that rape victims have been defiled and will bring great shame to their families. Because we do not believe as he does, we have no trouble seeing his beliefs as culturally bounded rather than naturally or divinely sanctioned. And what of our own most cherished beliefs? Are they fundamentally "true," in a noncontingent, noncultural, nonhistorical sense, or are they what Rorty likes to call sentences to which we pay the compliment of calling them "true"?

OK, now the students get it: *here's* the really noxious postmodernist stuff. Never mind that loopy Baudrillard and his simulacra; here we're finally getting to the stuff we read about in the newspapers! This is what we came for!

It is not true, in my experience, that college students are shrugging relativists. While they try to refrain from sweeping moral judgments, partly out of a sense of youthful humility and partly out of a sense that it's not their job to parse the entire world, they do tend to have a general skepticism of anything that smacks of open racism, sexism, or homophobia (if they're liberals) or hypersensitive, politically correct cant (if they're conservatives). And they tend to believe, when they have strong beliefs, that their beliefs have some basis in something—something, that is, other than other beliefs. I know precisely how they feel. When I first took a course with Richard Rorty in 1985 and heard him describe belief systems as "vocabularies" (much like Wittgenstein's "language games") and heard him describe entire "vocabularies" as "contingent," I naively asked, "Contingent on what?" Rorty blinked at me for a moment, cocked his head, knitted his brow, and said, "Not contingent *on*—just contingent." I had, of course, been using precisely the vocabulary he'd decided to leave behind; but surely, I thought in 1985, you can't say "X is contingent" without suggesting that there is something on which, or from which, X *depends*. After all, even in common parlance, when we say, "On what do you base that belief?" aren't we asking for nothing less than a basis, a factual or evidentiary ground for the belief in question?

Yeah, we sure are, my older self replies to the twenty-three-year-old who took Rorty's seminar and to the twenty-year-olds in my own seminar, but nothing about antifoundationalism banishes facts and evidence from consideration. We just have to specify what facts and evidence we're talking about, and why they matter. That really shouldn't be too much to ask. Beyond that, there are two other things to keep in mind when we deal with antifoundationalism. One, facts and evidence are rarely dispositive of moral disputes that proceed from principles rather than from empirical observations; few people change their minds about abortion or euthanasia, say, simply because they are introduced to certain facts. And yet, two, antifoundationalism is actually more open to new facts and evidence than are its competitors in the world of philosophy.[29] This second point—which I'll explain in more detail below—was finally the thing that made me begin to think, in the middle of my graduate-school career, that I would do better to think of cultures and their vocabularies as "contingent" rather than "contingent on something else."

First, though, I try to illustrate what an antifoundationalist approach to justice might look like,[30] since that's what bothers my students most: the idea that they will have nothing to say to the secret police and the torturers, all because they've made the terrible mistake of taking my class. I begin with the famous proposition, more familiar to my students even than *Pulp Fiction*, that "We hold these truths to be self-evident: that all men are created equal; that they are endowed by their Creator with certain inalienable rights; that among these are life, liberty, and the pursuit of happiness." It is, after all, one of the most important sentences ever written in the history of political philosophy, and it helped to change the course of the world. And so, begging my students' pardon, I set about revising it. I suggest instead that all humans should be considered to have equal claim to basic human rights such as food, shelter, education, health care, and political representation; and that we should endow each other with these rights, knowing full well that they are alienable and that we must work to interpret and to sustain them. And, finally, that none of the above is self-evident. Then I go a bit further, and point out that it was actually *not* self-evident in 1776 that all men were created equal, since almost nobody on the planet actually believed such a thing. On the contrary, most people who considered the matter at all, even in the educated, Christianized West, believed in natural hierarchies deriving either from the great chain of being or from the divine right of kings, which is why we Americans had to fight a war for principles that were allegedly self-evident. (So yes, I'm saying that Jefferson, drawing on John Locke, among others, made this stuff up.) And I am hardly the first to point out that the new nation, upon winning that war, practiced slavery for another fourscore and nine years, or that we continue to debate today, as we must, the meaning of the word "equal" and the meaning of the word "rights." As for the Creator: we are often tempted to think it would be easier to engage in political deliberation if we could simply appeal to the Almighty for sanction. But the events of the recent past, not to mention the past six millennia, have shown us that it is quite impossible to compel assent to notions of human rights and dignity by appealing to the authority of the divine. I am not denying that many people ground their beliefs and their lives in religion, and I am not saying that it is illegitimate or illiberal or wrong for people to do so. I am merely saying that the strategy of appealing to the Creator doesn't solve the problems it wants to solve; it merely displaces the question onto how one interprets the word of the Creator and how one vests authority in those interpreters. It thus leaves us once again with the problem of how to recognize, in concrete political practice, the human rights and the human dignity with which we are supposedly self-evidently endowed.

Then I told my students the following story.[31] Once, after one of my lectures, I was asked whether I didn't think there were moral imperatives the content of which we do not yet know. Wow, talk about neo-Platonism, I thought at the time. Weirder still, the questioner believed that we *must* accept the possibility of unknown moral imperatives if we are to stave off fascism. I was genuinely puzzled by this—what if those unknown moral imperatives turned out to be fascist?—but I tried not to dismiss the question altogether in that way. Instead, I told the questioner, "I have good news and bad news for you. If you want noncontingent, transhistorical grounds for social justice, the bad news is that you can't have them—and the good news is that you don't need them." This reply then provoked another question: If that's really what I think, then if I were the only person on earth who believed in the human rights of my son Jamie, would he still have those rights after I died, or would he, as a person with Down syndrome, be effectively dehumanized, cast out of the human "conversation" altogether?

My students hummed back and forth with ideas. I let them hum for a good long while, and then I asked: Which way of thinking is more responsible, do you imagine, if you're a parent of a child with a disability, whose disability has often been—and might again be— grounds for barring him from the rest of the human community? Do you (a) assert that there are objective, "intrinsic" moral grounds for your belief in his "innate" humanity, hoping to persuade others that your belief is founded on something other than your mere belief, or (b) assert that there are no "innate" criteria for inclusion in the human family and no "intrinsic" grounds for your advocacy of his inclusion, but that he should be included anyway because we should try to understand "equal rights" as broadly as possible?

It will come as no surprise, I hope, that the vast majority of my students say (a). And this more than anything else challenges the notion that our classrooms are full of post-adolescent relativists; when serious matters are at stake—not just foot rubs and oral sex, but the very definition of the human—they prefer to have firm ground to stand on. Again, I do not tell them there is no firm ground; that would be to make precisely the mistake Rorty avoids, of insisting that antifoundationalism is intrinsically true regardless of what people believe about it. Instead, I ask them to imagine what it would be like to believe and act as if there were no firm ground. And now, they realize with varying degrees of dismay and delight, we're having a real argument. It's a meta-argument, yes, an argument about the necessity of grounds for belief, but they're dealing with someone who really does see this aspect of the world differently than they do. They're supposed to think or say, "Interesting point," before they decide whether to kill me. And they do. But I help them to keep arguing; it's my job. If I were to find myself in a classroom full of committed antifoundationalists, I would have to argue as a devil's advocate for foundationalism, just as I had to argue as a Habermasian in my graduate seminar in order to break up my students' nearly-unanimous consensus that consensus does violence to heterogeneity.

Besides, I understand my students' preference for (a). I think there's no question that in the world we know, claims about the intrinsic rightness of X have a certain purchase on the moral imagination that claims about the contingent plausibility of X do not. It appears that so far, Rorty's appeal is simply not sufficiently powerful on this count; when the secret police arrive, most people I know want to be able to tell the secret police that fascism is intrinsically wrong, and they want to be able to point to something more authoritative on the subject than *Consequences of Pragmatism*—just as I sometimes want to believe, despite my explicit intellectual commitments, that my child has intrinsic value whatever the world might think.

Now, I've learned over the years that it is a dicey thing to admit to that desire. It invites realists and their friends to say, aha, you see, this Bérubé has been to graduate school and has been indoctrinated by Richard Rorty, and yet "down deep, in his heart," as the saying goes, he really does want to have an objective, noncontingent moral philosophy. But actually, in such matters I do not have one desire that resides "more deeply" than another; I have lots of conflicting desires all at once. One of them entails the vain hope that someday we will no longer need to make the case for the human rights of every human born. That's the foundationalist part, the one that emerges whenever I get weary at the idea that we all have to keep arguing for the humanity of our fellow humans, especially for those of us like Jamie who aren't very good at things like arguing. But another of my desires runs directly contrary to that one, for it entails the imperative to keep arguing with moral foundationalists, to try to convince them, as I've already said but will surely have to say again and again before I die, that it is the height of folly to think that we can give up the diurnal fight, safe in the knowledge that some higher or deeper forces are ultimately on our side. If it is dangerous to speak antifoundationalist in a world most of whose citizens like to believe in objective moral grounds, it is also dangerous to speak foundationalist and think that such an argument about human rights can ever be won once and for all, in such a way that no one need ever worry about fascism or eugenics again.

I can be more specific about what it takes to win such an argument. The Individuals with Disabilities Education Act grants to my child a "free appropriate public education" in the "least restrictive environment." For the past fifteen years or so, the "least restrictive environment" has been understood to be the "regular" classroom, and the law has been interpreted as indicating that "inclusion" is the default position—that kids with disabilities should be included in classrooms with their non-disabled peers to the greatest extent possible. It may happen someday that the IDEA is not reauthorized by Congress, or that the meaning of "free appropriate public education" or "least restrictive environment" will be construed differently than it is now. In fact, in 1997, House Republicans made vague noises about refusing to reauthorize IDEA and its "unfunded mandates." They were prevented from going after the law, in part, by the realization that Trent Lott's chief of staff had a child with a disability, and that any attempt to undo IDEA would be stalled in the Senate—where, at the time, Lott was majority leader.

It would be nice, surely, if our rights did not hinge on such things. I believe that foundationalists desire to live in such a world, and I can't blame them. But I've learned—partly from Rorty, and partly from the rest of the world—that the only philosophical "foundation" underlying the IDEA and its various realizations is our own collective political will, a will that rests on nothing more or less than our intersubjective agreement. Jamie Bérubé currently has a right to an inclusive public education, but that right is neither intrinsic nor innate. Rather, Jamie's rights were invented, and implemented slowly and with great difficulty. The recognition of his human dignity, enshrined in those rights, was invented. And by the same token, those rights, and that recognition, can be taken away. While I live, I promise myself that I will not let that happen, but I also live with the knowledge that it may; to live any other way, to live as if Jamie's rights were somehow intrinsic, would be irresponsible. For what would it mean for Jamie to "possess" rights that no one on earth recognized? A fat lot of good it would do him, I think, so I don't even see the point of speaking in such a way. The conclusion may sound either monstrous or all too obvious: if, in fact, no one on earth recognized Jamie's human dignity, then there would in fact be no human perspective from which he would be understood to possess "intrinsic" human dignity. And then he simply wouldn't have it, and then so much the worse for the human race.

This is my version of Rorty's Sartrean warning about fascism: the day that fascism becomes the truth of man, so much the worse for us. The day that people with cognitive disabilities and developmental delays are barred—once again—from public life, so much the worse for us. But that day might arrive. If you believe that universal human rights should accrue to every human born, it's your job to try to make sure that day never comes—and you should operate as if it always might.

Now I've finally laid all my cards on the table. I teach a course in postmodernism, I'm fond of much of postmodern culture (even some of the trashy SF elements of it!), but I find some aspects of it to be intellectually vacuous or deluded. I give a serious hearing to arguments that universalism is a mere stalking horse for Eurocentrism and imperialism, and I acknowledge that these arguments have a good deal of merit when it comes to the historical record; but I do not see these arguments as grounds for giving up on the promise of a truly universal universalism. And yet I'm an antifoundationalist who does not believe that this potential universalism has to be grounded in anything other than the rights with which we agree to endow each other. I retain a healthy sense of postmodern Lyotardian skepticism about the incommensurability of language games, but I think there are ways we can become intelligible to each other, and even begin to speak of the rationales and protocols by which our language games allow us to "change our minds," even if we don't wind up changing them. I admit that mine is a minority report on the subject—indeed, a minority report from within a minority report. But then, I don't demand that any of my students, or any of my readers, agree with anything I've said so far.

No one is penalized, in my course, for emerging as a resolute foundationalist at the end of the semester.

In the 2001 class, at least one student emerged as a resolute foundationalist at the end of the semester—more resolute, I think, than when he came in, for my arguments about antifoundationalism provoked him quite severely. That student wasn't John in the back of the room, with his well-developed resistance to any discussion that had to do with race or ethnicity. Rather, it was a student I'll call Stan, who sat in the very middle of the classroom all semester, paying careful attention but not saying a word, and who practically erupted at Rorty (and me), saying that *this* was the moral rot he'd expected to encounter in this course. Of the students who objected to antifoundationalism as really noxious postmodernist stuff, Stan was by far the most impassioned and the most eloquent.

He opened by accusing me of denying the existence of objective foundations for belief. I told him that I couldn't have done that (or shouldn't have sounded as if I were doing that), because to do so would be self-contradictory; obviously, I can't say that objective grounds objectively don't exist. Instead, I could offer him what I think Richard Rorty would say if he were in the room, and it would go something like this: it is more useful, more pragmatic to speak and behave as if there are no ahistorical, intrinsic grounds for the most capacious possible definition of the human, and to promote our understanding of that definition nonetheless, aware both of its fictionality and of its potential for reducing the amount of wanton cruelty and greed in the world. Where did this idea of human rights come from? We don't know, though we do know that most humans in most epochs haven't subscribed to it. All we know is that it's here and we ought to try to get used to it, because it does seem like a very good idea, on balance.

"Fine, then, *Professor Rorty*," Stan shot back, "and if you were here I'd say that there's nothing you've told me, so far as I can see, that would lead anyone to be less cruel or greedy. All you've said is that 'things will be much as man has decided they are.' I don't see anything in your introduction to *Consequences of Pragmatism* that suggests that we should band together to fight to prevent the arrival of a world in which the secret police come to take us away."

That was a fair reply, and I told Stan that although I think it's implicit in *Consequences of Pragmatism* that Rorty does not want to live under the secret police, I could see why he might not see this, or might not agree to make the implicit explicit. In his later book, *Contingency, Irony, Solidarity,* Rorty is clearer and more emphatic about his opposition to authoritarianism,[32] but, as I told Stan, there are critiques of that book that claim that Rorty's commitment to "irony," by which he means an awareness of the contingent nature of all language games, undermines his commitment to "solidarity," by which he means the project of reducing the amount of cruelty and greed in the world.

Stan agreed with those critiques, insisting that appeals to secure moral grounds are the only kind of appeals that work; as he put it, people aren't motivated by arguments that say, "This isn't true but you should believe it anyway." He was, I recall, the class's most enthusiastic advocate of option (a), asserting that there are objective, intrinsic moral grounds for your beliefs. Moreover, he argued that foundationalism works better because it speaks to a profound human need to believe in something outside ourselves. It works not just because it's convenient, but because we find it emotionally satis-fying, and we find it emotionally satisfying for reasons we can't fully explain because they're so completely a part of our human makeup.

Possibly, possibly, I said; but what if that part of our human makeup turns out to be closely allied to that part of our human makeup that fears others and wants to kill them? Stan was offended by this move, because, as he put it, it implied that antifoundationalists are more highly evolved, in a moral sense, than anybody else on the planet. I had suggested that foundationalism draws on primitive human instincts, and that foundationalists are more or less dragging their knuckles on the sidewalk. I apologized for that implication (which I hadn't intended, but which Stan was right to identify), and proceeded to suggest that often, when someone appeals to "intrinsic parts of our human makeup," she (or he) winds up constructing a ground that consists of a selective reading of the available evidence. Some aspects of our evolutionary inheritance do seem conducive to the creation of a just and peaceful world. Others don't. Stan appealed to an aspect of our species that finds it emotionally satisfying to believe in something "outside ourselves," while I appealed to an aspect of our species that finds it emotionally satisfying to take responsibility for structures of our own creation. How is this possible? It's possible because the "human makeup" seems to be too rich, chaotic, and contradictory to serve as a self-evident ground for either altruism or selfishness; yes, we're a greedy and violent species, but we're also the only species we know of that's devised theories of justice. To me, it seems a shame to build a philosophical foundation on an appeal to precisely those aspects of the human makeup that antifoundationalists believe we'd be better off ignoring.

Stan's next move was an especially good one. Conceding my point about the complexity of the "human makeup," he asked me how I could have any faith in the future of a kind of universalism that has never existed on the planet. I told him that, quite honestly, I'm not really sure. All I can do is to recall what Gandhi said when he was asked what he thought of Western civilization. It is a famously wry remark, speaking simultaneously to the promise of universalism and its betrayal by the history of imperialism: "It would be a good idea."

There were three or four other students who played significant parts in the discussion at this point. They were far less perturbed by Rorty than was Stan, but skeptical nonetheless. For a variety of reasons and in a variety of ways, they wanted to know (a) what is to be gained by advocating a kind of pragmatic, unfounded universalism as "a good idea," and (b) why the idea is good in the first place. I'd explained, in the course of our reading of Rorty, that Rorty subscribes to William James's pragmatist definition of truth as that which is "good in the way of belief," and I'd indicated my own impatience with the elusiveness and/or circularity of this definition. But I hadn't indicated, except in the most general way, what I might mean by "good." Before we got to (b), though, we dug deeper into (a). One student, a young woman with a double major in English and women's studies, returned us to the question of fascism, and asked why antifoundationalists can't simply declare that something is just wrong. Let's say we want to condemn clitoridectomy or widow-burning or the stoning of adulteresses—three touchstones that commonly put Western feminists (and their allies, like me) in the uncomfortable position of advocating a kind of moral imperialism with regard to the cultural practices of non-Western societies. Or let's say we want to insist that women should be educated. Can't we say, in so many words, that denying education to women is just wrong? Do we really have to wade through reams of *Pulp Fiction*-meets-Rorty debate in order to establish the meta-meta-meta-grounds for deliberation on this one?

Rorty himself is unambiguous about this; he thinks that the institutions of the liberal West constitute the best form of human society yet devised, and he unabashedly counsels the rest of the world to liberate its women in order to unleash their (the women's, and the societies') full potential. He's happily moral-imperialist in this respect. He doesn't say you can't call something wrong, but he does counsel you against saying, "There is something within you that you are betraying. Though you embody the practices of a totalitarian society which will endure forever, there is something beyond those practices which condemns you." He opposes cruelty and favors Tennyson's "Parliament of Mankind," but he simply insists that the ideal of universal human flourishing is something we cooked up one day.

"Something we cooked up one day!" the student laughed. "But then what happens when a patriarchal society says, 'You cooked up your morals, we cooked up ours, so you don't have any basis for criticizing us? Do we say, 'Yes, but you cooked yours up *wrong*?'"

I loved this answer, and I still do. It makes me think of the scene in *Raiders of the Lost Ark* in which Harrison Ford is confronted by an adversary who deftly brandishes a sword with flourishes that suggest that our hero is in for yet another long, dramatic bout of hand-to-hand combat, whereupon Ford, exhausted and exasperated, simply takes out a gun and shoots him. OK, so you don't want to argue anymore; you just want to expel your interlocutor from the conversation. The next question, as I pointed out in response, is this: What force does that declaration have for the wrong party in question? Does it truly expel someone from the conversation, or does it just make us feel good about our rightness and their wrongness? And as the student deftly replied, you have that problem no matter what, foundations or no foundations.

Still, that's how we discussed (a), as to what is gained and lost in antifoundationalism: on the one hand, the possibility of advocating universalism not as a natural law, not as a divine edict, not as a possibility latent within ourselves and yearning to be free, but simply as a good idea that, like Western civilization, we might want to put into practice sometime in the future, preferably sooner rather than later; on the other hand, the desire, the need, to insist that, sometimes, X is simply wrong regardless of the current state of the world, regardless of the contingency of cultural practices, and regardless of whether all parties involved will agree with the judgment (since they almost certainly will not).

Here's how I play those hands: if antifoundationalists are sometimes too leery of declaring X to be wrong, foundationalists jump much too quickly to that conclusion. Let me put this a bit more polemically: antifoundationalists did not bring you the Spanish Inquisition—or the Crusades, or the Holocaust. I cannot see why foundationalists proceed in this debate as if their side, the side that appeals to objective facts and secure moral grounds, has nothing to answer for in the world's long and sorry history of civil butchery. While I understand the need and the desire to say "X is simply wrong" and to act accordingly—by embargoing X's trade or intervening in X's internal affairs or simply censuring X somehow—I have to insist that most of the crimes of human history have followed not from our reluctance to declare X wrong but from our willingness to do so with extreme prejudice. What, then, is gained by treating moral edicts as nothing more than good ideas, dreamt up by well-meaning humans? Well, for one thing, it helps protect us from the hubris of thinking that we're propounding something more or other than human ideas, and for another, it cautions us against too readily leaping to the conclusion that X is simply wrong and must be stopped or exterminated.

Rorty suggests as much in the final words of his essay "Trotsky and the Wild Orchids," which speak not of moral humiliation but moral humility:

> Despite my relatively early disillusionment with Platonism, I am very glad that I spent all those years reading philosophy books. For I learned something that still seems very important: to distrust the intellectual snobbery that originally led me to read them. If I had not read all those books, I might never have been able to stop looking for what Derrida calls "a full presence beyond the reach of play," for a luminous synoptic vision.
>
> By now I am pretty sure that looking for such a presence and a vision is a bad idea. The main trouble is that you might succeed, and your success might let you imagine that you have something more to rely on than the tolerance and decency of your fellow human beings. The democratic community of Dewey's dreams is a community in which nobody imagines that. It is a community in which everybody thinks that it is human solidarity, rather than knowledge of some-

thing not merely human, that really matters. The actually existing approximations to such a fully democratic, fully secular community now seem to me the greatest achievements of our species.[33]

In this passage, antifoundationalism appears as if it affords us a means for avoiding temptation; Rorty's suggestion that one "might succeed" in discovering immutable moral laws is ironic, of course, for what he means is that one might *think* one has succeeded. And what follows from that "success"? Rorty suggests, interestingly enough, that the consequences would be a kind of complacency; you might think you have the luxury of relying on something more than merely human tolerance and decency. But there is another, nastier possible consequence as well: you might think that you have exclusive access to those extra-human sources of truth, and you might conclude that people who disagree with you are not simply working from different moral premises but, rather, are alien—or opposed—to morality itself. It then becomes all the easier to exclude them from the conversation, from all forms of human community.

It does not always happen that moral foundationalists exclude their opponents from the human community, just as it does not always happen that antifoundationalists are willing to tolerate every form of human difference. Antifoundationalists can, in certain circumstances, be warmongers, and foundationalists can be pacifists. Two students picked up on this fairly quickly: if antifoundationalism isn't a guide for how to act, they said, it's just a form of "situated knowledge." Ah, situated knowledge: my English/women's studies double major had been using the term as well, seeing it as a necessary corollary to antifoundationalism. If we start from the premise that human affairs are guided by principles that have a human origin and can be altered by human deliberation, she argued, then all knowledge is inevitably situated. She cited, in support of this proposition, the work of feminist and science studies scholar Donna Haraway.

OK, I replied, but if you are saying that all knowledge is situated, are you willing to insist that your own claim is situated as well? My question was a version of the question of whether the relativist believes that relativism is unrelativistically true, and to help my student avoid the conundrum, I suggested to her that even Haraway's idea of situated knowledge relies on a kind of knowledge that, while it may be antifoundationalist, cannot be wholly situated. I directed the class back to the syllabus, this time to the concluding chapter of Steven Connor's *Postmodernist Culture*: "there is a lurking incoherence in the idea of situated knowledge," writes Connor:

> For what Haraway proclaims or at least enacts is something more than the advantage of situatedness as such. It is the advantage of recognizing and declaring yourself to be situated, the epistemological edge conferred by knowledge *about* the situatedness of knowledge. The injunction issued by Haraway and repeated by those who follow her is not "Be ye situated," but "Know and acknowledge thy situatedness." The question that then arises is where this knowledge of the situatedness of one's knowledge comes from, and what its status is.[34]

Connor's critique of "situated knowledge" is closely allied to my complaint about the academic left's fetishization of the "local." Stan liked this passage, and responded to it by nodding his head vigorously; I thought, at the time, that if you could make noise by nodding your head, Stan would be shouting. He insisted that Connor was echoing his earlier argument against Rorty, and I replied that this was about half right: yes, Connor's critique of the antiuniversalist position had something in common with Stan's, but Connor does not insist, as Stan did, that we must abandon antifoundationalism altogether in order to criticize the "lurking incoherence in the idea of situated knowledge." He doesn't argue for a return to moral certainties, derived from something other than human deliberation.

Another young woman chimed in. She had no problem seeing human laws as having a human origin, and she believed that feminist standpoint epistemology says the same thing. But she didn't see how anyone can get from there to universalism. "Feminist-standpoint epistemology," she said, "challenges universalism precisely because we *don't* all think the same way about values—"

"Or anything else," I added.

"Or anything else, and we shouldn't be required to. So I don't understand how you can suggest as a provisional 'good idea' something that would eventually produce that kind of mass conformity."

She had a point, one that Rorty's essay doesn't fully acknowledge in its evocation of an ideal Deweyan society in which "everybody thinks that it is human solidarity, rather than knowledge of something not merely human, that really matters." In a fully secular society we would have to give up the claim that anyone's moral imperatives derive from something other than human deliberation, so yes, there would be a very general agreement on that. But would that induce mass conformity of the kind my student rightly wanted to avoid? Possibly, religious people who do not want to live in a "fully secular" society, who want to appeal to the Deity not just as a matter of personal expression but as a matter of public policy, might make that objection. Nor are religious believers the only people who might object to such a society; so far, I've discussed incommensurability as if it's always a standoff between religion and reason, but sometimes it's a standoff between reason and the kind of oddball, secular skeptics of reason you find in literature and the fine arts. For, as I told the class in response to this young woman's comment, one of the reasons Lyotard regards Habermas as so toxic is that Lyotard is, among other things, a defender of the artistic avant-garde who wants to leave open the door to innovative thought of all kinds, especially the kinds that don't orient themselves toward consensus. He calls this kind of thought "paralogy," and he thinks of it as a form of resistance to all manner of intellectual tyranny. "Invention," Lyotard insists, "is always born of dissension." In defiance of all authorities, whoever they may be, Lyotard writes, "Postmodern knowledge is not simply a tool of the authorities; it refines our sensitivity to differences and reinforces our ability to tolerate the incommensurable. Its principle is not the expert's homology, but the inventor's paralogy."[35]

But I don't think I'm asking for all that much in the way of intellectual conformity, consensus, or (gasp) tyranny. The version of universalism I'm proposing *does* suggest that it *might* be good and useful to say, "No matter how or what you think, you fellow human, you are entitled to food and shelter and health care and education and political representation." You can be a Christian Scientist, a secular-humanist professor, or an avant-garde poet/sculptor/dancer, and we can let all those language games flourish. But underlying that commitment to paralogy and dissensus, let's imagine provisional agreement about human entitlements to food and shelter, freedom from torture, and so forth, regardless of what we think about anything else. Let's say that these are human rights to which you are entitled, and that your entitlement is not dependent on your ability to pay for them or on your beliefs about God or language; they are simply part and parcel of being born into the human community. And let's set that as our standard for just societies, be they in Alabama, Angola, or Afghanistan: the extent to which such a society realizes these rights and gives them flesh, so to speak.

I asked the young woman if she had any complaint about that kind of universalism—and, if so, to what end she would want to forward such a complaint. Her worry, basically, was that we wouldn't be able to agree on even this provisional form of human rights unless we *were* all thinking in the same way. I think that's a worry worth having, and I told her so. Even still, the point remains that universalism holds out the possibility that you or anyone else can contest it in its own terms so as to change its own terms; anyone

can show up at the door one day and say, "Your so-called universalism is not, in fact, universal enough."

Which leads me finally to thing (b), what I mean by "good" in a
"good idea." Drawing on my experience with my son Jamie and
my readings in the history of eugenics and disability activism, I
think it might be a good idea for all of us to treat other humans as if
we do not know their potential, as if they just might in fact surprise
us, as if they might exceed our expectations. It might be a good idea
for us to check ourselves whenever we think we know what "normal" human standards of behavior and achievement might be.
Here, I'm taking up a debate in queer theory, one that starts with
scholars working in the wake of Michel Foucault: the idea that any
invocation of the normative will inevitably be normalizing. There's
no question that it usually is; for most of the past few centuries,
we've defined human norms in order to try to exclude significant
deviations from the norm from the human family altogether, and
that's what the project of eugenics—from the first glimmerings of
Social Darwinism to the mass exterminations of the Holocaust—
was all about. But I part ways with most queer theorists on this
question, because I think there's a way to separate "normative"
from "normalizing." I call it the normative paradox: I imagine the
queer-theory critique of the normative in the form of the self-
canceling sentence, "People ought not to issue normative judgments."[36] Then I retool it in such a way as to affirm a moral norm
that opposes such things as eugenics, misogyny, racism, homophobia, and (yes) discrimination against political conservatives:
"Norms ought not to normalize people in such a way as to stigma-
tize and dehumanize them." There, now, we've got ourselves a
normative sentence that takes a stand against normalizing.

But why be so agnostic about the "normal," and so committed in
principle to the idea that our fellow humans might surprise us,
even when they seem to be severely disabled? I think there's a very
good reason to extend the domain of the universal, to widen the

conversation, to democratize our social debates, and to see anti-foundationalism as central to the entire enterprise. The reason is this: a capacious, supple, and revisable sense of what it is to be human is better than a narrow, fixed, and parochial sense of what it is to be human, and the more participants we as a society can incorporate into the deliberation of what it means to be human, the greater the chances that that deliberation will enhance our collective capacities to recognize each other as humans entitled to human dignity. This last point is absolutely critical; it's the engine that drives the rest of my beliefs. And it wasn't just cooked up in some seminar room, either; it comes to us straight from recent US history. Most Americans had no idea what people with Down syndrome and other intellectual disabilities could achieve until we'd passed a law entitling them all to a free appropriate public education in the least restrictive environment. So just as women and minorities, when finally given access to the terrain of universalism, led universalists to rethink the terms of universalism, so too, when more and more formerly excluded groups are given access to the conversation, will we be impelled to rethink what access itself means. I use the word "access" carefully, because people with disabilities are still not sufficiently included in the debate about universalism, and sometimes it turns out that you need to build access ramps just so they can get in the door and tell you that your previous ideas about "access" to universalism were inadequate.

Last but not least, I can say all this without appealing to any idea of innate human dignity or objective moral value; all I would be doing in appealing to such things is saying that my beliefs are something more than my beliefs, thereby paying myself the flattering but delusional compliment of claiming to be incontestably in the right.

I am aware that many professional philosophers don't see things this way, and I have noticed that some of them can get quite territorial on the subject; carrying on an intellectual rivalry that reaches all the way back to Plato's *Republic*, they would prefer that the poets and the literary critics stay out of the *polis* altogether. They complain that we literary types like to "reduce" everything to texts and discourses, and we don't understand that they are searching for the immutable, nondiscursive truths of the universe. This position can crop up even in the most unlikely places, in the work of philosophers who are otherwise hostile to the idea of immutable truths. In his 2004 book, *The End of Faith: Religion, Terror, and the Future of Reason*, philosopher Sam Harris skewers all forms of religious belief yet holds on to the faith that philosophy can "discover"—not invent—new moral principles yet unknown to any humans:

> In philosophical terms, then, pragmatism can be directly opposed to *realism*. For the realist, our statements about the world will be "true" or "false" not merely in virtue of how they function amid the welter of our other beliefs, or with reference to any culture-bound criteria, but because reality simply *is* a certain way, independent of our thoughts. Realists believe that there are truths about the world that may exceed our capacity to know about them; there are facts of the matter whether or not we can bring such facts into view. To be an ethical realist is to believe that in ethics, as in physics, there are truths waiting to be *discovered*—and thus we can be right or wrong in our beliefs about them.[37]

This makes sense, I think, only if you don't consider things like gravity and slavery to be qualitatively different kinds of objects: the first a natural phenomenon whose laws can be discovered by humans with great diligence (and which we still haven't quite gotten the hang of, as the string theorists search for the principles of quantum gravity, and the advocates of a point theory of space search for principles that don't involve vibrating strings),[38] the other a cultural object created by humans, contested by humans, and gradually—and fitfully, and still not universally—abolished by humans. The reason I disagree with Harris, the reason I am not what he calls an "ethical realist," is that I believe that gravity and slavery are different kinds of things, and that objective, observer-independent knowledge about gravity is possible but should not be taken as a model for knowledge about human affairs. I believe there are mind-independent entities, and that you can check this for yourself by kicking a stone; but I do not understand how people like Harris, who are so stringently skeptical about religious belief, can insist on the existence of mind-independent concepts. And this, as my students gradually come to understand, is an incommensurability. It is not an incommensurability about slavery itself; both the ethical realists and I are against it. It is an incommensurability with regard to how one justifies one's being against it.

I wrapped up this part of the course by telling my students that if they wanted to pursue this further, with real philosophers, they should consult Richard Rorty for (most of) my end of the discussion, and Thomas Nagel—in *The View from Nowhere,* for a start—for one of the most salient responses to Rorty. (Today, I would also mention Simon Blackburn's 2005 book, *Truth: A Guide*. I added, back in 2001, that many philosophy professors don't even bother to consider Rorty a "real" philosopher, and that this too was evidence of the depth of the impasse.)[39] For now it was time for us to get back to literature; Richard Powers's *Prisoner's Dilemma* was on deck, and we were more than ready to talk about Powers's treatment of reciprocity and global conflict (the very next week, John would launch his stunning defense of the Japanese-American internment camps, thus giving us yet another example of incommensurability). Besides, there wasn't much more to do once we'd finally reached a real impasse, except to say, "Interesting point": one side says you can't even speak the language of praise or blame—or outright moral condemnation—without relying on absolutes and foundations; the other side says, oh yes, we do have a language of praise and blame, you other people just aren't crediting it in *your* language-game of praise and blame. One side says that there are moral truths out there and that we should search for them just as we try to discover the physical laws that govern the universe; the other side says that it is dangerous to think of moral laws as analogous to physical laws, because it ignores the human origin of human beliefs and practices. I prefer the latter side, as I've suggested above, because I think it better anticipates and accounts for the phenomenon of human disagreement than foundationalism does. Whenever I disagree with a foundationalist about the status of moral law, they think I'm disagreeing not just with some provisional suppositions about the good and the true, but with the very existence of goodness and truth themselves—not just with their beliefs but with Moral Law in capital letters, or, as some people like to put it, God's law. And when it comes down to the day when everyone on the planet believes in the rightness of Hitler, really and truly a planet-wide pro-Hitler consensus, ethical realists such as Sam Harris would insist that there would still be some extra-human perspective from which to condemn that planet-wide consensus. The foundationalists think I'm standing on shaky ground, and I think they're appealing to the ether, looking to the stars for moral edicts yet undiscovered. Me, I prefer to keep this debate right here on earth.

My appeal to disability issues as an example of how to be an antifoundationalist who still Believes In Things wins over some students; but, over the years, two or three undergraduates and a chorus of graduate students have pointed out that my ideal of a supple, capacious definition of the human is only a definition of the human. For animal-rights advocates, my weird quasi-postmodern humanism is still just a humanism, a reaffirmation that the human is the measure of all things. Here too, though, antifoundationalist universalism holds that door open; it leaves it up to us to answer the question of what constitutes a rights-bearing entity, and it insists that to such a question there is no final answer. I say "every human born," but others—pro-life conservatives, for example—would include potential humans (fetuses, embryos, zygotes), and still others—utilitarian philosopher Peter Singer, for example—would include sentient animals (though I think the definition of "sentient" is as slippery as the definition of "potential humans") but not intellectually disabled humans. (This is why Peter Singer is considered evil incarnate by disability activists.) Still, I ask those students who disagree with me about the boundaries not to think of the answer as given but as something we devise, drawing as best we can on the opinions of all members of the human family even if we eventually extend the domain of rights outside the human family.

I SHOULD PULL BACK and make a general remark about all these exchanges before I conclude this chapter with the story of Stan's vigorously combative final paper and how I responded to it. One remark I want to direct to everyone who might have a hard time believing that my honors students are really this nimble and eloquent. I assure you that they are. I have stylized the discussions I've described above, and I've taken out a lot of "um"s and assorted verbal stumbles (on their part and on mine). The students I've mentioned here are quite real, however, and I have reproduced their comments to the best of my ability. Penn State's Schreyer Honors College really does contain extraordinary students who could attend any university in the country, and I have to say I'm quite tired of people—inside and outside academe—who sneer at the idea that students at places like Penn State and Illinois can really be as bright as all that. With regard to undergraduates who are not quite so nimble and eloquent as my honors students, I have the following modus operandi: whenever they say something I personally disagree with, if they phrase it infelicitously, I refer them to the best possible version of their position that I am aware of, or I paraphrase them as best I can, with their approval. If I know of a reply to that position, I offer it; if I am unsure or agnostic about that position, I say that too. But I consider it part of my job to let students know where to go to reinforce or expand their beliefs as well as to challenge them. Should they write papers with which I disagree in any way, if their arguments are plausible, I do not respond by saying, "I wouldn't make this argument, myself"; I try to say, instead, "this argument is problematic as it stands—here's how to make it better."

As for Stan: his final paper continued our in-class debate by arguing that antifoundationalists exclude foundationalists from the discussion even as they suggest that they (the antifoundationalists, that is) are open to discussion from all quarters. Unfortunately, Stan's essay opened by declaring that antifoundationalists were the moral equivalents of tumors that need to be removed for the health of the body politic. He was fortified in this belief by conservative thinker Roger Scruton, who, in a *City Journal* essay of 1999, "Whatever Happened to Reason?," accused Richard Rorty of hypocrisy insofar as the Rortyan world apparently excludes the deeply religious from the outset. Stan cited Scruton's complaint that

> In place of objectivity we have only "inter-subjectivity"—in other words, consensus. Truths, meanings, facts, and values are now regarded as negotiable. The curious thing, however, is that this woolly-minded subjectivism goes hand in hand with a vigorous censorship. Those who put consensus in the place of truth find themselves distinguishing the true from the false consensus. Thus the consensus Rorty assumes rigorously excludes all conservatives, traditionalists, and reactionaries. Only liberals can belong to it; just as only feminists, radicals, gay activists, and anti-authoritarians can take advantage of deconstruction. . . . The inescapable conclusion is that today's gurus advocate subjectivity, relativity, and irrationalism not in order to let in all opinions but precisely to exclude the opinions of people who believe in old authorities and objective truths.[40]

Here, postmodernists are charged with having no principles, with being woolly minded subjectivists; but then, when it turns out that in fact we do have principles which we regard as defensible, we are charged with hypocrisy. This is the philosophical version of the right-wing culture wars argument: liberals claim to be tolerant, but they're not very tolerant of those of us who refuse to tolerate the homosexual lifestyle! Sure enough, Scruton argues that postmodernism is the basis for political correctness, and that politically correct postmodernists have been vigorous censors outside academe as well as inside. This is Scruton's example of such censorship:

> Recently Glen Hoddle, the English soccer coach, expressed the view (perfectly acceptable when uttered by a representative of some ethnic minority) that disabled people are suffering in this life for sins committed in another. He was at once castigated by his employers, by the media, and by the government, in a remarkable series of show trials. He was then fired. Such witch trials are more and more frequent in Britain, conducted outside the courts by bureaucrats and quasi-independent commissions like the Commission for Racial Equality.

Scruton has a point: progressive postmodernists like me do indeed want to help create a society in which it is widely considered inhumane to say publicly that people with disabilities are suffering in this life for sins committed in another. We would also like to help create a society in which it is widely considered inhumane to support bans on interracial marriage (and universities that ban interracial dating), and we would like to persuade our fellow humans that it is neither wise nor compassionate nor admirable to speak of homosexuality as an abomination in the sight of God. Truth be told, some of us would prefer that our fellow humans not claim divine sanction for any of their desires to persecute, eradicate, or simply "change" other people, but, being postmodernists, we know we're never going to achieve a universal consensus on this.

So I couched my reply to Stan partly as an indirect reply to Scruton, hoping to persuade him that his reliance on Scruton was not serving him well. I marked up the margins of his paper with the usual array of queries and annotations, and wrote the following in my formal comments at the end of the paper (what follows are lightly edited excerpts from my remarks):

First, Stan, a word about rhetorical strategies. It is neither useful nor right, in substantive intellectual debate, to open by calling your opponents tumors. This may seem to give your argument the urgency of a crusade, and it may stir the blood of your fellows-in-arms, but it will make your opponents think, "OK, this guy comes to take up the cause of reason, but he uses an eliminationist rhetoric that suggests he wants to exterminate his adversaries." Quite apart from the injustice you do to the human dignity of your adversaries, you should consider the injustice you do to the remainder of your essay.

As for your wholehearted admiration of Scruton, I have two cautions for you, both of which come from the essay you cite.

One, about Scruton's discussion of Glen Hoddle. When I read things like this, I wonder, *whatever happened to reason?* Is this really the kind of rigorous thinking with which you want to align yourself? And what, seriously, *should* one say about someone who blames people with disabilities for their disabilities?

Two, and far more important: "that is why, paradoxically, the postmodern curriculum is so censorious—in just the way that liberalism is censorious. When everything is permitted, it is vital to forbid the forbidder." Here, alas, we're on precisely the ground you want to attack. Scruton's claim here is that secular liberalism (and its postmodern avatar, Rorty) is "censorious" because it excludes censors. But then, you see, his imperative to include the "forbidders" gives a seat at the table not only to the Conservative Party in Britain but to the Taliban he affects to despise throughout the essay. Some forbidders, it turns out, have to be forbidden, and this is a problem for foundationalists and antifoundationalists alike. But stick with Scruton's argument, and you'll have all kinds of trouble forbidding the forbidders you don't care for.

Stan had not spent his entire paper arguing with me by way of Scruton; rather, he used his initial argument in favor of foundationalism as a scaffolding for a more specific argument about the "universal" status of language and literature. In response, I asked him how he was using the term "language," and whether it would cover some nonverbal forms of animal behavior, and I told him I thought he was using the term "universalist" in two different ways: first, to argue for a universal conception of human rights grounded in objective moral truths, and second, to argue that literature is great to the extent that it speaks to (or enunciates) those objective moral truths.

As for your paper's argument about language: is it just words, words, as Hamlet says, or is it an interdependent, weblike system of relations encompassing all of the world we know? Good question. I'll tell you what Rorty's criterion is: in order to exclude from consideration such things as cows facing all one way on a hillside, swallows returning to Capistrano, and amoebas moving around, Rorty suggests that we call "language" all those systems of communication, verbal and nonverbal, that have self-referencing, autocritiquing devices, such as "That was a cool sign" and "You don't make that gesture in here, young man." Just FYI. It's a handy tool—sometimes. [Here I should also have directed him to Ludwig Wittgenstein's arguments against the possible existence of a "private language" in *Philosophical Investigations*.]

Finally, your argument about literature and the universal: it's perfectly possible to read literature as an art form, among other art forms, that speaks beyond its specific time and place, even if (say) we no longer have quite as much invested in establishing the lineage of Rome as Virgil did. In fact, the proposition is (as you almost say) damn near tautological: if the stuff wasn't transcultural to some extent we simply couldn't read it at all. But (to quote a rye bread ad from my youth) just as you don't have to be Jewish to love Levy's, you don't have to be a universalist to love literature, and literature doesn't have to be universal to be great. Between the realm of the local and the realm of the universal is the realm of the *transcultural*, where certain art forms, moral systems, sports entertainments, and what-have-you are intelligible across many cultures *but not all*. For example, let's not forget how much of the *Iliad* really is utterly alien to us. We'll just never understand all of it, particularly with regard to how pre-Socratics understood the relations of the gods to human affairs. You can see Aeschylus's *Oresteia* working with one nettlesome aspect of this problem, namely, the conflict between newly emergent abstract forms of justice and older revenge codes. But back before Aeschylus, who's already weird enough to modern ears, we enter a strange and partly incomprehensible world which is different in kind from the strange and partly incomprehensible world of Confucius or of (for that matter) the world of Milton or the world of Ngugi wa Thiong'o. If we welcome all manner of thinking other than our own, then, including that of ancients and distant moderns, we can embrace the possibility of the transcultural (otherwise, what would be the point of reading, or conversing, at all?) without leaping immediately to the conclusion that all transcultural forms of knowledge and belief are potentially universal.

OK, enough for one semester. It's been a pleasure and a challenge, and perhaps next semester we can continue to hone each other's wits. Oh, yes, the paper: the paper is smart, energetic, cogent, wide-ranging, provocative, and too fond of the word "manifestly." Other than that, it's exceptionally well written. Aside from the moments I've mentioned above, in which your argument presents fairly easy targets for critique, the bulk of your defense of capital-P Philosophy is quite strong.

Good luck on the final, and have a peaceful holiday break.

Grade: A

The reason I mentioned "next semester" was that Stan had expressed interest in doing an independent study with me in the following semester, and he reiterated the request when he came to speak with me about my comments on his essay (during which I referred him to other opponents of Rorty); and I did not hear from him again—until, as fortune would have it, I was finishing a draft of this book in the last weeks of 2005. In the intervening years, Stan said, he has thought often of the course he took with me, and he has read and reread my comments on his paper. While he does not find my counterarguments entirely persuasive—he describes himself today as an "intuitive realist"—he told me that he considers the course one of his most rewarding classes at Penn State. He even thinks I made an interesting point or two. I really can't ask for much more; it's not my job to change Stan's mind, and, as I admitted to him more than once in the course of our conversations, it's not as if I'm searching for the immutable moral laws of the universe.

In the spring of 2006, Stan and I conducted an independent study course on the various schools of twentieth-century interpretive theory, and I wrote an enthusiastic letter of recommendation for Stan's application to graduate study in English.

7. More Liberalism

ARE UNIVERSITIES REALLY THE LAST BASTION OF liberalism in the United States? It sometimes seems tempting to think so, amid a decade of defeats in national and state elections and after many decades of labor's decline as a progressive force in American politics. Looking out from my office window onto the political landscapes of rural Illinois and Pennsylvania over the past seventeen years, I've often been struck by the contrast between the overwhelmingly white, conservative, Christian countryside and the little campus bubble in which my colleagues and administrators (sometimes) try to enhance the racial diversity of the local environs and (sometimes) offer same-sex partner benefits to faculty and staff. That contrast is so stark, at universities like mine, as to make liberal professors (and their conservative critics) think of campus towns as tiny oases of blue in the vast red prairie of middle America. And yet, in some ways, American society is significantly more liberal than it was forty years ago. To those who are inclined to doubt it, I offer the example of Sherri Finkbine, the host of *Romper Room* whose abortion rocked the nation in 1962 and eventually led to the liberalization of American abortion laws over the next decade. It is nearly impossible to imagine a scenario in 2006 under which a popular female figure in children's television learns that she is carrying a fetus with severe abnormalities caused by thalidomide, chooses to terminate the pregnancy, flies to Sweden for the abortion, and is scandalized by the national press at home (despite having four children already), hounded by death threats, and eventually fired from her job.[1] I don't mean to suggest that American women could never again find themselves in the position of facing two to five years in jail for aborting a fetus that does not present a risk to the mother's life (as the relevant Arizona law stipulated at the time); I mean only that American conservatives have lost the broad social consensus that enabled them to mount a campaign against Finkbine, just as they have lost the broad social consensus that Negroes are not ready for integration and the broad social consensus that gay men and lesbians are not to appear in public as gay men or lesbians.

It is similarly impossible to imagine a national scandal over a televised interracial kiss on the order we experienced in 1968, when, just one scant year after the Supreme Court decision of *Loving v. Virginia* finally struck down the nation's miscegenation laws, Captain Kirk kissed Lieutenant Uhura on *Star Trek* and got the show banned throughout the South—though *Star Trek* fans will note that the kiss took place during a sequence in which neither Kirk nor Uhura were acting under their own power, and cultural critics like me might add that in a weird way, television's first representation of an interracial kiss took place in science fiction, which displaced it into the twenty-third century. To be sure, cultural conservatives still fulminate about these things on a regular basis; anyone who's familiar with the jeremiads of the religious right knows that they locate our national spiritual decline from the moment the Supreme Court ruled against school prayer in 1962, and there are still plenty of Southern partisans who believe the Court overstepped its bounds in 1954's *Brown v. Board of Education*. And though Kirk and Uhura are tame by today's standards, the right-wing outrage over Justin Timberlake and Janet Jackson at the 2004 Super Bowl or Terrell Owens and Nicollette Sheridan in a promotional spot for *Monday Night Football* probably reverberates, in some quarters, with that tiny remaining segment of the population which believes that *Loving v. Virginia* was wrongly decided. But such cultural conservatives know that their fulminations are increasingly unlikely to win popular consent, which is one of the reasons they portray themselves as lonely voices in the wilderness even though they have ready access to all three branches of government and a good deal of the fourth estate. And as for gay rights—at the moment, the single issue most likely to transform otherwise reasonable cultural conservatives into fuming, conspiracy-mongering fanatics, searching for gay subtexts in *Teletubbies* and advocacy of the homosexual agenda by cartoon characters in *SpongeBob SquarePants* and PBS's *Postcards from Buster*—how can I begin to catalog the ways in which American culture is infinitely queerer in 2006 than anyone could possibly have imagined—or dreaded—in 1966?

I don't want to sound too triumphalist about the cultural liberalization of the United States, because I'm well aware of how strong the backlash has been, and very well aware of the extent to which the backlash agenda now dominates the political life of my country. But I do want to suggest some intelligible reason for the volume and the passion of the conservative lament in an era when most liberals feel themselves powerless, hopeless, or friendless. Think of it this way: despite Reagan's two-term presidency and George W. Bush's reelection, *Queer Eye for the Straight Guy* and HBO's *Real Sex* are available on cable; women are having legal abortions; half of all married couples are filing for divorce; rappers are grabbing their crotches in prime time; teenage girls are showing far too much midriff, and teenage boys are wearing ridiculously loose, baggy jeans; the Internet and satellite television are cesspools of porn; and Marxist and quasi-Marxist professors continue to ply their trades in the innocent Cedar Rapids and Terre Hautes of our fair nation.

For some "movement conservatives," therefore, the state of the union must be vexing indeed, all the more so when one realizes how far to the right they have managed to pull one of the nation's

two major political parties. Movement conservatism has trans-
formed national politics in half a generation, regrouping from
Barry Goldwater's epochal defeat in 1964 to elect Reagan sixteen
years later and then—under shady circumstances, to be sure—to
squeeze George Bush into the White House twenty years after that.
Once Bush took office, movement conservatives finally got themselves a conservative presidency unhindered by the Democratic
Congress that had forced Reagan to be a political pragmatist
instead of the political visionary who promised to roll back the
New Deal even as he and Mikhail Gorbachev rolled up the Iron
Curtain. Movement conservatives have accomplished much, with
their combination of secular anti-tax zealots and religious anti-
gay/lesbian crusaders; they have swept through the Republican
Party, banishing its Rockefeller wing to a tiny corner of the north-
east, installing far-right fundamentalists like Tom DeLay and Rick
Santorum in the party leadership, appointing a swath of federal
judges whose allegiance to religious dogma sometimes supersedes
their allegiance to the Constitution, and creating a host of news and
opinion networks from the Heritage Foundation and the American Enterprise Institute to Clear Channel radio and Fox News. But
they have made comparatively little headway in academe. Conservative screeds about anti-American campuses thus have to be seen,
in part, as expressions of right-wing outrage and disbelief that liberalism still survives; in the think tanks, at Townhall.com, on *The
O'Reilly Factor*, they simply can't believe it. They can't believe that
there are still so many annoying liberals out there with a substantial
presence in an institution that does not allow for a rapid rate of
turnover or takeover.

As far as the right is concerned, academic liberalism is an artificial liberalism, or perhaps a liberalism on life support—sustained
only by the fact of tenure, which prevents ideological purges and
legislative attempts to drive a truckload of Republicans into departments of literature, philosophy, political science, art history, and

biology. That's why conservatives inveigh so relentlessly against the institution of tenure, even though the institution of tenure is, strictly speaking, a profoundly conservative notion. But then, if conservatives are going to fantasize about achieving complete and total domination over every instititution of American life, I'd prefer that they fantasize about doing away with tenure than fantasize about doing away with liberals, as Rush Limbaugh mirthfully suggested in late 1995: "I tell people don't kill all the liberals. Leave enough so we can have two on every campus—living fossils—so we will never forget what these people stood for."[2]

Liberal sociologist Paul Starr named the game correctly over a decade ago; in his review of Martin Anderson's 1992 book, *Impostors in the Temple: The Decline of the American University*, he wrote, "Mr. Anderson seems to want to do for the universities what [Newt] Gingrich and his confrères have done for the Congress: bring the institution into such disrepute that conservatives, long stuck in minority status, will have a chance at gaining power."[3] Starr's words are compelling today, not least because he wrote them two years before the Gingrich Plan dramatically succeeded in delivering Congress to conservatives. But universities cannot be flipped quite so readily as was the House of Representatives in 1994. Over the ensuing decade, as the Gingrich Revolution set about institutionalizing itself, ensuring by means of gerrymandering and generous servings of pork that the GOP would not be so foolish as to lose the House of Representatives again, the Anderson Plan went nowhere. Conservatives have managed to create shadow universities-within-universities, like the Hoover Institution at Stanford, and they've managed to create a host of endowed programs and professorships here and there, but their presence in academe is nothing like their presence in the executive, legislative, and judicial branches of American government, nothing like their presence on radio and television and in mass media outside (and frequently inside) New York and Los Angeles. And they know it very well. "We won," they say. "So why haven't we cleared the field? Why do we still have dissenters and antagonists? And how can we get rid of them?"

In other words, they've won and yet they haven't; although movement conservatives established an enviable hegemony over America's political institutions, they don't have a comparable stranglehold over America's cultural life. Many of them still have to talk in code when they run for public office, signaling to each other by speaking in tongues that only fundamentalist Christians can understand; others have to lie low during Republican national conventions, letting Rudy Giuliani serve as the party's window dressing while the party's actual ideological operations are run by people more like Focus on the Family czar James Dobson. And when they stop to take a look back over the past forty years, or when they stop to gauge the opposition to gay marriage among voters under thirty as opposed to voters over sixty-five, they are haunted by the possibility that liberalism will find some way to survive and grow despite all their best efforts to stamp it out. They know that when *Loving v. Virginia* was decided, the Supreme Court flew in the face of public opinion, which strongly supported laws banning interracial marriage, and they are terrified that public opinion on such cultural matters can change so quickly.[4] And when cultural conservatives are horrified by liberal public opinion, they know very well who to blame. They blame "activist judges." They blame the "liberal media." They blame Hollywood. And they blame universities.

But perhaps there's still another reason why universities come in for such severe criticism from the right, and perhaps this reason has nothing to do with the preponderance of Democrats on the faculty or the preposterousness of fringe figures like Ward Churchill. At the outset of this book, I suggested that universities are, for one wing of the right, something like NPR, PBS, or the UN: favored fetish objects, things the right loves to hate so intensely that no liberal "defense" of them will suffice. But there's another sense in which the most appropriate analogy for universities isn't *All Things Considered* or the General Assembly so much as Social Security. Conservatives have hated Social Security for seventy years; they began by decrying it as a socialist program, which it certainly is, and they are attempting to destroy it today by partially privatizing it—though they prefer to say "personalizing" instead of "privatizing," as if America's elderly will be afforded the opportunity to receive monogrammed Social Security checks for the first time. For many years I failed to understand why conservatives hated Social Security so intensely. It's the only non-means-tested, universally implemented welfare program in the country (as opposed to, say, Medicaid), but it's paid for by the most regressive tax in American law—as of 2005, not a penny over the $90,000 income level is taxed—and conservatives still hate it. It amounts to socialism American-style: paid for disproportionately by working people in the middle-income brackets and almost completely unsupported by wealthy wage-earners and the even wealthier Americans whose income derives mainly from investments (which, of course, are not subject to FICA taxes). If you're on the right, I thought, you should look upon Social Security taxes and weep for joy: a system in which billionaires Oprah Winfrey and Richard Mellon Scaife pay precisely the same amount of tax—not the same percentage, the same *amount*—as the computer programmer or middle manager clearing $90,000 a year. What's not to love? Only gradually did I realize the obvious, namely, that conservatives hate Social Security because it works. It's a vital component of the public sector, a last-gasp guarantee that American retirees will not be left penniless and destitute. The only major complaint most sane Americans have about Social Security is that they want more of it rather than less.

Something similar is at work with conservatives' distrust of American higher education—and it accounts for the remarkable phenomenon in which we find Ben Shapiro at Harvard rather than Pepperdine and John Leo's daughter graduating from Wesleyan

University rather than Hillsdale. On some level, the American right attacks universities not because they don't work but because, by and large, they do. I've already mentioned American higher education's "trade surplus" with regard to universities abroad, but that's not the least of the attractions of American universities. Economically, they're powerhouses; not only does a degree enhance the future earnings of college graduates for the rest of their lives even when liberal professors teach them about *The Rise of Silas Lapham* or the history of lesbianism, but universities do indispensable, basic research and development and technology transfer in their corporate and applied-science sectors as well. Universities employ millions of faculty and staff across the country in what are some of the most stable workplaces in America: Penn State is not packing up and heading for Mexico or India anytime soon, and neither are Harvard, Johns Hopkins, or the University of Pittsburgh. American campuses and campus towns thrive not despite things like tenure but because of them; universities have been economically successful precisely to the extent they have managed to resist the scorched-earth, "just-in-time" capitalism of the private sector and institute welfare-state protections for stable employment, stable tax bases, and stable communities. There's a good reason why the public school systems of State College, Pennsylvania, and Champaign, Illinois, are so much better funded than the starved districts of the white rural poor who surround us, and it has everything to do with the economic stability of university faculty and staff. Universities— even private universities—are thoroughly and complexly interwoven into what remains of the public sector of the United States, and their relative economic health, together with their extraordinary capacity to generate economic wealth (if you're interested in that kind of thing), provides powerful testimony to the wisdom and the long-term structural soundness of the mixed free-market/welfare- state economy. So America's cultural conservatives may despise us for the obvious reasons—our cosmopolitanism, our secularism, our corrosive attitude of skepticism about every form of received authority—but the economic conservatives, I think, despise us precisely because we work so well.

Personally, I wish we worked even better, and that our graduates emerged from our institutions even more cosmopolitan, less parochial, more willing to consider themselves citizens of (and responsible to) the entire world, more prepared for the moral and intellectual consequences of globalization; I wish our graduates were more fluent writers and more nimble thinkers; I wish more of them majored in the liberal arts, and that more of my fellow citizens appreciated the strength of liberalism, the power of the arts, and the appeal of liberal arts. But when I'm discouraged about such things, I take some solace in the fact, that despite it all, and despite the best efforts of the anti-academic right, universities remain among the most respected institutions in American life, ranking far above organized religion, big business, Congress, the legal profession, and the news media—and just above the White House and the Supreme Court.[5]

They despise us because we work so well. And that's why, just as Social Security is under assault by would-be privatizers, state universities have been partially privatized over the past thirty years. No fact is so well known inside academe and so little known outside it: your average state university now receives only a token amount of financial support from the state. Institutions like Penn State and the University of Michigan are nearly off the public books altogether, receiving only a tiny fraction of their budgets from state funds. The state provided 45 percent of Penn State's budget as recently as 1984-85, when in-state tuition was $2,562;[6] that figure is now down to 10 percent, and in-state tuition is $11,508. The correlation speaks for itself. The costs of college, in state after state, have been passed along to individual families, as higher education has gradually been reconceived as a private investment for individuals rather than as a social good for the entire nation. In this way, too, we are structurally analogous to Social Security; we're a good idea and a social boon, but we cost far too much for those who can least afford it.

I hesitate to say even this much on the subject of tuition, because there is so much demagoguery surrounding the issue, ranging from the merely annoying to the positively and creatively mendacious. Everyone hears about tuitions of thirty and forty thousand dollars, because those are the price tags of the elite schools; I have a child in one of those schools, and I can vouch for the fact that I am paying almost twice as much for his college education as I paid for my family's first house. But, in fact, most public-school tuitions are under ten thousand dollars, and even then, thanks to universities' financial-aid packages, very few students actually pay full fare (at the University of Illinois at Urbana–Champaign, for instance, 22 percent of students pay no tuition and fees at all).[7] Even during my time at Illinois, when the annual tuition rate for in-state residents went from $2,969 in 1990–91 to $4,994 in 2000–01,[8] I knew that many students were paying less for tuition than for their hideous, dilapidated "off-campus housing units"—that is, scuzzy apartments in buildings perched on stilts. Nonetheless, the rate of tuition increases at both public and private universities has seriously outstripped the rate of inflation for two decades, and many middle- and working-class families have been priced out of college; even if financial aid packages manage to whittle a $10,000 tuition bill down to $5,000, there are still millions of ordinary Americans who don't have $5,000 to spare this year or next. Public universities aren't supposed to cost that much; but then, public universities are supposed to be supported largely by public funds. All I can tell you is that the faculty aren't pocketing the extra change. Over the past fifteen years, I've seen public university tuition rates climb by 8, 10, 12 percent a year; but every year, the faculty raise pool remains at 2 to 4 percent.[9] These basically amount to cost-of-living increases for most professors, who are merely keeping pace with inflation.

The real scandal of Social Security is that the truly rich are largely exempt from contributing to it; the real scandal of public universities is that they have become increasingly beholden to right-wing demagoguery with respect to "the public" (as in, "why should your taxes pay the salaries of these America-hating liberals") even as right-wing demagogues in elected office have managed to cut our funding from the states. The result is a weird and thoroughly dishonest political two-step, whereby your local Republican state legislator or Democratic (but not that tax-and-spend kind of Democratic) governor alternates between (a) cutting funds for public colleges, demanding that State U. find ways of "doing more with less" in the name of fiscal austerity, and (b) crying that it is an outrage that State U. staged *The Vagina Monologues* with the tax money of the good God-fearing people of upper Appalachia or rural Oklahoma, regardless of whether that venerable Eve Ensler standby was sponsored by any public funds. It's a neat trick, invoking the public with one hand and privatizing the enterprise with the other. But it works, and, as a result, tuitions are higher than they should be. That's what "partial privatization" is all about: passing the social costs of public goods onto individuals, leaving students and families to fend for themselves as best they can. If this is fine with you, so be it: you're a conservative or a libertarian. If you think this is a suspect or foolhardy enterprise, you may already be a liberal or progressive. In that case, more power to you.

BUT WHAT IS IT we believe, we stubborn ones who continue to call ourselves liberals and progressives? First and foremost, we believe that a person's prospects and life chances should not depend on accidents of birth. We think it is a good idea to wriggle free of long-conventional beliefs about class and caste, Pharaoh and slave, lord and serf, and to imagine that each of us has an equal moral claim on the rest of us. But we think we haven't yet wriggled free enough, because even today too many humans' life chances depend far too heavily on whether one is born man or woman, dark-skinned or light-skinned, Alabaman or Angolan or Afghan, a resident of a comfy exurban collar county or a denizen of a polluted and ravaged industrial pit. That's why we believe in progressive taxation on both incomes and investments as a way of trying to compensate or ameliorate some of those accidents of birth. We advocate progressive taxation not because we resent the rich—on the contrary, a fortunate few of us are among the rich—but because we fear that the concentration of great wealth in few hands effectively undermines the project of democracy, and (on our happy days) we do not want to believe that the American experiment in democracy, which has included African-Americans only in the past forty years (and hardly satisfactorily at that) and has yet to be extended to gay men and lesbians, has already degenerated into a foul combination of oligarchy and plutocracy. And we advocate progressive taxation not because we like government and bureaucracy—on the contrary, most of us distrust the IRS and don't like dealing with the Department of Motor Vehicles, either, even as we know these things are necessary—but because we know that the state is the very last resort for the weak, the disabled, and the impoverished. It's not necessarily the best resort—far from it. Liberals know this well, having worked for decades to reform everything from labor laws to mental institutions. But we think it's immoral (yes, *immoral*) for free-market conservatives to leave our weakest citizens to depend on the whims of private charities, and to leave our wealthiest and most powerful citizens with the mere option of deciding whether or not to contribute to the common weal today or tomorrow or the next day. When liberals say we're all in this together, or that we should be, we mean that we have obligations to one another—and that we should collectively, democratically devise the means for realizing those obligations. That this is not broadly understood as a moral position says a great deal about the poverty of our public discourses of morality.

Some of us like to say that taxation is the price you pay for living in a civilized society. That's true as far as it goes, but it doesn't go nearly far enough. Rather, we should say that taxation is the price you pay for living in a free society, because this strikes more directly at the heart of libertarian economic mythologies. The reason a successful American entrepreneur should contribute to the common weal is that even if (as happens only rarely) her success is due only to her own individual talents, she couldn't have achieved that success in Saudi Arabia or Namibia or Kazakhstan. Americans who strike it rich—bless their clever hearts—do so in part because they live in a society that makes such things possible. It is in their long-term interests, and the interests of their associates and descendants, that the free society that enabled their success remain stable and secure, lest it turn slowly into a North American banana republic in which a constellation of overlords and apparatchiks live in gated communities with armed sentries overlooking the *favelas* below. Liberals like me tend to see George W. Bush's economic policies, with their massive public deficits and massive shifts of taxation from investment to income, as the force that will not only undo the American social contract but will eat away at the very idea of a social contract. We know that conservative anti-tax crusaders and political organizers like Grover Norquist say as much in so many words when they speak of shrinking government to the size at which it can be drowned in the bathtub, and we pay Norquist and his Norquistas the compliment of believing them. But when the Norquista version of the United States actually plays out in practice, we liberals don't see a government drowned in a bathtub; we see hundreds of poor and disabled Americans drowned in the streets of New Orleans.

In response, conservatives and libertarians typically complain that raising marginal tax rates will stifle growth, because if a multimillionaire entrepreneur or investor thinks that he's only going to see 50 cents from the next dollar he makes, he won't bother making the dollar. That's possible, though I have trouble imagining the scenario at work here—not merely because I have no personal experience with it, but more seriously because I find it hard to imagine a Clever Entrepreneur who thinks, "Well, I've made ten million this year, but if I make another two million I only get to keep one million of it, so I'm going to stop developing and promoting my product right about now." This sounds to me more like a rational-choice-theory textbook exercise than like actual human behavior, but even if it isn't, I am surprised that liberals and progressives haven't made a more forceful case that it might in fact be a good thing to have a tax system that does discourage the ultrawealthy from becoming ultra-ultra-ultrawealthy. Conservatives and libertarians claim that progressive-tax "disincentives" will lead entrepreneurs to create fewer jobs than they might otherwise, but that clearly wasn't the case in the bad old days of the 1950s and 1960s, when the top tax rate for individuals was 70 percent. If indeed such "disincentives" are a problem for exceptionally high wage-earners, then perhaps some clever tax attorneys could devise very steep rates for very high income levels along with tax credits and cuts for very wealthy people who actually create jobs with their money instead of hoarding it, moving it into offshore tax shelters, or donating it to electoral campaigns and political action committees (just to name three other popular avenues for significant wealth). I'm a literature professor, not a tax specialist. But the arguments I've heard from the right against progressive income and investment taxes just don't add up; they sound to me like the rationalizations of people who have already decided they don't like the idea of "social welfare" or the "common weal" or "obligations to one's fellow citizens," and are looking for convenient excuses to opt out of public systems altogether. Liberals and progressives, by contrast, sound to me like people who still care about our social infrastructure—our transportation systems, our disability services, our schools, our hospitals, our parks, our air, our water, our food industry—but who still haven't figured out ways of preventing the public good from being misadministered and subverted by inefficient or corrupt government bureaucracies (though we have learned that fully nationalized economies give rise to behemoth state apparatuses which function efficiently only when it comes to political repression). But when it comes to the actual conduct of the state and its many agencies, I'll take the flawed but fixable attempts of liberals any day over the deliberate malice of conservatives, who serve in the offices of the Department of Energy, the Environmental Protection Agency, or the Equal Employment Opportunity Commission chiefly in order to make sure that the foxes run the henhouse.

On cultural issues, I believe liberals and progressives have nothing to be ashamed of. Yes, we're sometimes self-righteous (as in the preceding sentence!) and sometimes too dismissive or snotty toward those who disagree with us, but then again, I have to admit that I really do think there's something wrong—not just "culturally relative" or "different," but *wrong*—with a form of morality that condemns the depiction of a same-sex couple on *Postcards from Buster* but says not a word about the atrocities committed at Guantánamo and Abu Ghraib (except to deny or defend those atrocities). We don't understand people who claim to value freedom but will not grant the freedom of other adults to fall in love and choose their life partners if those life partners are of the same gender. We don't see why they grant nine-day embryos the same moral status as living human children. We don't understand why they think any useful purpose is served by displaying the Ten Commandments in schools and courthouses. We're horrified that George Bush conducted his reelection campaign by means of loyalty pledges, chants of allegiance, and threatened arrests of schoolteachers wearing T-shirts reading, "Protect our civil liberties."[10] We think this kind of behavior in a free election, and this attitude of reverence for a national leader, is best suited to forms of government other than democracies or republics. And we just don't trust cultural conservatives' track record over the long term, to be honest. We think they're the heirs of the people who spent decades dehumanizing African-Americans and immigrants, arguing chapter and verse that the Bible endorses slavery and the subjection of women. We think they're the ones who hounded Sherri Finkbine and who called their NBC affiliates throughout the South a few years later to protest Kirk kissing Uhura. I see no way to soft-pedal the impasse between the religious right and the secular left; the conflict I describe in my postmodernism class—the conflict between reason and faith—is an utterly intractable one, because there's no way to negotiate between people who insist on the scientific evidence for evolution and people who insist on the scriptural evidence for Armageddon.

There's another asymmetry here, as well, and it goes back to the question I broached in my postmodernism class: namely, how to understand and manage intractable disagreement. Liberals and progressives tend to be suspicious of people too far to their left, because those people, like the religious right, have a bad track record when it comes to devising policies for fostering pluralism and decentralizing decision-making authority in civil society. But there aren't too many of those people in the United States, and none of them are anywhere near actual sites of decisionmaking authority in civil society—or the state.

By contrast, the religious authoritarians of the right occupy some of the most powerful positions in the country, and their attitude toward those who disagree with them is not that they must be accommodated and debated but that they must be converted or vanquished. To put this asymmetry another way, there is nothing in the modern liberal canon from Mill to Rawls that licenses the kind of evangelism that remains central to Christian (or Islamic) fundamentalism; there is nothing in the liberal canon that compels us to go out and preach among the people until they relinquish their beliefs and join us in our interpretations of texts written a couple of millennia ago, lest they be cast into the outer darkness. There are no secular liberals who believe that their opponents in political debate are condemned to eternal perdition; we tend not to believe in the immortality of the soul and we don't believe in perdition, either. In any standoff between secular liberals and religious conservatives, then, each side will have a drastically different conception not only of the issues at hand in the standoff but also of the consequences of the dispute itself: the liberals believe that the religious conservatives will craft social policies that will hurt gay men, atheists, and rape victims, whereas the religious conservatives believe that a just and omnipotent deity will consign the liberals to unending torment in hell, where they belong. Surely you don't have to be a secular liberal to see that, in this game, the deck is stacked.

Ultimately there are two kinds of liberalism that need defending, on campus and off. One has to do with the ideal of egalitarian human rights I mentioned in the previous chapter, the one in which all humans should be considered to have equal claim to basic human rights such as food, shelter, education, health care, and political representation, and that we should endow each other with these rights, knowing full well that they are alienable and that we must work to interpret and to sustain them. We have not yet devised the political means to realize this utopian vision, and perhaps we never will; utopia, to date, is a place we know only by way of speculative fiction. But, over the years, as we've developed family/clan relations, city-states, empires, kingdoms, caliphates, constitutional monarchies, theocracies, military dictatorships, communist autocracies, and liberal democracies, we've come to learn that liberal democracies stand the best chance of realizing some approximation of that ideal, and—just as importantly—the best chance of changing the collective mind, so to speak, about how to approximate the ideal as we go along. Because they allow for plural, disparate, multiply competing political constituencies and modes of advancing political argument, liberal democracies seem best suited to realizing the kind of social self-reflexivity necessary for any significant political—or personal—change of understanding with regard to human rights. When liberal democracies decline into oligarchies and plutocracies in which "the people" are invoked in direct proportion to the degree to which they are betrayed, liberalism has been traduced; for that matter, when liberal campuses tolerate administrative show trials, liberalism has been traduced. And wherever people are not permitted to disagree about the meaning of human rights and the best means by which to realize them, the proper solution, it seems to me, is more liberalism rather than less.

Which brings me to my second kind of liberalism. The first has to do with content: promoting egalitarian human rights, and declaring that access to those rights shall not be contingent on any individual's accidents of birth. The second has to do with form: ensuring that wide, vigorous, and meaningful discussion about the first kind can actually take place. This is the procedural or intellectual liberalism we should properly associate with institutions like universities, where any reasonable proposition can and should be debated from any reasonable angle. When universities are criticized for failing to provide that kind of intellectual liberalism—whether at Penn State or Colorado or Columbia or Brigham Young—we liberal professors should agree that our nation's academic institutions exist partly to ensure that plural perspectives and unpopular opinions get a fair hearing, whether those perspectives and opinions are antifeminist, pro-Palestinian, venture-capitalist or neo-Marxist. And we should seek to agree (if we're good secular liberals and want to avoid predetermining the goal of debate in advance, whether this be Habermas's "consensus" or my own "egalitarian human rights") that every participant in the conversation is entitled, at least at first, to challenge all received notions of what is reasonable, what is egalitarian, what is human, and what is a right, just as he or she can challenge the very idea that human societies ought to be advancing egalitarian notions of human rights. But we cannot and should not try to ensure that those plural perspectives and those unpopular opinions will be immune to criticism once they are aired; if people want to argue, for example, that it is a Christian's moral obligation to try to save people from the sin of homosexuality, they may do so, but they should not expect to be shielded from criticism and disagreement, and they should not resort to the intellectually dishonest claim that criticism and disagreement constitutes an infringement of their rights under the First Amendment. Most important of all, we cannot and should not be held to a shallow, relativist conception of "intellectual diversity" in which Holocaust deniers, al-Qaeda operatives, creationists, and people who believe in telepathy, astrology, and/or magic dolphins are given equal weight with people who have studied deeply in subjects for decades and know what constitutes the boundaries of "reasonable" dispute in their fields. One of the reasons American universities are such lightning rods for debate—quite apart from all the reasons I've enumerated already—is that they are the points at which the democratic desire to entertain and discuss all reasonable ideas meets the (properly) elitist demand for intellectual depth and rigor. To put this in simpler terms: everyone is entitled to his or her opinion, and yet some opinions are more informed by the weight of empirical evidence and the historical record than others.

Nothing demonstrates this tension so well as the contemporary dispute over the legitimacy of intelligent design as a scientific theory. Advocates of intelligent design, invoking the democratic ideal of reasoned debate, present their case as a matter of intellectual diversity and healthy open-mindedness: "It doesn't seem as if evolution can fully account for the staggering variety and complexity of living organisms," they say, thoughtfully. "Perhaps we ought to consider whether the life we see all around us is in fact evidence of design in the universe. Let's discuss this further, shall we?" So posed, the question strikes many Americans as reasonable: the proper thing to do in such debates, we think, is to let the debaters have at it, and may the most persuasive and compelling theory win.

But aside from a few outliers like Michael Behe, there are almost no scientists who regard intelligent design as a *scientific* theory. It does not offer evidence, and is susceptible neither to verification (unless we can conduct experiments that will induce the designer to step forward and accept the credit for her work) nor to falsification (which Karl Popper famously proposed as the criterion for science: if it cannot be false, Popper argued, it cannot be a scientific theory, and we cannot subject the hypothesis of a designer to this standard, for it would involve "proving" that no such designer exists). Intelligent design simply hangs around at the margins of Darwinism, pointing out sundry evolutionary lacunae and saying, "Well, what about that? And what about that?" As a result, the seemingly democratic appeal of intelligent design—"Let's teach it together with evolution, and let students make up their own minds"—runs up against what it means to have professional expertise in an academic discipline. It is altogether reasonable to behold the universe and wonder where it all came from and whether it testifies to the existence of a governing intelligence, but it is not reasonable to suggest that a discipline in the natural sciences should include material that relies on an idea of the supernatural and does not respond to ordinary protocols of scientific inquiry.[11]

By contrast, if proponents of intelligent design wanted to promote their work as a form of philosophical or religious speculation, that would strike me as altogether reasonable. The fact that they do not, together with the fact that they focus exclusively on evolution rather than on the far more basic fact that the relations among the elemental forces of the universe have to be *just so* in order for matter to exist at all, suggests that secularists and evolutionary theorists are right to think of ID as a stalking horse for creationism. (In

other words, it is entirely possible to accept the Big Bang account of
the origins of the universe and still wonder why the universe exists
at all; ID advocates, by contrast, concentrate exclusively on the
development of life on earth, because at bottom they share with
creationists some version of the belief that God hath made us in His
image.) One of the reasons I am a pragmatist and antifoundationalist, after all, stems from the (practical, mundane) realization that
humans will never achieve consensus in such philosophical matters,
and that we should, accordingly, devise social forms in which a
healthy pluralism about human affairs can be accommodated. The
university is nothing if not one of those social forms—one of the
most important, precisely because of its complex independence
from and interdependence with the state. The question of whether
the universe speaks of design is thus an appropriate one for academic pluralists in the humanities, along with such other perennials
as the problem of evil and the nature of free will. I may hold out
the possibility of a provisional universalism when it comes to
endowing each other with basic rights to food, shelter, education,
health care, and political representation, but I cannot imagine that
all of us would ever manage to agree about why, in this world,
there is *something* rather than *nothing*. Universal agreement about
the meaning of the universe seems not to be a goal worth trying for.
As I see it, therefore, the question presented by intelligent design is
how best to keep religious and philosophical speculation out of the
realms of physics and biology, so that scientists can go about their
business without entertaining the proposition that the hand of the
Maker is readable in the fossil record or the proposition that the
universe is balanced on the back of an infinitely large turtle, while
allowing the widest possible latitude for religious and philosophical
speculation elsewhere in the university. Once again, the standard
should be that of reasonable accommodation: where such speculation is not reasonable, as in the natural sciences, it should not be
accommodated; where it is reasonable, it should be allowed to

flourish. Last but not least, it should flourish in fields that afford the widest possible latitude for debates about what constitutes the "reasonable" part of "reasonable accommodation."

Just as the social welfare state is the guarantor of last resort when it comes to human rights, insofar as it operates as an institution to which the powerless can appeal for redress, so too are universities the guarantor of last resort when it comes to the kind of procedural liberalism in which every argument is required to meet and parry its most powerful antithesis, for there is no other institution that makes intellectual independence its very raison d'être. This is not to say that either institution is doing its job properly; it is only to say that they have jobs worth doing and defending, and that these jobs are indelibly, undeniably liberal. Whenever the social welfare state rebuffs and punishes the powerless, requiring a disabled man to crawl up two flights of courthouse stairs simply to appear on his own behalf,[12] it is not serving the social welfare; whenever universities fail to promote reasonable debate or to honor the injunction that every proposition is open to every kind of reasonable challenge, they are not serving the cause of intellectual independence. There are times when academic factions turn into bastions of groupthink rather than havens and habitats for the incurably intellectually curious. But here, too, the solution is not less liberalism but more. For if universities want to claim intellectual independence from the state, as they must, even as they assert their profound economic and social interdependence with the state, then they have to demonstrate that they are committed to fostering intellectual independence on campus and off. Most of the time, we liberal professors do precisely this, and conservatives attack us because we do precisely this. When they complain that taxpayers are subsidizing us liberal professors (even when taxpayers are doing no such thing), as if professors' teaching and research should be answerable directly to the state, they are complaining about our intellectual independence; when they complain that we give poor grades to students like Nicole Krogman or Ahmad al-Qloushi, they are complaining about our intellectual rigor. They are, in short, attacking us for doing our jobs, for when we do them well, there is inevitably something liberal about the enterprise. No doubt that's why we spend so much of our time and energy trying to promote a lively critical pluralism in our classrooms, and trying to ensure that every reasonable proposition is open to reasoned debate, even when we feel strongly about the subject under discussion: we believe that this enterprise, in and of itself, is a truly liberal art.

And why should you support such a liberal art, even if you don't consider yourself a liberal? Because the liberal arts teach people how to think deeply and reflectively about the good life, the good society, and the very idea of the "good." The liberal arts do their work by acquainting students with at least some of the history of how humans have thought about such things, thereby giving them a richer and more complex language in which to speak and with which to think. The liberal arts do their work by encouraging students to think of lifelong learning as an integral part of a good life; as you may have heard before, we humanists believe in the superiority of the examined life to the unexamined life, and we believe that nothing human should be alien to us. And, finally, the liberal arts do their work by combating every kind of parochialism, reminding us by way of a plenitude of human counterexamples that any one of us may be wrong or only partially right. Even the postmodernist ideas of "situated knowledge" and "local knowledge" participate in this enterprise, for what they value is the acknowledgment of one's own perspective as partial and situated, even though they're unfortunately less than clear on where that acknowledgment might come from. But the values of the liberal arts can't be transmitted simply by opening the great books and reciting key passages. Classroom discussion and debate is an indispensable part of our pedagogy, not only because it gives students a chance to try out ideas and gut reactions on each other in a relatively safe space, but also because it serves as a form of deliberation in which each of us participates according to his or her abilities and desires. To be a professor in the liberal arts—to be a professor *of* the liberal arts, someone who professes those arts—is to try to enhance one's students' abilities and desires to participate in substantive discussion on and off campus, and to enhance their abilities and desires to compose written arguments about all kinds of complex texts. Professors who do these things may or may not promote the causes of Democrats in their lives as citizens; that should be irrelevant to their bearing in the classroom. But professors who do these things will find that, whatever else they do in their lives as citizens, they promote the cause of democracy.

Notes

CHAPTER 1: REASONABLE DISAGREEMENTS

This chapter is an extensively revised version of an essay that first appeared in the *Chronicle of Higher Education*, December 5, 2003, under the title, "Should I Have Asked John to Cool It? Standards of Reason in the Classroom": B5–7, http://chronicle.com/free/v50/i15/15b00701.htm.

1. Ishmael Reed, *Mumbo Jumbo* (New York: Atheneum, 1972), 38.
2. For a brief introduction to the Republic of New Africa, see William L. Van Deburg, *New Day in Babylon* (Chicago: University of Chicago Press, 1992), 144–49.
3. Edward Rothstein, "Attacks on US Challenge Postmodern True Believers," *New York Times*, September 22, 2001: A17.
4. Eric Hoover, "Death Threats and a Sit-In Divide Penn State," *Chronicle of Higher Education*, May 11, 2001: A43, http://chronicle.com/weekly/v47/i35/35a04301.htm. The "Christian conservative" quoted in the report is Professor David Warren Saxe.
5. Professor Vaidhyanathan posted his remarks on Eric Alterman's MSNBC *Altercation* weblog on May 4, 2005, at http://www.msnbc.msn.com/id/772 0654/#050504.
6. Throughout the novel, Powers treats the internment camps as forms of "tit for tat," an abrogation of freedom undertaken in the name of freedom. One such passage reads as follows:

> Disney sits at his drawing board and wrestles up a pen and ink cel of the Mouse. "What do you say to fighting fire with fire?" he mumbles to the image. With a few deft strokes, he blows a talk bubble above Mickey's head reading, "That makes a *big* fire, Walt." Disney puts his pens down and sighs. He knows the size of the blaze we are up against. He has heard Murrow's London broadcasts. He has seen what the Imperial Navy accomplished in the Philippines. He knows about roundups far more hideously

evil than the local one. Terminally evil. And other than retaliation he cannot think of a weapon large enough to put this fire out.

Richard Powers, *Prisoner's Dilemma* (New York: Harper Perennial, 1988),
176.

7. At the time, I was thinking of Michi Weglyn, *Years of Infamy: The Untold
Story of America's Concentration Camps* (New York: Morrow, 1976; repr.,
Seattle: University of Washington Press, 1996). Today, I would add Eric L.
Muller, *Free to Die for Their Country: The Story of the Japanese American
Draft Resisters in World War II* (Chicago: University of Chicago Press, 2001);
Greg Robinson, *By Order of the President: FDR and the Internment of Japan-
ese Americans* (Cambridge, MA: Harvard University Press, 2003); and
David Neiwert, *Strawberry Days: How Internment Destroyed a Japanese
American Community* (New York: Palgrave, 2005).

8. In a variety of ways, one of which involves comparing the treatment of
Americans of Japanese ancestry with that of Americans of Italian or German ancestry:

> Walt rubs his ears for hours, wondering if Huston and Capra, at this very
> minute making documentaries and cheer films for the army, are having
> half as much difficulty overcoming the technical obstacles to believability as
> he. Capra's making *Why We Fight*. Disney must make the far more prob-
> lematic and unpopular *Why We Shouldn't Have To*. It occurs to him that
> Capra is a first-generation Italian. *We're at war with the Eye-ties too, right?
> What are THEY doing walking around free while we're locked up?* The sug-
> gestion is clear: national security is not separable from budding hatred.
> (Powers, *Prisoner's Dilemma*, 218.)

I don't imagine that I have to elaborate on the resonance of the final sentence for debates over national security after September 11. All I can say is
that I didn't plan things that way; I drew up my syllabus many months
before the attacks, and had planned to discuss the experimental aspects of
Prisoner's Dilemma, in which an apparently realistic novel turns out to be
both a Nabokovian hall of mirrors and a quasi-autobiographical account of
a midwestern family.

9. Colson Whitehead, *The Intuitionist* (New York: Anchor, 1999). I have since
written an essay on the novel, titled "Race and Modernity in Colson Whitehead's *The Intuitionist*," in *The Holodeck in the Garden: Science and Technology in Contemporary American Fiction*, ed. Peter Freese and Charles B.
Harris (Normal, IL: Dalkey Archive Press, 2004), 163–78.

10. Dinesh D'Souza, *The End of Racism: Principles for a Multiracial Society*
(New York: Free Press, 1995), 147.

11. Michelle Malkin, *In Defense of Internment: The Case for "Racial Profiling" in
World War II and the War on Terror* (Washington, DC: Regnery, 2004).

12. See, e.g., Ana Marie Cox, "More Professors Said to Be Off Tenure Track," *Chronicle of Higher Education*, July 6, 2001: A12: "John Lee, president of JBL Associates, a group in Bethesda, Md., that analyzed the data for the [National Education Association], says the drop to 32 percent from 35 percent of all faculty members (full- and part-time) who hold tenure 'is mostly due to the increased number of part-timers, and the great number of professors working at institutions that don't offer tenure.' " The *Chronicle* report is available online (for subscribers) at http://chronicle.com/weekly/v47/i43/43a 01201.htm; the NEA report is available at http://www.nea.org/he/heup date/vol7no3.pdf. The most recent and comprehensive data set on faculty employment (through fall 2003) is available from the National Center for Education Statistics and can be found in the *IPEDS Dataset Cutting Tool*, National Center for Education Statistics (accessed January 3, 2006), http://nces.ed.gov/ipedspas/dct/download/index.asp?Year=2003&Survey=9.

CHAPTER 2: CONSERVATIVE COMPLAINTS

1. Kathy Lynn Gray, "Bill Could Limit Open Debate at Colleges: Lawmaker Says Profs Are Pushing Agendas," *Columbus Dispatch,* January 27, 2005, http://www.dispatch.com/election.php?story=dispatch/2005/01/27/20050127 -C1-04.html.

2. General Assembly of Pennsylvania, House Resolution 177, Session of 2005, http://www.legis.state.pa.us/WU01/LI/BI/BT/2005/0/HR0177P2553.htm.

3. Ohio Senate Bill 24, http://www.legislature.state.oh.us/bills.cfm?ID=126_ SB_24.

4. Reported in David Steigerwald, "The New Repression of the Postmodern Right," *Inside Higher Education*, February 11, 2005, http://www.inside highered.com/views/2005/02/11/steigerwald1.

5. James Vanlandingham, "Capitol Bill Aims to Control 'Leftist' Profs: The Law Could Let Students Sue for Untolerated Beliefs," *Independent Florida Alligator*, March 23, 2005, http://www.alligator.org/pt2/050323freedom.php.

6. For background on Bachmann, see G. R. Anderson, Jr., "Somebody Say Oh Lord! Michele Bachmann Heads an All-Star Cast of GOP Christian Flat-Earthers in the Sixth District," *Minneapolis/St. Paul City Pages*, February 23, 2005, http://www.citypages.com/databank/26/1264/article12984.asp.

7. "The Professors' Orwellian Case," *FrontPage*, December 5, 2003, http:// www.frontpagemag.com/articles/ReadArticle.asp?ID=11154. A useful discussion of the case and of Horowitz's spinning of it can be found on the History News Network in a post by Jonathan Dresner, "Fact-Checking Cuts Both Ways," *Cliopatria: A Group Blog*, http://hnn.us/blogs/entries/ 10712.html. See also Simon Maloy, "Media Repeat Unsubstantiated Horowitz Tale of Anti-conservative Bias on Campus," *Media Matters*, March 7, 2005, http://mediamatters.org/items/printable/200503080001.

8. The passage that follows is from Scott Jaschik, "Tattered Poster Child,"

Inside Higher Education, March 15, 2005, http://www.insidehighered.com/ news/2005/03/15/horowitz3_15. See also Scott Jaschik, "The Poster Child Who Can't Be Found," *Inside Higher Education*, March 14, 2005, http:// www.insidehighered.com/news/2005/03/14/ horowitz3_14, and Mano Singham, "That Liberal Fiend Can't Be Found," *Cleveland Plain Dealer*, March 4, 2005.

9. David Horowitz's reply, "Correction: Some of Our Facts Were Wrong; Our Point Was Right," *FrontPage*, March 15, 2005, http://www.front pagemag.com/Articles/ReadArticle.asp?ID=17370.

10. On al-Qloushi, see *"Hannity and Colmes*, Horowitz Ignored Facts Undermining GOP Student's Claim that Professor Failed Him for 'Pro-American' Paper," *Media Matters for America*, February 22, 2005, http://mediamatters .org/items/200502220005, which not only summarizes the case but provides links to Professor Woolcock's question and al-Qloushi's essay (http:// www.studentsforacademicfreedom.org/archive/December2004/Ahmad'ses say 121004.htm). The *Media Matters* post includes links to responses from two political science professors who are also conservative-leaning bloggers: James Joyner (http://www.outsidethebeltway.com/archives/8841) and Steven Taylor of Troy University (http://www.poliblogger.com/index.php?p=5923). It was Joyner who gave the essay an F, calling it a "poorly written, error-ridden, pabulum-filled essay that essentially ignores the question put forth by the instructor"; Taylor gave it a low D. Woolcock's response is available online at http://mypetjawa.mu.nu/archives/066832.php.

11. On Nicole Krogman: Krogman's press release is available at http://www .studentsforacademicfreedom.org/archive/2005/May2005/Wellspressrelease republicansuspended051605.htm?%20id=ryelwiqfnqjd08rezz244grrc nbbw2pn. Morton Blackwell's letter to "Friends of the Leadership Institute" is reprinted in full at http://www.dailykos.com/story/2005/5/20/01429/ 7721. Krogman's plagiarism was reported by John Stith, "Student at Wells Denies Plagiarism: Paragraphs Were Identical. She Says It Was Her Politics that Got Her Suspended," *Syracuse Post–Standard*, May 21, 2005. http:// www.highbeam.com/library/doc3.asp?docid=1G1:132655681&ctrlIn fo=Round18%3AMode18c%3ATYF%3AContinue (registration required).

The liberal blogger who Googled Krogman's May 7, 2005, *Cornell American* essay is S.Z. of "World o' Crap," a *Salon* website devoted chiefly to parsing the work of right-wing writers, and is available at http:// blogs.salon.com/0002874/2005/05/23.html. The uncredited sources in Krogman's essay include an Accuracy in Academia talk by Bill Lind (http:// www.academia.org/lectures/lind1.html), an online wiki-like encyclopedia entry on "Political Correctness" (http://www.everything2.com/index.pl? node_id=37246&lastnode_id=650481), and another online essay by Philip Atkinson (http://www.ourcivilisation.com/pc.htm). In each case, Krogman's plagiarism of these texts is word for word.

12. The complaints can be read in full at http://www.studentsforacademicfree dom.org/comp/viewComplaint.asp?complainId=370, http://www.students foracademicfreedom.org/comp/viewComplaint.asp?complainId=374, and http://www.studentsforacademicfreedom.org/comp/viewComplaint.asp?co mplainId=166.

13. Gray, "Bill Could Limit Open Debate at Colleges."

14. "Bill Targets Colleges' Liberal Bias," *Washington Times*, February 14, 2005, http://washingtontimes.com/national/20050214_121804-9020r.htm.

15. Guy Kovner, "SRJC Uproar Over Republican Protest: Several Instructors Targeted by Student's Posting of Red Stars, State Code on Teaching of Communism," *Santa Rosa Press Democrat*, March 2, 2005, http://www .pressdemocrat.com/apps/pbcs.dll/article?AID=/20050302/NEWS/5030203 03/1033/NEWS01.

16. The Higher Education Research Institute study is available at "UCLA Study Finds Growing Gap in Political Liberalism Between Male and Female Faculty," http://www.gseis.ucla.edu/heri/act_pr_02.html. The 2005 Harris poll was released on March 9, 2005: "Party Affiliation and Political Philosophy Show Little Change, According to National Harris Poll," http://www.harrisinteractive.com/harris_poll/index.asp?PID=548.

17. The Horowitz–Zinsmeister study was published in *American Enterprise*, September 2002, accompanied by (among other articles) Zinsmeister's "The One-Party Campus" (http://www.theamericanenterprise.org/issues/ articleid.17443/article_detail.asp) and Kenneth Lee's "Time to Fight Back" (http://www.theamericanenterprise.org/issues/articleid.16857/article_detail .asp).

18. Mark Bauerlein, "Liberal Groupthink Is Anti-Intellectual," *Chronicle of Higher Education*, November 12, 2004: B6–7, http://chronicle.com/weekly/ v51/i12/12b00601.htm.

19. Plissner, "Flunking Statistics," *The American Prospect* 13.23 (December 30, 2002), http://www. prospect.org/print/V13/23/plissner-m.html.

20. For the visual accompaniment to "One Last, Leftist Lecture," see http:// www.mattbettis.com/Articles/FrontPage%20magazine_main.htm. The accompanying article, published on September 9, 2003, is available at http:// www.frontpagemag.com/Articles/ReadArticle.asp?ID=9738.

21. Abigail Thernstrom, "Guinier Miss," *New Republic*, June 14, 1993: 18. I also discuss Thernstrom's attack in *Public Access: Literary Theory and American Cultural Politics* (New York: Verso, 1994), 7–10, 16. Clint Bolick's op-ed was titled "Clinton's Quota Queens," and appeared in the *Wall Street Journal* on April 30, 1993: A12.

22. Kathleen Quinn, "Author of Her Own Defeat: Lani's Lesson for Academia," *Lingua Franca* 3.6 (September/October 1993), 54.

23. For a good overview of the complex Bellesiles case, see Joyce Lee Malcolm, "Disarming History: How an Award-Winning Scholar Twisted the Truth

about America's Gun Culture—and Almost Got Away with It," *Reason* 34.10 (March 2003), 22–29, http://www.reason.com/0303/fe.jm.disarming .shtml. For an in-depth examination of academic plagiarism, see the *Chronicle of Higher Education*'s special report on the subject: Thomas Bartlett and Scott Smallwood, "Four Academic Plagiarists You've Never Heard Of: How Many More Are Out There?" *Chronicle of Higher Education*, December 17, 2004, http://chronicle.com/weekly/v51/i17/17a00802.htm, and "Mentor vs. Protégé: The Professor Published the Student's Words as His Own. What's Wrong With That?" *Chronicle of Higher Education*, December 17, 2004, http://chronicle.com/weekly/v51/i17/17a01401.htm. See also David Glenn, "Judge or Judge Not," *Chronicle of Higher Education*, December 17, 2004, http://chronicle.com/weekly/v51/i17/17a01601.htm.

24. For the story of David Horowitz's invitation to Hamilton (and subsequent "fib for truth" on the *O'Reilly Factor*), see Maurice Isserman, "Whose Truth?" *Academe* 91.5 (September/October 2005), 32–33, http://www.aaup .org/publications/Academe/2005/05so/05sofight.htm#isser. Horowitz's September 18, 2002, blog entry is available at http://www.frontpagemag.com/ blog/BlogEntry.asp?ID=52; his admission of the "fib" is dated February 23, 2005, at http://frontpagemag.com/blog/BlogEntry.asp?ID=423. That admission is (in part) a response to my blog entry of February 23, 2005, http:// www.michaelberube.com/index.php/weblogclumpy_v_smooth/.

    Horowitz's obsessions with academic legitimacy—as well as his salary and speaking fees—were reported in an extensive *Chronicle of Higher Education* profile: Jennifer Jacobson, "What Makes David Run," *Chronicle of Higher Education*, May 6, 2005: A9–11, http://chronicle.com/weekly/v51/ i35/35a00801.htm.

25. "Alabama Bill Targets Gay Authors," *CBS Evening News*, April 27, 2005, http://www.cbsnews.com/stories/2005/04/26/eveningnews/main691106.shtml.

26. Scott Smallwood, "Web Site Lists Professors Accused of Anti-Israel Bias and Asks Students to Report on Them," *Chronicle of Higher Education*, September 19, 2002, http://chronicle.com/daily/2002/09/2002091902n.htm. The "Solidarity with Apologists" webpage (and resulting controversy) is discussed in a *Washington Square News* article that is republished on Campus Watch itself: Christine Amario, "Profs Protest Campus Watch: Watchdog Web Site Lists Accused 'Apologists to Terrorism'," November 21, 2002, http://www.campus-watch.org/article/id/352. The "Solidarity with Apologists" page itself (with my name included) is cached at http://web.archive .org/web/20030201110834/www.campus-watch.org/apologists.php.

    The language about how Campus Watch "fully respects the freedom of speech of those it debates" can still be found on the "About" page of the Campus Watch site, http://www.campus-watch.org/about.php.

27. My own position on Israel and Palestine, insofar as it is relevant to this discussion, is as follows. While I support the creation of an independent Pales-

tinian state and oppose the extraordinary brutality of the Israeli occupation, I also support the existence of Israel and oppose the civilian-targeting tactics of the Second Intifada. There are, therefore, scholars in Middle Eastern studies who are too stridently pro-Palestinian for my political taste, just as there are conservative scholars and pundits whose knee-jerk defenses of Israel I find morally and intellectually dishonest. My position on such matters is roughly that of Michael Walzer, *Dissent* editor and professor at Princeton's Institute for Advanced Study, whose 2002 essay "The Four Wars of Israel/Palestine" (*Dissent* 49, Fall 2002: 26–33, insists that both sides must repudiate their "rejectionists" if there is to be any hope of peace in the region. I know that the politics of the region are profoundly desperate and bloody; I have been taken to task more than once by pro-Palestinian critics for writing sentences like these, on the grounds that they imply some kind of symmetry between Israel and Palestine. I do not understand this complaint. I am familiar with the kill ratios in the Israel–Palestine conflict, and I know which side is fighting with state-of-the-art weaponry and which side is fighting with rocks and suicide bombs, yet I do not see how this knowledge bars me from denouncing political tactics with which I have no sympathy. I am especially concerned with any statement, tactic, or development—on the Israeli right, on the Palestinian left, or in the rest of the world—that threatens to alienate liberal and progressive Jews, because I cannot imagine a peaceful settlement of Israeli and Palestinian claims that does not include the mediation of liberal and progressive Jews who remain sympathetic to the Palestinian cause.

28. Scott Sherman, "The Mideast Comes to Columbia," *Nation*, April 4, 2005: 18–24, http://www.thenation.com/doc/20050404/sherman.

29. Massad's reply to Sherman, and Sherman's response, appeared in the Letters section of the May 16, 2005, issue, http://www.thenation.com/doc/2005 0516/exchange.

30. Deena Shanker's remarks appear in Sherman's April 4 article, p. 22; Massad's website includes a letter (signed by twenty students) which insists that Shanker's claims about her exchange with Massad in spring 2002 are false, http://censoringthought.org/twentystudentpetition.html.

31. Jon Wiener, "When Students Complain About Professors, Who Gets to Define the Controversy?" *Chronicle of Higher Education*, May 13, 2005: B12–13, http://chronicle.com/weekly/v51/i36/36b01201.htm.

32. The testimony is available at http://edworkforce.house.gov/hearings/108th/ sed/titlevi61903/kurtz.htm. See also Martin Kramer, *Ivory Towers on Sand: The Failure of Middle Eastern Studies in America* (Washington, DC: Washington Institute for Near East Policy, 2001).

33. Stephen Burd, "House Panel Approves Bills on Graduate and Area Studies," *Chronicle of Higher Education*, October 10, 2003: A25, http://chronicle .com/weekly/v50/i07/07a02501.htm. For the 2005 reauthorization and the

language of "diverse and balanced perspectives," see Stephen Burd, "Notable Provisions in the Senate Version of the Higher Education Act," *Chronicle of Higher Education*, September 23, 2005: A33, http://chronicle .com/weekly/v52/i05/05a03301.htm.

34. Martin Kramer, "Why We Don't Need More Students Majoring in Middle Eastern Studies," *History News Network*, May 19, 2003, http://hnn.us/ articles/1454.html.

35. See Scott Smallwood, "A Weblog Starts a Fire: At Indiana U., a Professor's Comments on Gay Schoolteachers Cause a Controversy," *Chronicle of Higher Education*, November 7, 2003: A10–11, http://chronicle.com/weekly/ v50/i11/11a01001.htm. Rasmusen's remarks, some of which are reproduced in Smallwood's essay, include the following from August 26, 2003: "A second reason not to hire homosexuals as teachers is that it puts the fox into the chicken coop. Male homosexuals, at least, like boys and are generally promiscuous. They should not be given the opportunity to satisfy their desires." And these from September 2, 2003: "How about homosexual males? (I don't have much idea about lesbians.) I think they are attracted to people under age 18 more than heterosexual males are. . . . Men are attracted to a young but physically mature woman. But what is the ideal for homosexual men? For some it is certainly the mature, broad-shouldered, hairy 25-year-old. But my impression is that the 16-year-old beardless boy would attract more votes. And the 16-year-old beardless boy is not so different from an 8-year-old beardless boy as the 16-year-old girl is from the 8-year-old girl, so we should expect homosexuals to be far more tempted by 8-year-olds than heterosexuals are. I could check this by looking up a large enough sample of pornography—but I'd rather not."

36. Ann Marie B. Bahr, "The Right to Tell the Truth," *Chronicle of Higher Education*, May 6, 2005: B5, http://chronicle.com/weekly/v51/i35/35b00501 .htm.

37. George M. Marsden, *The Soul of the American University: From Protestant Establishment to Established Nonbelief* (New York: Oxford University Press, 1994).

38. See Dan Lewerenz, "Blackface Photo on Web Riles Black Caucus at Penn State," *Pittsburgh Post–Gazette*, December 5, 2003, http://www.post-gazette .com/localnews/20031205psublacklocal6p6.asp. The picture of the hooded student, complete with caption, is archived at http://www.geocities.com/ immortal1st/index2.htm.

39. Richard Epstein, *Takings: Private Property and the Power of Eminent Domain* (Cambridge, MA: Harvard University Press, 1985).

40. Associated Press, "Education Chief Rips PBS for Gay Character: Network Won't Distribute Episode with Animated 'Buster' Visiting Vt.," January 26, 2005, http://www.msnbc.msn.com/id/6869976.

41. For a scathing critique of the corporate wing of campus and its encroach-

ment on every other wing, see Jennifer Washburn, *University Inc.: The Corporate Corruption of Higher Education* (New York: Basic Books, 2005).

CHAPTER 3: IN THE LIBERAL FACULTY LOUNGE

1. George Will, "Academia, Stuck to the Left," *Washington Post*, November 28, 2004: B7, http://www.washingtonpost.com/wp-dyn/articles/A15606–2004Nov26.html.

2. Howard Kurtz, "College Faculties a Most Liberal Lot, Study Finds," *Washington Post*, March 29, 2005: C1, http://www.washingtonpost.com/wp-dyn/articles/A8427–2005Mar28.html.

3. Quoted in Joyce Howard Price, "Study Finds Liberals Dominate Faculties," *Washington Times*, March 30, 2005, http://www.washtimes.com/national/20050329–115949–1594r.htm.

4. Fairness and Accuracy in Reporting, "Study of Bias or Biased Study? The Lichter Method and the Attack on PBS Documentaries," May 14, 1992, http://fair.org/index.php?page=2515. Lichter's line about "journalists seeing themselves as citizens of the world rather than patriotic Americans" is quoted in this article as well.

5. See Cathy A. Trower and Richard P. Chait, "Faculty Diversity: Too Little for Too Long," *Harvard Magazine*, March/April 2002, http://www.harvard-magazine.com/on-line/030218.html.

6. Lee, "Time to Fight Back."

7. Terry H. Anderson, *The Pursuit of Fairness: A History of Affirmative Action* (New York: Oxford University Press, 2004). "only one was tenured": 145. "minefield of blatant inequality": 144.

8. Terry Teachout, "When Theater Becomes Propaganda: The Problem of Political Art," *In Character* 3 (Spring 2005), 60, http://www.incharacter.org/article.php?article=32.

9. Quoted in Gray, "Bill Could Limit Open Debate at Colleges."

10. National Center for Education Statistics, *2004 Digest of Education Statistics* (Washington, DC: US Department of Education, 2005), table 252, http://nces.ed.gov/programs/digest/d04/tables/dt04_252.asp.

11. Definite figures on the state of the job market for PhDs are harder to come by than most people think, not least because the supply side of the job market, every year, includes many of the PhDs who did not get jobs in previous years. In other words, there's no simple way to compare the number of degrees awarded to the number of jobs filled on a year-by-year basis. But Maresi Nerad and Joseph Cerny have conducted a "PhDs ten years later" study which found that of 814 English PhDs who received their degrees between July 1, 1982, and June 30, 1985, and who replied to Nerad and Cerny's survey questions, 53 percent had tenure by 1995. That figure might actually be cheerier than today's job market for new PhDs, since PhD production in English during the years 1982–85 was especially low. Nerad and

Cerny, "From Rumors to Facts: Career Outcomes of English PhDs," *Association of Departments of English Bulletin* 124 (Winter 2000), 43–55. Likewise, salary levels vary dramatically by region and by type of institution, so it's hard to come up with a general "wage floor" for new assistant professors. But the overall level of compensation in the field can be gauged by the fact that the average salary for all English professors, in every rank from assistant to full professor, was $52,894 in 2002–03. See Katherine S. Mangan, "The Great Divide: Concerns Grow Over Pay Gaps Between Professional-School Professors and Everybody Else," *Chronicle of Higher Education*, May 30, 2003: A10–12. Salary table available online at http://chronicle.com/weekly/v49/i38/38a01202.htm.

12. According to the National Center for Education Statistics, my workload conforms to the national average. "Across all types of postsecondary degree-granting institutions," noted the NCES in its summary of a 1999 survey, "the average full-time faculty member with any instructional responsibilities worked 53 hours per week." National Center for Education Statistics, *The Condition of Education, 2001* (Washington, DC: NCES, 2001), 84, http://nces.ed.gov/programs/coe/2001/section5/indicator51.asp.

13. Steven H. Gale, "1983–84 Average Salaries in Nationally Rated Graduate English Departments," *Association of Departments of English Bulletin* 78 (Summer 1984), 43–44. Salary levels in departments that were not "nationally rated" were undoubtedly somewhat lower.

14. Susanne Dumbleton, "Special to *The DePaulia*: SNL Seeks to Resolve Situation," *DePaulia*, October 8, 2004, http://www.thedepaulia.com/story.asp?artid=118&sectid=1.

15. As is often the case in such encounters, some observers came away with the impression that Klocek was threatening rather than conversing with the students. See Michael Gallo, "Goodbye, Klocek. Thanks, DPU," *The DePaulia*, April 26, 2005, http://www.thedepaulia.com/story.asp?artid=685&sectid=4; Kelsey Snell, "Loop Professor Takes Heat for Conduct," *DePaulia*, March 4, 2005, http://www.thedepaulia.com/story.asp?artid=77&sectid=1. The Foundation for Individual Rights in Education (FIRE) has taken up Klocek's case, and in June 2005 Klocek sued DePaul for defamation. See David French, "Klocek Files Suit," *Torch*, June 17, 2005, http://www.thefire.org/index.php/article/5790.html.

16. See Dan Skinner, "Ever Vulnerable Adjuncts," *Inside Higher Education*, June 7, 2005, http://www.insidehighered.com/views/2005/06/07/skinner.

17. American Association of University Professors, "Policy Statement: Contingent Appointments and the Academic Profession," http://aaup.org/statements/SpchState/Statements/contingent.htm: "Through the 1990s, in all types of institutions, three out of four new faculty members were appointed to non-tenure-track positions." Citing Martin J. Finkelstein and Jack H. Schuster, "Assessing the Silent Revolution: How Changing Demographics

Are Reshaping the Academic Profession," *American Association of Higher Education Bulletin* 54 (October 2001), 5, figure 2. More recent information suggests that the pace of "adjunctification" has only increased. As Scott Jaschik wrote in *Inside Higher Education*, in response to a report released in May 2005 by the National Center for Education Statistics, "Between 2001 and 2003, the number of full-time faculty jobs at degree-granting institutions rose to 630,419, from 617,868—a gain of 12,551 jobs. But the number of part-time jobs rose to 543,137, up from 495,315—a gain of 47,822 jobs. And as a percentage of faculty jobs at degree granting institutions, part-time positions increased to 46 percent, from 44 percent, over those two years." Scott Jaschik, "The Shrinking Tenure Track," *Inside Higher Education*, http://www.insidehighered.com/news/2005/05/19/data.

18. According to one study, Syfers's essay is the seventh most frequently anthologized essay in English, behind "A Modest Proposal" (Swift), "Politics and the English Language" and "Shooting an Elephant" (Orwell), "The Declaration of Independence" (Jefferson), "Once More to the Lake" (E. B. White), and "Salvation" (Langston Hughes). See Lynn Z. Bloom, "The Essay Canon," *College English* 61.4 (March 1999), 401–30.

19. Quoted in Cindy Yee, "DCU [Duke Conservative Union] Sparks Various Reactions," *Duke Chronicle*, February 10, 2004, http://www.chronicle .duke.edu/vnews/display.v/ART/2004/02/10/4028d1724320b?in_archive=1.

20. John McGowan, *Democracy's Children: Intellectuals and the Rise of Cultural Politics* (Ithaca: Cornell University Press, 2002), 40–41.

21. Viktor Shklovsky, "Art as Technique," *Russian Formalist Criticism: Four Essays*, trans. and intro. by Lee T. Lemon and Marion J. Reis (Lincoln: University of Nebraska Press, 1965), 3–24.

22. Brian Leiter, "The Right-Wing Attack on the Universities is Going Mainstream," *Leiter Reports*, November 23, 2004, http://leiterreports.typepad .com/blog/2004/11/the_rightwing_a.html.

23. Louis Menand, "Dangers Within and Without," *Profession 2005*: 10–17, citing *Elapsed Time to Degree for Master's and Doctoral Degrees: Results by Discipline College and Degree Program*, University of Colorado, Office of Planning, Budget, and Analysis, August 26, 2004, http://www.colorado.edu/pba/degrees .tdtbl.htm. As Nerad and Cerny observe in their "PhDs ten years later" study, English graduate programs have the dubious distinction of having longer time-to-degree averages than programs in biochemistry, computer science, electrical engineering, mathematics, and political science: "Over half (51%) of the English PhDs took more than 9 years to complete the degree, 44% took between 5 and 9 years, and 5% took 3 to 5 years." Nerad and Cerny, "From Rumors to Facts: Career Outcomes of English PhDs": 44.

24. Bauerlein, "Liberal Groupthink Is Anti-Intellectual."

25. Ross Douthat, *Privilege: Harvard and the Education of the Ruling Class* (New York: Hyperion, 2005).

26. Ross Douthat, "Bill of Wrongs," *New Republic Online*, May 24, 2005, http://www.tnr.com/doc.mhtml?i=w050523&s=douthat 052405.

27. See Jane Gallop, *Around 1981: Academic Feminist Literary Theory* (New York: Routledge, 1991).

28. See VèVè Clark, Shirley Nelson Garner, Margaret Higgonet, and Ketu H. Katrak, eds., *Antifeminism in the Academy* (New York: Routledge, 1996).

29. MLA Committee on the Status of Women in the Profession, "Women in the Profession, 2000," *Profession 2000*: 191–217, http://www.mla.org/pdf/wip00.pdf. For data on women in engineering and the sciences, see Cathy Ann Trower, "Women Without Tenure, Part Two: The Gender Sieve," *Next Wave* (*Science* magazine's online journal, published by the American Association for the Advancement of Science), January 25, 2002, http://sciencecareers.sciencemag.org/career_development/issue/articles/1400/women_without_tenure_part_ii_the_gender_sieve/.

30. Gerald Graff, *Beyond the Culture Wars: How Teaching the Conflicts Can Revitalize American Education* (New York: W. W. Norton, 1992), and *Clueless in Academe: How Schooling Obscures the Life of the Mind* (New Haven: Yale University Press, 2004).

31. Thomas Frank, *One Market Under God: Extreme Capitalism, Market Populism, and the End of Economic Democracy* (New York: Doubleday, 2000).

32. Bauerlein's descent into caricature, however, is far less objectionable than his descent into outright disingenuousness. He closes his essay by suggesting to *Chronicle of Higher Education* readers that he would never sign on to a Horowitzian campaign against academe: "We can't open the university to conservative ideas and persons by outside command. That would poison the atmosphere and jeopardize the ideals of free inquiry." A commendable remark, surely. Earlier that year, however, Bauerlein had appeared before the Georgia state legislature to testify on behalf of the Georgia version of Horowitz's "bill of rights," arguing that universities have broken their "social contract" to serve as "a full marketplace of ideas, with all respectable viewpoints represented," and therefore must be made subject to legislative oversight. His account of his testimony is available on Horowitz's website. It reads, in part:

> For administrators to discourage conversative speakers, while paying radical Leftists five-figure fees, is to throw a mainstream aura around but one narrow range of belief.
>
> The educational costs of such bigotry are obvious, and the ethical example it sets is deplorable. Such behaviors belong outside the campus, not inside, and there is no reason why outsiders should countenance universities that break the terms of the social contract. To be sure, academic Leftists will perceive outside pressure as an infringement of academic freedom. They think that the university is an independent enclave

accountable only to itself, and that any incursions from beyond by definition threaten the integrity of higher eduction. But, in truth, outside pressure arises precisely in order to do the opposite. It is the faculty who have
abandoned the ideal, who stifle dissent no matter how learned, who under
the guise of a rearguard, adversarial, protest posture rule the campus
intellectual world and apportion its many comforts and securities to a slim
ideological spectrum.

In other words, we *must* open the university to conservative ideas and persons by outside command. Mark Bauerlein, "Securing Academic Freedom
on Campus," FrontPage.com, March 3, 2004, http://www.frontpagemag
.com/Articles/ReadArticle.asp?ID=12452.

33. See Associated Press, "Speak Up at Your Own Risk," September 26, 2001,
republished by the First Amendment Center at http://www.fac.org/
news.aspx?id=4602. The AP article also notes that "Rep. William Fuller,
R–Albuquerque, is among those calling for Berthold's resignation. He said
the First Amendment offers Berthold no protection because he is paid by
the state and teaches at a public university." Berthold was forced to resign
his position at the University of New Mexico a year later. Jennifer W.
Sanchez, "UNM's Gadfly Says Life Goes On," *Albuquerque Tribune*, September 29, 2003, http://64.233.187.104/search?q=cache:ZX5iZ43yHfIJ:www
.abqtrib.com/archives/news03/092903_news_berthold.shtml+%22Richard+
Berthold%22%2B%22has+my+vote%22&hl=en.

34. Ward Churchill, "Ward Churchill Responds to Criticism of 'Some People
Push Back.'" January 31, 2005, http://www.kersplebedeb.com/mystuff/s11/
ward_churchill_responds.html. "Some People Push Back: On the Justice of
Roosting Chickens" is available at http://www.kersplebedeb.com/mystuff/
s11/churchill.html and in Ward Churchill, *On the Justice of Roosting Chickens: Consequences of American Conquest and Carnage* (Oakland, CA: AK
Press, 2003).

35. In his January 31, 2005, defense of "Some People Push Back," Churchill
insisted that he was not defending the attacks of September 11 or advocating violence, and concluded, "the gross distortions of what I actually said
can only be viewed as an attempt to distract the public from the real issues
at hand and to further stifle freedom of speech and academic debate in this
country." It is true that Churchill did not defend the attacks in so many
words. But I find it impossible to read "Some People Push Back" without
concluding that Churchill did, in fact, say in so many words that the World
Trade Center dead deserved to die for, among other things, the crimes of
"arranging power lunches and stock transactions":

> True enough, they were civilians of a sort. But innocent? Gimme a break.
> They formed a technocratic corps at the very heart of America's global
> financial empire—the "mighty engine of profit" to which the military

dimension of U.S. policy has always been enslaved—and they did so both willingly and knowingly. Recourse to "ignorance"—a derivative, after all, of the word "ignore"—counts as less than an excuse among this relatively well-educated elite. To the extent that any of them were unaware of the costs and consequences to others of what they were involved in—and in many cases excelling at—it was because of their absolute refusal to see. More likely, it was because they were too busy braying, incessantly and self-importantly, into their cell phones, arranging power lunches and stock transactions, each of which translated, conveniently out of sight, mind and smelling distance, into the starved and rotting flesh of infants. If there was a better, more effective, or in fact any other way of visiting some penalty befitting their participation upon the little Eichmanns inhabiting the sterile sanctuary of the twin towers, I'd really be interested in hearing about it.

Somewhat literal-mindedly, I take the language of "penalty befitting their participation" to mean "penalty befitting their participation," hence my insistence that this essay assigns profound moral culpability to the dead.

36. Paul Berman, *Terror and Liberalism* (New York: W. W. Norton, 2003), 16. Berman's exact words are: "A thousand commentators have pointed out, in retrospect, that Ronald Reagan's policy in Afghanistan back in the 1980s did lead to difficulties in later years, which is indisputable. In Afghanistan, just as in Saudi Arabia, America's beneficiaries turned out to be America's worst enemies. The world is full of back-stabbing sons-of-bitches: such is the lesson of modern history."

37. Sidney Hook, *Academic Freedom and Academic Anarchy* (New York: Cowles Book Co., 1970), 36. Genovese's right to teach: 42. I briefly discuss Hook's conception of academic freedom in the opening of the essay "Intellectual Inquiry and Academic Activism," in *Academic Questions: The Journal of the National Association of Scholars* 10.4 (1997), 18–21, from which the following paragraph is adapted.

38. Chris Bush, "Support Our Truths!" *Printculture: A Daily Blogzine on Culture, Politics, and Academic Life*, May 24, 2005, http://printculture.com/index.php?itemid=177.

CHAPTER 4: STUDENTS IN AND OUT OF CLASS

1. National Center for Education Statistics, *2004 Digest of Education Statistics* (Washington, DC: US Department of Education, 2005), table 250, http://nces.ed.gov/programs/digest/d04/tables/dt04_250.asp.

2. Jeffrey R. Young, "Homework? What Homework? Students Seem to be Spending Less Time Studying Than They Used To," *Chronicle of Higher Education*, December 6, 2002: A35–36, http://chronicle.com/weekly/v49/i15/15a03501.htm. 2004 survey: "Students Study Less Than Expected, Survey Finds: Report on 'Engagement' Says More Seniors Find College Offi-

cials Helpful," *Chronicle of Higher Education*, November 26, 2004: A1, http://chronicle.com/weekly/v51/i14/14a00101.htm.

3. For an argument that the US does have such a national culture, see Michael Lind, *The Next American Nation: The New Nationalism and the Fourth American Revolution* (New York: Free Press, 1995). For an argument that American multiculturalism is little more than burritos and San Gennaro festivals, see Christopher Clausen, *Faded Mosaic: The Emergence of Post-Cultural America* (Chicago: Ivan R. Dee, 2000).

4. My framing of "culture" and "society" in this course owes everything to Raymond Williams, *Culture and Society: 1780–1950* (New York: Columbia University Press, 1958; 2nd ed. 1983).

5. Richard Poirier, *Robert Frost: The Work of Knowing* (New York: Oxford University Press, 1977).

6. As Travis McDade argues, these well-intentioned exercises can wind up having an effect precisely counter to the intention behind their design:

> Before coming to Ohio State University, I spent the better part of a decade working in residence-life departments, and I have been both a participant and facilitator in privilege walks. At every walk I have ever been a part of, the winner has been an athletic white male who, egged on by similar students, achieved his victory with the help of giant leaps and surreptitious scoots forward.
>
> While the white males are urging each other toward the finish line, the African-Americans—particularly the females, the group supposed to do the worst in the exercise—form another clique, sequestered off in one segment of the court, usually chatting about something unrelated to the walk. Despite the fact that not every student of color grew up in the ghetto—in fact, the majority of African-Americans at the universities where I have studied or worked came from the middle class—they all know what roles they are expected to play.
>
> In the end, the privilege walk builds barriers that might not have otherwise existed. Persons of color rapidly develop an us-against-them mentality and refuse to move forward or backward except in lockstep. African-Americans who didn't grow up in dire circumstances feel that responding to the statements correctly would be both a betrayal of their group and a public admission that they are not "authentic." That is not the sort of choice we ought to be foisting on to students who just want to be resident assistants.

Travis McDade, "For Resident Assistants, A Race for Inequality," *Chronicle of Higher Education*, August 6, 2004: B5, http://chronicle.com/weekly/v50/i48/ 48b00501.htm.

7. Eerily enough, this has happened at both Illinois and Penn State in the past eight years, under very similar circumstances. On June 25, 1998, Ernest

Seri, a graduate student from the Ivory Coast, went to a local bar with his fiancée, allegedly became violent, and was attacked by bouncers, each of whom outweighed him considerably; he died two days later of blunt-force injuries to the head. See Cindy Gearhart, "Suit's Damages Meant for Victim's Son," *Daily Illini Online*, May 5, 2000, http://www.illinimedia.com/di/apr_00/apr07/news/news03.shtml. On October 26, 2003, Filipino-American student Salvador Peter Serrano went to a local bar with his fiancée, allegedly got involved in a tussle with bar employees, each of whom outweighed him considerably; he was pinned to the ground, where he asphyxiated. See Sarah Rothman, "Bouncers Will Go to Trial for Involuntary Manslaughter," *Digital Collegian* (online version of Penn State's *Daily Collegian*), January 16, 2004, http://www.collegian.psu.edu/archive/2004/01/01-16-04tdc/01-16-04dnews-08.asp.

8. See Alex Muller, "Lawsuit Filed Over Use of Funds for Moore Speech," *Digital Collegian*, January 10, 2005, http://www.collegian.psu.edu/archive/2005/01/01–10–05tdc/01–10–05dnews–07.asp.

9. "The Iraqis who have risen up against the occupation are not 'insurgents' or 'terrorists' or 'The Enemy.' They are the REVOLUTION, the Minutemen, and their numbers will grow—and they will win." "Heads Up . . . From Michael Moore," April 14, 2004, http://www.michaelmoore.com/words/message/index.php?messageDate=2004-04-14. This is a regrettable proclamation any way you slice it, and it leads me to conclude that Moore would be better off focusing on exposés of corporate America and leaving foreign policy to more capable progressive commentators.

10. On the Democratic Party's cluelessness about the youth vote, see Danny Goldberg, *Dispatches from the Culture Wars: How the Left Lost Teen Spirit* (New York: Miramax Books, 2003).

11. See, e.g., Edward S. Herman, "The Politics of the Srebrenica Massacre," *ZNet,* July 7, 2005, http://www.zmag.org/content/showarticle.cfm?SectionID=74&ItemID=8244, and Bill Weinberg's splendid rejoinder, "Why Does Z Magazine Support Genocide?" *ZNet,* July 19, 2005, http://www.zmag.org/content/showarticle.cfm?SectionID=4&ItemID=8327. For a sample of Parenti's shameful defenses of Milošević and dismissal of what he calls "the media-hyped story of how the Serbs allegedly killed 7,000 Muslims in Srebrenica," see Michael Parenti, "The Demonization of Slobodan Milošević," December 2003, http://www.michaelparenti.org/ Milošević.html.

12. Ezra Klein, "Wild for Guy," March 8, 2005, http://ezraklein.typepad.com/blog/2005/03/wild_for_guy.html.

13. Eugene D. Genovese, "Heresy, Yes—Sensitivity, No," *New Republic*, April 15, 1991: 30–35.

14. See Deirdre Henderson, "Admissions: Worse Than Ever," *Inside Higher Education,* July 11, 2005, http://www.insidehighered.com/views/2005/07/11/henderson.

15. Paul M. Weyrich, "The Start of an Academic Revolution?" *Free Congress Foundation*, August 30, 2001, http://www.freecongress.org/commentaries/2001/010830PWfcc.asp.

16. See Richard J. Bishirjian, "New Conservative Internet University," June 22, 2002, http://www.freedomwriter.com/issue22/consumer.htm.

17. Ben Shapiro, *Brainwashed: How Universities Indoctrinate America's Youth* (Nashville, TN: Nelson Current, 2004). Nelson Current is an imprint of Thomas Nelson, Inc., a self-described Christian publishing house which manages to publish, alongside the Bible, three books by far-right radio ranter Michael Savage.

18. John Leo, "Campus Life, Fully Exposed," *U.S. News and World Report*, January 10, 2005, http://www.usnews.com/usnews/opinion/articles/050110/10john.htm.

19. For Jacobowitz's case, see Alan Charles Kors and Harvey A. Silverglate, *The Shadow University: The Betrayal of Liberty on America's Campuses* (New York: Free Press, 1998); for Hinkle, see the Foundation for Individual Rights in Education, "Major Victory for Free Speech at Cal Poly: University Settles Lawsuit, Abandons Effort to Defend Censorship," May 6, 2004, http://www.thefire.org/index.php/article/152.html.

20. David Horowitz, "In Defense of Intellectual Diversity," *Chronicle of Higher Education*, February 13, 2004: B12–13, http://chronicle.com/weekly/v50/i23/23b01201.htm.

CHAPTER 5: RACE, CLASS, GENDER

1. William Dean Howells, *The Rise of Silas Lapham*, intro. by Kermit Vanderbilt (New York: Viking Penguin [Penguin Classics], 1986), 40.

2. Ernest Hemingway, *Green Hills of Africa* (New York: Charles Scribner's Sons, 1935), 22.

3. Jonathan Arac, *Huckleberry Finn as Idol and Target: The Functions of Criticism in Our Time* (Madison: University of Wisconsin Press, 1997).

4. Howells, *The Rise of Silas Lapham*, 24.

5. Ibid., 28.

6. Ibid., 25.

7. Ibid., 30.

8. Ibid., 113.

9. F. Scott Fitzgerald, *The Great Gatsby* (New York: Charles Scribner's Sons, 1925), 45–46.

10. Howells, *The Rise of Silas Lapham*, 264.

11. Ibid., 166.

12. Ibid., 129.

13. Ibid., 327.

14. Ibid., 79.

15. The full passage reads as follows:

"I hate to see them stirring up those Southern fellows again," said the Colonel, speaking into the paper on his lap. "Seems to me it's time to let those old issues go."

"Yes," said the young man [i.e. Tom Corey]. "What are they doing now?"

"Oh, stirring up the Confederate brigadiers in Congress. I don't like it. Seems to me, if our party hain't got any other stock-in-trade, we better shut up shop altogether." (Ibid., 79.)

Clearly, the "stirring up" has something to do with the Civil War (those old issues) and Reconstruction, which was nearing its end when this scene occurs. (The contested election of 1876, in which the presidency was awarded to Rutherford B. Hayes in exchange for the Republican Party's promise to withdraw federal troops from the South and put an end to Reconstruction, is just around the corner.) But note that Lapham's reply is no reply at all; when asked how his party, the GOP, is "stirring up those Southern fellows," he says simply, "Oh, stirring up the Confederate brigadiers in Congress." This is hardly an explanation of what's at issue in the national political debates of the day.

16. Howells, *The Rise of Silas Lapham*, 194.
17. See Jeffory A. Clymer, *America's Culture of Terrorism: Violence, Capitalism, and the Written Word* (Chapel Hill: University of North Carolina Press, 2004).
18. Howells, *The Rise of Silas Lapham*, 272.
19. Ibid., 92.
20. Ibid., 145.
21. Ibid., 67.
22. Ibid.
23. Ibid., 358–89.
24. Ibid., 336.
25. Ibid., 37.
26. Ibid., xv.
27. Ibid., 366–67.
28. W. E. B. DuBois, *The Souls of Black Folk*, intro. by Randall Kenan (New York: Signet, 1995), 139.
29. Ibid., 45.
30. Zora Neale Hurston, *Their Eyes Were Watching God*, foreword by Mary Helen Washington, afterword by Henry Louis Gates, Jr. (New York: Harper Perennial, 1990), 123.
31. See Melville Herskovits, *The Myth of the Negro Past* (1941; repr., Boston: Beacon, 1990). "Nothing remains": E. Franklin Frazier, *The Negro Family in the United States* (Chicago: University of Chicago Press, 1939), 22. For a representative overview of the debate, see Kevin A. Yelvington, "The Anthropology of Afro-Latin America and the Caribbean: Diasporic Dimensions," *Annual Review of Anthropology* 30 (2001), 227–60.

32. Gates, Jr., *The Signifying Monkey: A Theory of African-American Literary Criticism* (New York: Oxford University Press, 1988).

33. Hurston, *Their Eyes Were Watching God*, 122.

34. Ibid., 124.

35. Ida B. Wells, "Southern Horrors: Lynch Law in All its Phases" (1892), repr. in *Man Cannot Speak For Her: Key Texts of the Early Feminists*, ed. Karlyn Kohrs Campbell, vol. II (New York: Praeger, 1989), 385–419. The statistic appears on 403.

36. See James Allen, *Without Sanctuary: Lynching Photography in America* (Santa Fe, NM: Twin Palms, 2000).

37. James Weldon Johnson, *The Autobiography of an Ex-Colored Man*, intro. by William L. Andrews (New York: Viking Penguin, 1990), xxxiv.

38. Ibid., 137.

39. Ibid., 139.

40. Ibid., 154.

41. Ibid., 108.

42. Ibid., 107.

43. Ibid., 107–8.

44. See "Limbaugh's Remarks Touch Off Controversy," *ESPN.com*, October 1, 2003, http://sports.espn.go.com/nfl/news/story?id=1627887; "Game Over for Limbaugh," *CBS News*, October, 2, 2003, http://www.cbsnews.com/stories/2003/10/02/entertainment/main576353.shtml. McNabb's remarks to the *Philadelphia Daily News*, and Limbaugh's resignation statement, are quoted in "Limbaugh Resigns from NFL Show," ESPN.com, October 2, 2003, http://espn.go.com/gen/news/2003/1001/1628537.html.

45. Actually, as ESPN noted in "Limbaugh's Remarks Touch Off Controversy," "This season, 10 of the 32 teams will have started black quarterbacks in at least one game." But I didn't quibble about this at the time.

46. Johnson, *The Autobiography of an Ex-Colored Man*, 106.

47. Ibid., 77.

48. Ibid., xv.

49. Willa Cather, *My Ántonia*, foreword by Doris Grumbach (Boston: Houghton Mifflin, 1977), 226–27.

50. Ibid., 238.

51. Ibid., 13.

52. Ibid., 14.

53. Ibid., 32.

54. Ibid., 7.

55. Ibid., 73.

56. Ibid., 74.

57. Ibid., 75.

58. Ibid., 52.

59. Ibid., 57.

60. Ibid., 58.
61. Ibid., 127.
62. Ibid., 128–29.
63. Ibid., 128.
64. Ibid., 142.
65. Ibid., 144.
66. Ibid., 216.
67. Ibid., 2.
68. Ibid.
69. Ibid., 142.
70. Ibid., 206.
71. Ibid., 143.
72. Ibid., 143–44.
73. Ibid., 144.
74. Ibid., 159.
75. Ibid., 173.
76. Ibid., 186.
77. Ibid.
78. Ibid., 153.
79. Ibid., 111.
80. Ibid., 106.
81. Ibid., 105.
82. Ibid., 201–2.
83. The first critic to emphasize the importance of gender and sexuality in *My Ántonia* was Blanche Gelfant, in "The Forgotten Reaping-Hook: Sex in *My Ántonia*," *American Literature* 43.1 (1971), 60–82; see also Deborah G. Lambert, "The Defeat of a Hero: Autonomy and Sexuality in *My Ántonia*," *American Literature* 53.4 (1982), 676–90. More recently, the question of Cather's sexual identity, and the possibility of "lesbian" and "queer" rereadings of *My Ántonia*, has become a major concern of Cather studies (I remain much more interested in the latter than the former). See, e.g., Sharon O'Brien, "'The Thing Not Named': Willa Cather as a Lesbian Writer," *Signs: Journal of Women in Culture and Society* 9.4 (1984), 576–99; Joanna Russ, "To Write 'Like a Woman': Transformation of Identity in the Work of Willa Cather," *Journal of Homosexuality* 12.3–4 (1986), 77–87; Timothy Dow Adams, "My Gay Ántonia: The Politics of Willa Cather's Lesbianism," *Journal of Homosexuality* 12.3–4 (1986), 89–98; Katrina Irving, "Displacing Homosexuality: The Use of Ethnicity in Willa Cather's *My Ántonia*," *Modern Fiction Studies* 36 (1990), 91–102; Frances W. Kaye, *Isolation and Masquerade: Willa Cather's Women* (New York: Lang, 1993); John P. Anders, *Willa Cather's Sexual Aesthetics and the Male Homosexual Literary Tradition* (Lincoln: University of Nebraska Press, 1999). Joan Acocella, in the course of rapping the knuckles of a few dozen feminist and gay readers

of Cather's work, comes to the conclusion that "Cather was homosexual in her feelings and celibate in her actions," as if to rebut (and yet, in a strange way, to affirm) the most reductive versions of the argument that the question of sexuality in Cather's work can be settled by reference to Cather's actual sex acts. Joan Acocella, *Willa Cather and the Politics of Criticism* (Lincoln: University of Nebraska Press, 2000), 48.

84. Ibid., 138.

85. My reading of Jim is inspired in part by the doctoral dissertation of T. Scott Herring, "Incognitos: Queer Slumming Narratives and the Unraveling of Sexual History," University of Illinois at Urbana–Champaign, 2004 (currently a book in progress with the working title *Queer Slumming*). Herring, starting from the queer-theory premise that "queer" moments in literary works involve forms of obliquity or partial opacity (precisely because homosexuality cannot be named or acknowledged), argues that such moments are paradoxically rendered less queer once they are positively identified as "gay" or "lesbian." Herring develops his argument in close readings of works by writers such as Djuna Barnes, Wallace Thurman, and Willa Cather, among others, who often created sexually elusive or ambiguous characters and narratives that, in Herring's reading, remain "incognito."

86. I'm thinking of Kushner's remarks on individualism and capitalism in the afterword to *Angels in America*: Tony Kushner, "With a Little Help from My Friends," *Angels in America: Part Two: Perestroika*, revised version (New York: Theatre Communications Group, 1996), 149–55.

87. F. Scott Fitzgerald, *The Great Gatsby*, 2.

88. Ibid., 154.

89. Ibid.

90. Ibid., 130.

91. Ibid., 60.

92. Ibid., 59.

93. Ibid., 20.

94. Ibid., 102.

95. Ibid., 65–66.

96. Ibid., 66.

97. Ibid., 2–3.

98. Ibid., 5.

99. Ibid., 18.

100. Ibid., 9–10.

101. Ibid., 120.

102. Ibid., 112.

103. Ibid., 148.

104. Ibid., 150.

105. Ibid., 148.

106. Ibid., 162.

107. Ibid., 2.
108. Ibid., 2. I owe some of this argument to an undergraduate course I took with Sacvan Bercovitch at Columbia University in 1982.
109. Ibid., 182.
110. Ibid., 182.
111. Ibid., 135.
112. Ibid., 3.
113. Ibid., 109.
114. Lionel Trilling, "What Is Criticism?" (1970), repr. in *The Last Decade: Essays and Reviews, 1965–1975*, ed. Diana Trilling (New York: Harcourt Brace Jovanovich, 1979), 86.

CHAPTER 6: POSTMODERNISM

The opening pages of this chapter draw on material from a previously published essay, "Teaching Postmodern Fiction Without Being Sure that the Genre Exists," *Chronicle of Higher Education*, May 19, 2000: B4–5, http://chronicle .com/weekly/v46/i37/37b00401.htm.

1. Partly because humanists' work does not proceed under the same protocols of falsifiability as those of the natural sciences, our interpretations of Kuhn have been somewhat looser than they should be. It is commonly charged that humanists embraced Kuhn so enthusiastically because he seemed to have undermined the authority and the objectivity of the sciences, and the charge may have some merit; but I believe humanists, as well as social scientists, were attracted primarily to the idea of paradigm shifts as a way of explaining epistemic change (for it is a very good explanatory scheme) and less concerned with what Kuhn calls "normal science," which, after all, is where all the important paradigm-building and -challenging work gets done. So, for example, humanists tend to overlook the specificity of Kuhn's examples with regard to the discovery of oxygen or X-rays, not least because we have no direct analogy for Roentgen's realization that, in the course of his experiments with cathode rays, something was causing a barium platinocyanide-coated screen to heat up across the room.

Because of his emphasis on the importance of "normal science" and the protocols under which it operates, Kuhn is not a relativist; on the contrary, he argues that there is such a thing as scientific progress, though he insists that it can only be gauged retrospectively, for it is not proceeding toward any preordained goal. For Kuhn, science is therefore evolutionary in precisely the same sense that evolution itself was evolutionary for Darwin: in an anti-teleological sense.

The developmental process described in this essay has been a process of evolution *from* primitive beginnings—a process whose successive stages are characterized by an increasingly detailed and refined understanding of nature. But nothing that has been or will be said makes it a process of evolution *toward* anything. Inevitably that lacuna will have disturbed many readers. We are all deeply accustomed to seeing science as the one enterprise that draws constantly nearer to some goal set by nature in advance. . . .

For many men the abolition of that teleological kind of evolution was the most significant and least palatable of Darwin's suggestions. *The Origin of Species* recognized no goal set either by God or nature. Instead, natural selection, operating in the given environment and with the actual organisms presently at hand, was responsible for the gradual but steady emergence of more elaborate, further articulated, and vastly more specialized organisms. Even such marvelously adapted organs as the eye and hand of man—organs whose design had previously provided powerful arguments for the existence of a supreme artificer and an advance plan—were products of a process that moved steadily *from* primitive beginnings but *toward* no goal.

T. S. Kuhn, *The Structure of Scientific Revolutions*, 2nd ed. (Chicago: University of Chicago Press, 1970), 170–72. This passage aligns Kuhn quite clearly with philosophers like Rorty, who similarly see human deliberations about things like "justice" in an anti-teleological way; though Rorty prefers trial by jury to trial by ordeal, he believes it is fruitless to conceive of this progress in human affairs as proceeding toward some antecedent goal. As we will see later in the chapter, this stance puts Rorty at odds with philosophical foundationalists for whom the idea of an antecedent goal provides a benchmark, a "ground," for notions of human progress.

In a recent complaint about humanists' appropriation of Kuhn's work, Thomas Nagel writes: "Much of what Kuhn says about great theoretical shifts, and the inertial role of long-established scientific paradigms and their cultural entrenchment in resisting recalcitrant evidence until it becomes overwhelming, is entirely reasonable, but it is also entirely compatible with the conception of science as seeking, and sometimes finding, objective truth about the world"; Thomas Nagel, "The Sleep of Reason," repr. in *Theory's Empire: An Anthology of Dissent*, ed. Daphne Patai and Will H. Corral (New York: Columbia University Press, 2005), 541–52. I agree with this if, and only if, "objective" is understood as "mind-independent," and (as I will explain in more detail in the course of this chapter) I decline to believe that this standard of objectivity, as it pertains to objects like quarks and quasars, can be usefully applied to mind-dependent matters such as justice or anxiety. See, e.g., my entry on "Objectivity" in *New Keywords*, ed. Tony Bennett, Lawrence Grossberg, and Meaghan Morris (Oxford: Blackwell, 2005), 244–46. Finally, like Kuhn, I see no need to tie this idea of mind-independent objectivity to a teleological idea of human or scientific progress.

2. Andreas Huyssen, *After the Great Divide: Modernism, Mass Culture, Postmodernism* (Bloomington: Indiana University Press, 1986); Charles New-

man, *The Post-Modern Aura: The Act of Fiction in an Age of Inflation* (Evanston, IL: Northwestern University Press, 1985).

3. Robert Venturi's *Learning from Las Vegas* (Cambridge, MA: MIT Press, 1972; with Denise Scott Brown and Steven Izenour) may be dated in the sense that Las Vegas itself has long since evolved beyond mere roadside stands and rhinestone-studded excess, but it decisively opened the postmodernism debate in architecture, and set the terms under which architects and social theorists are still working today.

4. This paragraph is drawn in part from my cover essay for the tenth anniversary edition of the *Village Voice Literary Supplement*, "Just the Fax, Ma'am: Or, Postmodernism's Journey to Decenter," *Village Voice Literary Supplement* 99 (October, 1991), 13–17, repr. in part in *Postmodern American Fiction: A Norton Anthology*, ed. Paula Geyh, Fred G. Leebron, and Andrew Levy (New York: W. W. Norton, 1997), and in full in *War of the Words: 20 Years of Writing on Contemporary Literature*, ed. Joy Press (New York: Three Rivers, 2001), 186–99.

5. For the Cindy Sherman profile, see Cathy Hainer, "For Cindy Sherman, Art Has Many Guises," *USA Today*, November 18, 1993, 6D. For Benjamin, see "The Work of Art in the Age of Mechanical Reproduction," *Illuminations*, ed. and introd. Hannah Arendt, trans. Harry Zohn (New York: Schocken Books, 1968), 217–51.

6. Hal Foster, "What's News," *Village Voice Literary Supplement* 99 (October, 1991), 25. The passage in full is this: "Postmodernism doesn't signal the closure of modernism as much as its complication, and it can do so for other periods too. That is, it can be used to *deperiodize* other periods, to open them up to uneven developments of many sorts (it is therefore less a chronological term than a computer virus in the history mainframe)."

7. Jean Baudrillard, *The Gulf War Did Not Take Place*, trans. Paul Patton (Bloomington: Indiana University Press, 1995); *Simulations*, trans. Paul Foss, Paul Patton, and Philip Beitchman (New York: Semiotext(e), 1983). Baudrillard does not, in fact, argue that the first Gulf War did not happen. But he argues about its representation on television and in mass media in ways that make telling points about television and mass media and attempt almost no useful analyses of the many geopolitical causes and consequences of that war.

8. Jean Baudrillard, "The Precession of Simulacra," trans. Paul Foss and Paul Patton; repr. in *Art after Modernism: Rethinking Representation*, ed. Brian Wallis, foreword by Marcia Tucker (New York: New Museum of Contemporary Art; Boston: David R. Godine, 1984), 262.

9. Lynne Cheney, *Telling the Truth: Why Our Culture and Our Country Have Stopped Making Sense—and What We Can Do About It* (New York: Simon and Schuster, 1997).

10. Baudrillard, "The Precession of Simulacra," 256.

11. Don DeLillo, *White Noise* (New York: Viking Penguin, 1985), 13.

12. Ibid., 139.

13. For a related—and far more substantial—development of this line of thought, see Peter Starr, *Logics of Failed Revolt: French Theory After May '68* (Stanford: Stanford University Press, 1995).

14. For Habermas, see especially Jürgen Habermas, *The Structural Transformation of the Public Sphere: An Inquiry into a Category of Bourgeois Society*, trans. Thomas Burger with the assistance of Frederick Lawrence (Cambridge, MA: MIT Press, 1989); *Moral Consciousness and Communicative Action*, trans. Christian Lenhardt and Shierry Weber Nicholsen (Cambridge, MA: MIT Press, 1990); and *The Theory of Communicative Action*, trans. Thomas McCarthy, 2 vols. (Boston: Beacon Press, 1984–87). For Lyotard, see especially Jean-François Lyotard, *The Postmodern Condition: A Report on Knowledge*, trans. Geoff Bennington and Brian Massumi, foreword by Fredric Jameson (Minneapolis: University of Minnesota Press, 1984); and *The Differend (Phrases in Dispute)*, trans. Georges van den Abbeele (Minneapolis: University of Minnesota Press, 1988).

15. Lyotard, *The Postmodern Condition*, 60.

16. Ibid., xxv.

17. I make this argument, as well as the link between Lyotard and Beckett, in "The Abuses of the University," *American Literary History* 10.1 (1998), 147–63. Review essay on *The University in Ruins*, by Bill Readings (Cambridge, MA: Harvard University Press, 1996), *The Academic Postmodern and the Rule of Literature: A Report on Half-Knowledge*, by David Simpson (Chicago: University of Chicago Press, 1995), *We Scholars: Changing the Culture of the University*, by David Damrosch (Cambridge, MA: Harvard University Press, 1995), and *Antifeminism in the Academy*, ed. VèVè Clark, Shirley Nelson Garner, Margaret Higgonet, and Ketu H. Katrak (New York: Routledge, 1996).

18. However, Meera Nanda argues that academic-left defenses of the heterogeneity of language games and critiques of the oppressiveness of Western ideas of Enlightenment and reason have, in fact, played directly into the hands of the far right in India; Meera Nanda, *Prophets Facing Backwards: Postmodern Critiques of Science and Hindu Nationalism* (New Brunswick, NJ: Rutgers University Press, 2003).

19. Martha Nussbaum, *Cultivating Humanity: A Classical Defense of Reform in Liberal Education* (Cambridge, MA: Harvard University Press, 1997); see also my review of Nussbaum's book, which touches on some of the themes I develop in this chapter: "Citizens of the World, Unite!" *Lingua Franca* 7.7 (September 1997), 54–61.

20. Ron Rosenbaum, "Staring into the Heart of the Heart of Darkness," *New York Times Magazine*, June 4, 2005: 36–44, 50, 58, 61, 72.

21. See, e.g., Ien Ang, *Watching Dallas: Soap Opera and the Melodramatic Imagination* (London: Methuen, 1985).

22. *Pulp Fiction: A Quentin Tarantino Screenplay* (New York: Miramax Books, 1994), 19–22.

23. John Keats, letter to George and Thomas Keats, repr. in *The Norton Anthology of English Literature*, ed. M. H. Abrams et al., vol. II, 5th ed., (New York: W. W. Norton, 1986), 863.

24. Samuel Beckett called attention to Joyce's "twosome twiminds" in his commentary on *Finnegans Wake* (known, at the time of publication, as "Work in Progress"), "Dante . . . Bruno . Vico . . Joyce," in Beckett et al., *Our Examination Round His Factification for Incamination of Work in Progress* (Paris: Shakespeare and Company, 1929), repr. in Beckett, *Disjecta* (New York: Grove, 1984), 19–33. The brief discussion of "doubt" occurs on page 29.

25. Andrew Sullivan, "Protocols," *New Republic*, November 5, 2001: 46, http://www.aijac.org.au/updates/Oct–01/281001.html.

26. Simon Blackburn, "The Professor of Complacence," *New Republic*, August 20, 2001: 39–43.

27. Richard Rorty, *Consequences of Pragmatism: Essays, 1972–80* (Minneapolis: University of Minnesota Press, 1985), xlii. Citing Jean-Paul Sartre, *L'Existentialisme est un Humanisme* (Paris: Nagel, 1946), 53–54.

28. Leon Kass, *Life, Liberty, and the Defense of Dignity: The Challenge for Bioethics* (San Francisco: Encounter Books, 2004).

29. See, e.g., the various arguments to this effect in Barbara Herrnstein Smith, *Belief and Resistance: Dynamics of Contemporary Intellectual Controversy* (Cambridge, MA: Harvard University Press, 1997).

30. Some of this argument is drawn from my essay, "Citizenship and Disability," in *Dissent* (Spring 2003), 52–57, as is the argument about extending the domain of the universal so as to include the perspectives of people with disabilities.

31. This paragraph, and some of what follows, is drawn from my essay, "The Return of Realism and the Future of Contingency," in *What's Left of Theory? New Work on the Politics of Literary Theory*, ed. Judith Butler, John Guillory, and Kendall Thomas (New York: Routledge, 2000), 137–56.

32. Richard Rorty, *Contingency, Irony, Solidarity* (Cambridge: Cambridge University Press, 1989).

33. Richard Rorty, "Trotsky and the Wild Orchids," in *Wild Orchids and Trotsky: Messages from American Universities*, ed. Mark Edmundson (New York: Viking Penguin, 1993), 50.

34. Steven Connor, *Postmodernist Culture: An Introduction to Theories of the Contemporary*, 2nd ed. (Oxford: Blackwell, 1997), 269.

35. Lyotard, *The Postmodern Condition*, xxv.

36. In *The Normal and the Pathological*, Georges Canguilhem, who sponsored Michel Foucault's doctoral thesis and was one of Foucault's most important intellectual influences, offers another version of this paradox: "normative men exist for whom it is normal to break norms and establish new

ones"; Georges Canguilhem, *The Normal and the Pathological*, trans. Carolyn R. Fawcett (Cambridge, MA: Zone Books, 1991), 164–65. Though much of queer theory has been devoted to critiques of the "normal," the most sustained and eloquent of which is surely Michael Warner's *The Trouble with Normal: Sex, Politics, and the Ethics of Queer Life* (New York: Free Press, 1999), it seems worth noting that the ideas of the normal, the normative, and the normalizing are, in fact, in constant conflict with one another.

37. Sam Harris, *The End of Faith: Religion, Terror, and the Future of Reason* (New York: W. W. Norton, 2004), 180–81.

38. My understanding of these matters derives chiefly from Brian Greene, *The Elegant Universe: Superstrings, Hidden Dimensions, and the Quest for the Ultimate Theory* (New York: W. W. Norton, 1999).

39. Thomas Nagel, *The View from Nowhere* (Oxford: Oxford University Press, 1986); Simon Blackburn, *Truth: A Guide* (Oxford: Oxford University Press, 2005).

40. Roger Scruton, "Whatever Happened to Reason?" *City Journal* (Spring 1999), http://www.city-journal.org/html/9_2_urbanities_what_ever.html

Chapter 7: More Liberalism

1. For a comprehensive history of pre–*Roe v. Wade* abortion policies and their consequences, see Leslie J. Reagan, *When Abortion Was a Crime: Women, Medicine, and Law in the United States, 1867–1973* (Berkeley: University of California Press, 1997).

2. Quoted in Bill Tammeus, "The Year of Talking Dangerously: Next Time, Folks, Consider Silence," *Denver Post,* December 29, 1995: B07. To those of my colleagues who are horrified by this remark, and horrified by the fact that Limbaugh made it eight months *after* far-right American terrorists attacked Oklahoma City, I explain that Limbaugh, the self-described harmless, lovable little fuzzball, was only making a little joke. And yet, underneath the good-natured humor of the remark, I hear a plaintive note of pathos. We are accustomed to thinking of the 1960s as a polarizing time in American history, and we often imagine that the left is nostalgic for those days of rage and riots while the right recoils in horror from the sex, drugs, rock and roll, and political chaos of the time. But might it be possible that conservatives like Limbaugh, too, harbor a kind of sixties nostalgia, a yearning for a simpler time when right-wing maniacs could simply kill prominent liberals rather than going through all the tedium of mounting expensive, time-consuming smear campaigns against them?

3. Paul Starr, "Pummeling the Professors," review of *Impostors in the Temple*, by Martin Anderson (New York: Simon and Schuster, 1992), *New York Times Book Review*, August 9, 1992: 10–11.

4. "In 1968—the year after the U.S. Supreme Court struck down anti-

miscegenation laws in Loving v. Virginia—Gallup reported that only 20% of Americans approved of interracial marriage while 72% disapproved. It wasn't until 1991, 23 years later, that for the first time more Americans (48%) approved than disapproved (42%) of such marriages." "In Depth: Public Opinion and Polls," Gay and Lesbian Alliance Against Defamation Media Reference Guide, http://www.glaad.org/media/guide/indepthpolls .php. See also David E. Rosenbaum, "Race, Sex, and Forbidden Unions," *New York Times*, December 14, 2003: IV.4: "The last Gallup Poll on the topic, in 1997, showed that two-thirds of adults approved" of interracial marriage.

5. The Harris Poll, "Overall Confidence in Leaders of Major Institutions Declines Slightly," March 17, 2005, http://www.harrisinteractive.com/har ris_poll/index.asp?PID=550. Perhaps the most interesting (if also the most ephemeral) finding in the 2005 Harris poll is that confidence in the military plunged between 2002 and 2005; in 2002, 71 percent of respondents professed "a great deal of confidence" in the military, while in 2005, 47 percent did so—a return to 1996 levels. Conversely, the percentage of respondents who professed "a great deal of confidence" in "major educational institutions such as colleges and universities" hit a six-year low in 2003, at 31 percent, only to rebound in 2005 to 39 percent. Meanwhile, the White House went from 21 percent in 2001 to 50 percent in 2002 to 31 percent in 2005.

6. Michael Bezilla, *Penn State: An Illustrated History* (University Park: Penn State University Press, 1985), 361, http://www.libraries.psu.edu/speccolls/ psua/psgeneralhistory/bezillapshistory/083s13.htm.

7. The University of Illinois publishes this, and many other remarkable, myth-deflating numbers about tuition and university budgets, at http:// www.uillinois.edu/budget/faq.html#1.

8. Purdue University Data Digest 2000–01, http://www.purdue.edu/datadi gest2001_02/pages/2000–01/pages/bigten/big_res.htm. The truly astonishing numbers, however, don't kick in until after 2001: $5,754 in 2001–02, $6,704 in 2002–03, $7,010 in 2003–04, $7,922 in 2004–05, and $8,624 in 2005–06. See Arienne Thompson and Breanne Gilpatrick, "Double-Digit Hikes Are Down," *USA Today*, October 4, 2005, http://www.usatoday.com/ news/education/2005–10–04-tuition-survey_x.htm.

9. More specifically, in 1994–95 faculty salaries increased by 3.4%, in 1995–96, 2.9%; in 1996–97, 3%, in 1997–98, 3.3%, in 1998–99, 3.6%; in 1999–2000, 3.7%, in 2000–01, 3.5%; in 2001–02, 3.8%; in 2002–03, 3%; in 2003–04, 2.1%; and in 2004–05, 2.8%. Scott Smallwood, "Faculty Salaries Rose 2.8%, but Failed to Keep Pace with Inflation for the First Time in 8 Years," *Chronicle of Higher Education*, April 4, 2005: A12–13, http://chronicle.com/weekly/ v51/i33/33a01201.htm#annual.

10. "Teachers' T-shirts Bring Bush Speech Ouster," Bend.com, October 14, 2004, http://www.bend.com/news/ar_view.php? ar_id=18712, repr. in *Com-*

mon Dreams, October 18, 2004, http://www.commondreams.org/headlines 04/1015–06.htm.

> Three Medford school teachers were threatened with arrest and escorted from the event after they showed up wearing T-shirts with the slogan "Protect our civil liberties." All three said they applied for and received valid tickets from Republican headquarters in Medford.
>
> The women said they did not intend to protest. "I wanted to see if I would be able to make a statement that I feel is important, but not offensive, in a rally for my president," said Janet Voorhies, 48, a teacher in training.
>
> "We chose this phrase specifically because we didn't think it would be offensive or degrading or obscene," said Tania Tong, 34, a special education teacher.

Little did they realize that the phrase "Protect our civil liberties" would be regarded by the Bush campaign as a form of sedition. Nor were these schoolteachers the only threat Bush–Cheney 2004 faced in Oregon. From the same article:

> When Cheney visited Eugene last month, the Register–Guard newspaper reported that Perry Patterson, 54, was cited for criminal trespassing for blurting out the word "No" after Cheney claimed that the Bush administration had made the world safer.

11. The conservative attack on evolution should be seen as part of a larger and more corrosive skepticism toward science and rationality on the American right, as Chris Mooney argues in *The Republican War on Science* (New York: Basic Books, 2005).

12. See Bill Mears, "Court Debates Disabled Access Liability," *CNN.com*, January 13, 2004, http://www.cnn.com/2004/LAW/01/13/scotus.disabled. George Lane had to crawl up two flights of stairs to attend his own hearing on a misdemeanor charge; as Mears writes, "he refused to do so for a second hearing and was arrested for failing to appear, even though he had told the judge beforehand of his situation." Lane sued the state of Tennessee for $100,000 in damages. The Supreme Court ruled five to four in his favor (and in favor of court reporter Beverly Jones, who uses a wheelchair) in *Tennessee v. Lane and Jones* (2004).

Index